TREES
FOR THE
YARD, ORCHARD,
AND WOODLOT

TREES
FOR THE
YARD, ORCHARD,
AND WOODLOT

Propagation • Pruning
Landscaping • Orcharding • Sugaring
Woodlot Management • Traditional Uses

Edited by

ROGER B. YEPSEN, JR.

RODALE PRESS, INC.
EMMAUS, PENNSYLVANIA 18049

Library of Congress Cataloging in Publication Data

Main entry under title:

Trees for the yard, orchard, and woodlot.

  Includes index.
  1. Tree crops. 2. Trees. 3. Trees, Care of.
4. Arboriculture. I. Yepsen, Roger B.
SB170.T73   634   76-18890
ISBN 0-87857-130-2
ISBN 0-87857-229-5 pbk.
Printed in the United States of America on recycled paper

      4 6 8 10 9 7 5 3

Contents

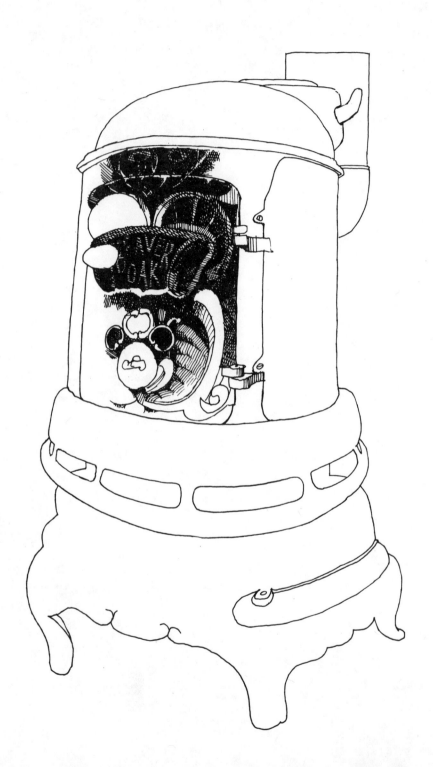

Introduction

As I write this, I am warmed by a fire of sweet gum in our Beaver Oak. The heat is such that the stove paint glistens, as if the stove sweats from exertion. As firewood, sweet gum isn't much—certainly not the peer of hickory, ash, or oak—but the windfall gum was in sight of the house. And the wood has a delicate, almost perfumy odor as it burns, unlike the clinging bacony odor of the nut woods.

I mention the fire here as a real, tangible benefit accrued from getting involved with trees. Although Saturday mornings with a Swedish saw may not seem like serious business, our electric heating system will stay inert as long as there's an orange flicker behind the mica windows.

Do the savings justify the time and labor invested? I'd say yes, if satisfaction is tallied as part of the wage. I have gotten out of the habit of evaluating my performance in terms of dollars-per-hour. Looking at things in that light can be pretty discouraging.

I got to know the woods surrounding our place largely through cutting wood. Otherwise, that nearly impenetrable stand of trees might have remained little but a scenic backdrop. Cutting up trees may not be a rite of nature worship, but sawing, splitting, and lugging these huge plants around is actually an intimate experience.

After addressing a huge fallen oak with a handsaw it's hard not to come away impressed. Trees are noble even in repose, lying on the forest floor like beached serpents.

The Beaver Oak is putting off enough heat that I have siphoned off a big mug of apple mead from a barrel in the dining room. And this leads me to more talk of trees. Last fall my wife Claire and I filled our pickup at an abandoned apple orchard, drove to a nearby cider mill, and had the squeezings poured into a couple of forty-two-gallon barrels. To encourage the juice to metamorphose into better things, we added a hundred pounds of honey. The fat barrels have been hissing and sighing for four months now, yielding a different drink every week. Starting off as apple juice, the liquid followed its natural course and became cider, and since has matured into a mildly carbonated drink—somewhere between a beer and a wine—with a slight bitter edge that we find to be an improvement on young cider. The nose and all of the tongue are pleased by this mead. And the bubbles: these are real bubbles from respiring yeast plants, not the empty excitement of artificial carbonation.

Just as there is more to our stove fires than heat and smoke, there is more to this mead than CO_2, ethyl alcohol, water, and fruit essence. In each mug is the memory of shovelling the huge mound of apples from the back of the truck into the hopper at the cider press, and of the seemingly endless flow of sweet stuff that flowed from the hose at the other end.

Our experiences are hardly unique, but just go to introduce what this book is all about: trees are great for gazing upon, but most of the fun comes from getting involved with them—harvesting, managing, identifying, topping, studying, or climbing them. This book was written as a guide to doing just that.

A Preview of What Follows. Trees are beautiful and splendidly massive. This you know for yourself, and just in case you didn't there is a spate of books in libraries, bookstores, and on coffee tables waiting to clue you in.

Trees are also useful, but the pretty picture books don't say too much about that. The text likely gives a tip of the hat to the lumber and pulp industries ("Why, if it weren't for trees, what would this book be printed on?") and likely pays tribute to man's self-expression through the medium of wood (furniture, exposed wood beams, and so on).

Trees for the Yard, Orchard, and Woodlot is the practical sister to such pretty books. It gets down to the business of working with trees in the yard, orchard, and woodlot, and does so with a minimum of fanfare.

The most obvious way to get involved with trees is to plant them in your yard to destroy the illusion that the lawn is a carpet. See Chapter 1. From there it's an easy step to plant a fruit or nut tree instead of the typical pretty, but barren, ornamental. Chapters 2 and 3 show how. If the suburban landscape is devoid of bees, you will learn how to pollinate the fruit tree blossoms yourself. In time you will probably graduate to the point of risking a few grafts or trying a hand at layering, and a chapter is given to propagating and pruning chores. The following chapter details how to keep trees healthy without toxic chemicals.

You can increase your enjoyment of a patch of woods by learning more of its mysteries, and the "Woodslore" chapter was written with this in mind. This chapter assumes that you still contain something of the curious, imaginative child you once were—otherwise, you aren't likely to get very excited over making persimmon pudding, hunting wood witches, or pursuing other bits of woodslore.

The chapter on maple sugaring isn't for everybody. You've got to have sugar maples (or at least maples, or nut trees, or sweet birches), and you should live in the northeastern or north central states, or adjacent Canada. If you qualify, you can look forward to a yearly harvest, as first conducted by the Indians with implements of birch bark.

Families are learning once again that gardens ease one's dependence on store-bought goods. The next step is to apply the wealth of vegetation in the woods to earning a measure of self-sufficiency, and the chapter called "Trees and Homestead Economics" suggests ways of putting trees to work.

If you have a woodlot and aren't really sure what to do with it, the chapter on new trends in woodlot management is for you. For those of you who didn't even know that there were *old* trends in woodlot management, these at one time involved mindless clear-cutting and the destruction of animal homes. Luckily, the new trends are more enlightened, providing for both income from the family woodlot and recreation and aesthetic value at the same time.

Plastic trees aren't very cheap or very good looking, helping to explain why there continues to be a market for real live (or recently deceased) evergreens. If you have some land to spare, consider planting it to Christmas trees. They don't require a great deal of your time, and you only have to wait six to ten years for the harvest. Chapter 10 tells how it's done.

Finally, *Trees for the Yard, Orchard, and Woodlot* closes with an attempt to pull together hundreds of obscure, interesting, and even important uses of trees of the United States. Did you know that you can raise pork on a ration of acorns and mulberries, that an excellent black ink can be made from rusty nails, water, and pin oak galls, or that a wine can be fermented from sycamore sap? So that you don't waste your time getting excited about a tree that has never been seen in your state, many of the profiles have a map showing just where that species grows.

Throughout the book are drawings of what the trees look like, how to plant and care for them, and things you can make from them. As for pretty color photographs—well, put down the book and have a good long look around you.

A Word About the Contributors. *Trees for the Yard, Orchard, and Woodlot* was to cover such a variety of topics that no one person could be found to handle them all. So, people from all walks of life have contributed. Helpful in pulling the pieces together was Jim Ritchie, a homesteader and writer from Missouri. Jim also wrote three chapters. Ohioan Gene Logsdon also is a homesteader-writer; among his books are *The Gardener's Guide to Better Soil*, *Homesteading*, and *Successful Berry Growing*, all published by Rodale Press. Our authority on the orchard is John Vivian, a Massachusetts homesteader who has written two Rodale titles, *The Manual of Practical Homesteading* and *Wood Heat*. Harry V. Wiant, Jr., is Professor of Forestry at West Virginia University at Morgantown. Richard A. Jaynes is a geneticist with the Connecticut Agricultural Experiment Station. Lester A. Bell is Professor Emeritus of Forestry at Michigan State University. Guy Thompson taps three hundred maples in upstate New York. Nevyle Shackelford is an information specialist for the Cooperative Extension Service of the University of Kentucky. Roger B. Yepsen, Jr., the editor, filled in the rest and did the drawings, save those in Chapter 11.

The identification drawings in this last chapter were taken from three books: 1) *Pennsylvania Trees*, by Joseph S. Illick.

Harrisburg: Pennsylvania Dept. of Forestry, 1923. 2) *Forest Trees of the Pacific Slope,* by George B. Sudworth. Washington: U.S. Government Printing Office, 1908. Drawings by Margaretta Washington. And 3) *Delaware Trees,* by William S. Taber. Dover: Delaware State Forestry Dept., 1937. Drawings by the author.

The range maps are courtesy of the USDA.

R.B.Y.

CHAPTER **1** Trees
for the Yard

by HARRY V. WIANT, JR.
and GENE LOGSDON

Deciding just which trees to plant around a home requires careful thought, as the choices are many and the mistakes long-term. But assuming that you do not intend to surround your home with a formal garden filled with rare and priceless plants, there are only two really serious mistakes you can make: planting a tree that does not fit your climate, soil, or ecological environment; and over-crowding—either planting too many trees or trees that grow too large for the space they occupy. If you avoid both mistakes, you can't go too far wrong.

The ideal lawn tree does not exist, as all species have both desirable and undesirable traits. The trick is to find trees that possess as many of the desirable qualities as possible, in line with the purpose you want your trees to fulfill. Generally, the purposes for planting trees around your home can be reduced to three: for beauty, for protective screening, and for food, fuel, and other products. If you are a suburban homeowner, beauty and screening may be the priority functions for the trees you plant. A homesteader might put equally high priority on the products of his trees, namely fruit, nuts, fuel, and timber. In this chapter, we'll consider briefly the more aesthetic purposes for planting trees.

TREES FOR BEAUTY

Many of us are inclined to bow before expert opinion on matters of beauty, perhaps because we fear being branded as having poor taste. But in fact, *all* trees are intrinsically beautiful. Their beauty can be discussed in terms of form, color, and texture.

Remember, good landscaping is primarily a matter of common sense. If you will sit down and determine the uses to which various areas around your home will be put, and the size of each area involved, you'll be well on your way to planning a functional, pleasing arrangement that suits your own situation. We'll discuss landscape planning in more detail later.

Trees, especially when in leaf, have silhouettes that can be described as more or less oval, pyramidal, columnar, mounding (or weeping), round, or irregular.

Oval is possibly the most common form in deciduous shade trees and resembles closely an egg, small end up, sitting on a golf tee. Ovals look good standing alone where space is ample. Good examples are white oak, red oak, buckeye, red elm, ash, most maples, walnut, hickory, yellow poplar, beech, and basswood.

Pyramidal forms include most conifers. Blue spruce is the perfect example. Among deciduous trees, the pin oak often grows with a marked pyramidal form, as does the sweet gum.

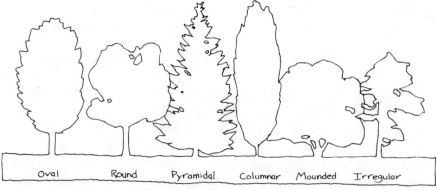

Oval   Round   Pyramidal   Columnar   Mounded   Irregular

The basic tree forms and shapes.

Columnar trees are nearly as narrow at the bottom as at the top. Due to the popularity of this form where ground space is limited (or for screening), horticulturists have developed columnar types of several tree varieties not originally of this shape. There is a columnar (fastigiate) arborvitae (Douglas), a pyramidal arborvitae (Ware), and columnar forms of English oak, cedar, and beech cypress. An offbeat tree noted for its columnar form is the Japanese umbrella pine.

The mound form includes the drooping and weeping trees, whether low to the ground like Sargent hemlock, or broad and massive like a weeping beech. Weeping willow is perhaps the most common tree in this category, but it grows so large that many suburban lots are too small for it. Weeping Japanese cherry is an in-between size adaptable to small- and medium-sized yards.

Truly round trees are rare, though globular types of Norway maples, sugar maple, black locust, and smooth-leafed elm have been developed. The green ash is somewhat rounded in form.

Trees without geometric shape—those irregular forms that defy description—appeal to many people. These are bonsai-like species that display a certain picturesque, unbalanced quality. Examples include old Scotch pines, dogwoods, true cedars, and some hawthorns.

Color is an important consideration. North Americans enjoy spectacular autumn colors not seen as vividly elsewhere in the temperate zones. Fall color is triggered when summer heat is followed swiftly by autumn's chill. It's not really Jack Frost that paints northern trees red, orange, and gold. Bright clear days of autumn cause leaves to produce large amounts of plant sugars, and cool nights slow down the movement of these sugars from the leaves to the roots. Sugars trapped in the leaves trigger increased production of chemicals that cause bright coloration, while at the same time the production of green chlorophyll declines.

The sugar maple, in her red and gold robes, is the queen of the fall show. Oaks range from red to russet to brown, depending on the species. Hickories turn a blazing yellow; red, yellow, orange, and even purple sweet gums may be seen; sassafras becomes a brilliant orange; dogwoods turn red; and aspens and birch display rich yellow leaves. (Colorful tree names usually do not refer to leaf coloring. White oak refers to the pale wood, and there's a white, a blue, a red, and a green ash. Credit these names to perceptive lumbermen who noticed subtle differences in wood coloring.) Leaf color is not entirely a matter of seasonal changes with all trees. The leaves of some trees are never green. The copper beech is one example—and in this case, the "copper" does refer to leaf color.

All but a few broad-leafed and needled evergreens stay green all year. They provide color when winter gray and white snow rule the landscape. Many shades of green are seen, from the light green of the underside of yew needles to the dark green of the hemlock.

The texture of bark and the patterns made by denuded branches get little attention from most landscapers. This is a mistake, because it's the tree's trunk that you see most often. We live with the bare branches of deciduous trees nearly as long as with limbs clothed in leaves, explaining the great popularity of the paper birch. The white bark with its black bands would be beautiful even if the tree never leafed out at all. The gray birch is almost as elegant but has a shorter life.

The smooth bark of the yellowwood tree has earned it a place on many lawns. Although not originally native to a great part of United States, the yellowwood can be grown in most areas. In addition to bright yellow fall color, the tree sports clusters of white flowers in early summer.

The sycamore's striking light and dark patches of smooth bark are well known across much of America. The Korean stewartia has similar bark. Exfoliation from the lacebark pine and shagbark hickory makes a distinctive trunk pattern. (You can peel the shags off the hickory and use them to charbroil steaks for a hickory flavor.) The smooth bark of beech trees has its own special charm if the temptation to carve initials in it can be resisted.

Before leaving the subject of tree beauty, mention should be made of trees that produce a shower of blossoms each year. All trees blossom, but some show off more than others. The early spring blossoms of sugar maple (yellow green) and Norway maple (reddish) are delicate and fascinating, but not as flashy as the lavender blossoms of the tamarack. Other large trees with colorful flowers include the southern magnolia, saucer magnolia, serviceberry (Juneberry), yellowwood, catalpa, Japanese pagoda tree, and yellow poplar. Smaller flowering trees are the dogwood, redbud, black locust, mimosa (silk tree), the hawthorns, Carolina silverbell, goldenrain tree, sourwood, flowering crab, several cherries, and—of course—all of the other fruit trees.

PLAN BEFORE PLANTING

How do you orchestrate trees with different shapes, sizes, colors, and textures into a pleasing, functional whole? Start with a sketch of your home and grounds. Determine the uses you will make of various areas around the home and how large those areas need to be. Lay out the traffic patterns needed to serve those areas.

If you are building a new home, go through the same exercise, but plot in the location, species, size, and vigor of any trees on the site. You probably won't be able to save *all* the trees on your property, but if a tree is worth saving, your cost and work involved in protecting it may be well spent. Good shade trees can add thousands of dollars to the value of residential property, and yet most contractors bulldoze the land bare and start from scratch. The U.S. Forest Service reports that, on a half-acre lot, the first six-inch-diameter tree adds $300 to the appraised value of the property, the tenth adds $200, and the twentieth, $100. Trees can contribute as much as twenty-seven percent of the appraised land value.

Consider that trees you do want to save will need protection from damage by construction equipment and supplies, grade changes (either raising or lowering the existing grade), excavations for sewer and water lines, and so on.

Now, back to the drawing board. Once you have the use areas roughly diagramed on the sketch of your property, you will need to familiarize yourself with the trees that do well in your region. Em-

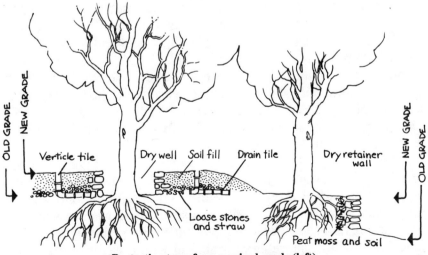

**Protecting trees from a raised grade (left)
and a lowered grade (right).**

phasize *do well,* rather than survive. If you want your yard planting to succeed, steer away from borderline trees and exotics. The plantings on your property are supposed to improve year after year, not die out the first season. You'll find range maps of many species in Chapter 11. Your extension forester or county agent can also be of valuable help in preparing a list of trees adaptable to your area.

Now you are ready to sketch in the plantings. Do your planning carefully, before you start planting. Remember, trees are not furniture. You can't just pick them up and rearrange them when the mood strikes. In designing a yard planting, you might consider one or more of the following functions: to screen or protect; to shade; or to define activity areas. What shape, size, and type tree will best suit the purpose?

Screening. Columnar trees make good screening; a row of round-shaped trees often contrasts nicely with a long squarish building; a pyramidal tree may act as the visual focal point of your homesite.

Using trees to screen as windbreaks and shelterbelts is more important in the country than in towns and suburbs where other houses and buildings serve as windbreaks. But in these days of fuel shortages, windbreaks are valuable everywhere. It has been found that twice as much fuel is required to heat the average house at an outdoor temperature of 32°F. and a wind of twelve miles per hour as is needed to heat it with the same outdoor temperature and a wind of only three miles per hour. The fuel used to heat at 32°F. and a twelve-mile wind would more than heat it at 0°F. and a three-mile wind. In the summer, tree shade on a roof and west wall can reduce temperatures there as much as 20° to 40°F. Gardens, too, can benefit from judicious placement of trees and shrubs. Even on a lot that slopes only slightly, well-placed shrubs can direct cold air away from vegetable or flower gardens and can provide some protection from the first frosts of fall. The frost stratum in the air may reach but three inches above ground.

Establishing a shelterbelt around a farm or homesite is a rather technical undertaking, and you may want to get advice from your local soil conservation officer before you design one. On smaller homesites, a double row of evergreens spaced between your house and the prevailing winter wind can cut heating bills significantly. Your yard will be more comfortable in windy weather, too. Red cedar, Canadian spruce, Norway spruce, red spruce, Austrian pine, western yellow pine, pitch pine, white pine, Scotch pine, Japanese black pine, and hemlock are good choices for smaller windbreaks. Good deciduous trees for windbreaks include Amur maple, boxelder, Osage orange, white mulberry, white poplar, balsam poplar, and pin oak.

Privacy is another important reason for planting screening trees—in fact, more important than shade for many homeowners. Some trees, such as Canadian hemlock and upright yew, make good hedges. A row of any kind of conifer will eventually screen out the public eye effectively, or screen *your* eye from an unsightly view. Most conifers do not take heavy trimming, but some, particularly hemlocks and yews, thrive with prudent trimming and also grow well in the shade of other trees.

Large decaying trees can be a hazard if close to a roof. In windstorms, they are liable to topple onto the house. Trees planted directly south and southeast of the house are less likely to hit the roof than trees planted to the southwest of the house, as strong winds come most often from westerly directions.

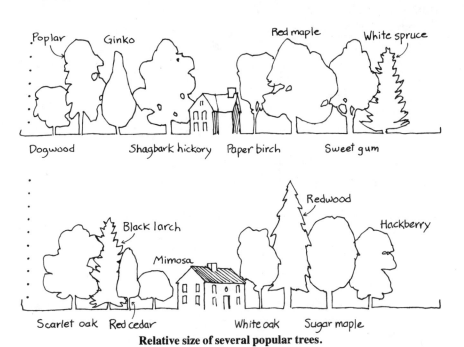

Relative size of several popular trees.

Shading. Shade trees can be used to shield the house. Happily, among the best shade trees are those mentioned earlier for their fall colors: maples, oaks, ashes, sweet gum, beeches, and others. In general, any tree you can walk under, and whose leaves form a canopy overhead, is adequate for shade. Bear in mind, however, that the better the shade, the more leaves you'll have to rake.

Dense shade trees cut out sunlight enough so that grass has a difficult time under them. A cure is to keep trimming off lower branches as the tree grows taller, so that sunlight can angle to the ground under the branches. Or, you can grow a shade-loving ground cover, such as ivy or pachysandra, under these trees in lieu of grass.

Grass grows green under honey locust trees, for the fine, small leaves allow enough sunlight through for most lawn grass varieties. Also, the locust tree is a legume that fixes nitrogen from the air to help feed the turf below. The pods of the honey locust make good feed for cattle and hogs, as well as food for humans, as discussed in Chapter 8. Grass does well under black walnut trees too.

Shade trees can also cut down on road noise and dust. On the leeward side of a belt of trees the dust count may be reduced as much as seventy-five percent.

Defining Activity Areas. In sketching a plan for the yard, keep in mind that you can engineer how the grounds will be used by where trees are placed. While it may be argued that such planning makes the environment unnecessarily artificial or constrained, the benefits should be considered.

A border of trees can define: the public area, or that side of the house presented to the street or road; the service area, including drying yard, gardens, tool sheds, compost piles, and animal pens; and the living area, incorporating patios, pool, picnic area, and adjacent porches.

To test out the landscape that's in your imagination, you might develop a landscape model using either model trees or inserting plant clippings in a box of sand.

By studying trees wherever you find them growing, whether in a forest or in a yard, the selection of the right tree for the right site becomes an easier task. The first step, logically, is identification. Identification of tree species is as much art as science, and those who develop this ability greatly increase their enjoyment of the outdoors.

IDENTIFYING TREES

To study and understand nature, man has devised classification schemes, with compartments in which to place the organisms he finds. These compartments are based more or less on obvious relationships. For example, a genus or family is comprised of apparently related species, such as the various pines in the genus *Pinus*. Each species within a genus has its own species name: the eastern white pine is *strobus*, and its complete scientific name is *Pinus strobus*.

Unfortunately, common names are not consistent. That same eastern white pine is known as northern white pine, soft pine, pumpkin pine, and Weymouth pine. That's why scientific names were developed to clearly specify a particular species.

You may be able to get an inexpensive and useful booklet describing native forest trees by writing to your state's department of natural resources or forestry. Other guides are available from the library or a good bookstore. Identifications are made by flipping through the pages and matching drawings, photographs, or verbal descriptions with the specimen in question. This is a slow process, however. Keys are usually faster.

Keys emphasize certain major identifying features and lead the tree watcher step-by-step through numbered statements to the correct identification. The following simple key can help identify the genus (family) of most coniferous trees. (Conifers often are called softwoods to distinguish them from broad-leafed trees, which are often called hardwoods; however, some so-called softwoods actually have harder wood than some hardwoods.)

Key to the Conifers. To use the key for some of the more common coniferous trees, pick any conifer that you are familiar with and follow it through. The numbers after each description refer you to a following numbered description. If the tree were a spruce *(Picea)*, for example, the second number 1 statement would lead you to the second number 2, in turn directing you to the first part of number 4, which tells you to go to number 5. The first statement of that step fits the sample's description, and identifies it as a spruce. Some runs through a key are quite brief, involving only a few steps, while others are a more lengthy process.

1. Foliage needlelike in shape and mostly in bundles of 2 to 5; cone woody . . . . .pine *(Pinus)*
1. Foliage neither needlelike in shape nor in bundles of 2 to 5 2
   2. All foliage shed in winter 3
   2. All foliage not shed in winter 4
3. Foliage on older twigs (not those near the end of the branch) clustered on short woody knobs .larch *(Larix)*
3. Needle arrangement resembles a feather . .baldcypress *(Taxodium)*
   4. Foliage attaches to twigs on short peglike projections 5
   4. Foliage does not attach on short peglike projections 6
5. Foliage stiff and usually sharp to the touch . . . . .spruce *(Picea)*
5. Foliage flexible and not sharp to the touch . . . . . . .hemlock *(Tsuga)*
   6. Fruit berrylike 7
   6. Fruit woody, not berrylike 8
7. Fruit cuplike in shape, with a hole in the center . . . . . . .yew *(Taxus)*
7. Fruit round . . . . .juniper *(Juniperus)*
   8. Three-pronged bracts extend between cone scales . . . . .Douglas Fir *(Pseudotsuga)*
   8. Three-pronged bracts not present 9
9. Closed fruit resembles a duck's bill . . . .incense cedar *(Libocedrus)*
9. Closed fruit does not resemble a duck's bill 10
   10. Barrel-shaped cones clustered near the top of the tree and stand upright . . . . .fir *(Abies)*
   10. Cones neither barrel shaped nor upright 11
11. Foliage featherlike in appearance, or if scalelike, cones average 2 inches long . . . . .redwood *(Sequoia)*
11. Foliage not featherlike in appearance, and cones less than 2 inches long 12
   12. Cones oblong, not round . . . . .cedar *(Thuja)*
   12. Cones round . .cypress or cedar *(Cupressus* or *Chamaecyparis)*

Key to the Broad-leafed Trees. After a couple of trial runs, the simplicity of the system should become apparent. Here is a key to some of the better-known, native broad-leafed trees. Again, pick the leaf of a tree you are familiar with and follow it through.

1. The stem of the leaf, with a bud in the axis where it attaches to the twig, supports only one leaf (a simple leaf) .2
1. The stem of the leaf, with the bud as previously described, supports more than one leaflet (a compound leaf) .23
   2. Leaves opposite each other on the twig .3
   2. Leaves not opposite on the twig but alternate 5
3. Leaves heart shaped . . . . .catalpa *(Catalpa)*
3. Leaves not heart shaped 4
   4. Leaf margins have obvious teeth or points . . . . . . .maple *(Acer)*
   4. Leaf margin entire or nearly so . . . . .dogwood *(Cornus)*

5. Fruit resembles a small pine cone ....birch *(Betula)*
5. Fruit does not resemble a small pine cone 6
    6. Fruit a nut 7
    6. Fruit not a nut 9
7. Fruit an acorn, a "nut with a cap" ....oak *(Quercus)*
7. Fruit a nut within a burr 8
    8. Burr covered with sharp, rigid, branched
       spines.................................chestnut *(Castanea)*
    8. Burr covered with weak, unbranched spines; buds long and
       sharp pointed ....beech *(Fagus)*
9. Leaves long and slender ....willow *(Salix)*
9. Leaves neither long nor slender 10
    10. Many of the lobed leaves have the outline of mittens 11
    10. Leaves, if lobed, do not have the outline of mittens.........12
11. Broken twigs and roots have a strong, agreeable
   odor ....sassafras *(Sassafras)*
11. Broken twigs and roots do not have a strong
   odor ....mulberry *(Morus)*
    12. Leaves star shaped in outline ....sweet gum *(Liquidambar)*
    12. Leaves not star shaped in outline 13
13. Fruit falls from tree attached to a leaflike bract ...basswood *(Tilia)*
13. Fruit not attached to leaflike bract 14
    14. Fruit berrylike 15
    14. Fruit not berrylike 19
15. Bark on tree has corky warts or ridges ....hackberry *(Celtis)*
15. Bark does not have corky warts or ridges 16
    16. Pimplelike glands present near the base of the margin of the
       leaf or on the leaf stem ....cherry *(Prunus)*
    16. No pimplelike glands 17
17. Leaves on most common species dark green and thick with spines
   around the margins ....holly *(Ilex)*
17. Leaves without spines 18
    18. Berrylike portion of fruit scattered in a football-shaped cone-
       like arrangement ....magnolia *(Magnolia)*
    18. Fruit not in conelike arrangement; a lengthwise cut up the solid
       pith of a twig reveals white lines at regular
       intervals ....tupelo *(Nyssa)*
19. Leaves heart shaped; fruit resembles a bean pod ...redbud *(Cercis)*
19. Leaves not heart shaped; fruit does not resemble a bean pod 20
    20. Fruit resembles a ball or old-fashion button; bark a mixture of
       brown and white ....sycamore *(Platanus)*
    20. Fruit not ball-like 21
21. Outline of leaf resembles a tulip......yellow poplar *(Liriodendron)*
21. Outline of leaf does not resemble a tulip 22
    22. Leaves generally have long and somewhat flattened stems,
       allowing them to flutter in the slightest
       breeze ....poplar *(Populus)*

22. Leaves do not have long, flattened stems; open-grown trees have vase shape; seed flat and more or less circular in outline . . . . .elm *(Ulmus)*
23. Compound leaves attach opposite each other on the twig 24
23. Compound leaves alternate on the twig 25
   24. Winged seeds attached in pairs; young twigs deep green . . . . .boxelder *(Acer)*
   24. Winged seeds not in pairs . . . . .ash *(Fraxinus)*
25. Twigs have sharp thorns . . . . .locust *(Robinia)*
25. Twigs without thorns 26
   26. Leaflets of each leaf radiate from one point (palmately compound) . . . . .buckeye *(Aesculus)*
   26. Leaflets attached at intervals along the leaf stem 27
27. A lengthwise cut through the pith of a twig reveals an essentially hollow pith with solid walls at regular intervals (a chambered pith) . . . . .walnut *(Juglans)*
27. Pith solid . . . . .hickory *(Carya)*

Keys given on these pages serve only as an introduction to serious tree study. A more complete key is required to identify either species within a given genus or not-so-common specimens. Many popular field guides describing native trees do not contain keys, while keys in botanical publications often are so complicated that they are of little use to laymen. An illustrated, rather simple but complete key is contained in Richard J. Preston, Jr.'s *North American Trees* (MIT Press, 1961).

Keys such as those presented in this chapter have real limitations. For instance, the fruit or leaves needed for positive identification may not be present on the specimen you wish to identify. The best—and most practical—way to learn the native trees is to go into the field with someone who already knows them.

MEETING A TREE'S REQUIREMENTS

Knowing the correct name for a species is just a beginning. You need to learn enough about a particular species to know the conditions in which it grows best. Of the many environmental factors influencing the growth of a tree, some are controllable while others are not. The concentration of carbon dioxide in the air, which is combined with water in the leaf to produce sugars, limits the growth of trees. We can do little to alter this environmental factor, but we can control others.

Light, Moisture, and Soil. Trees need light, of course. It is necessary for the photosynthetic process, which produces sugars. Some species, however, are more tolerant of shade than others.

Seedlings of pines are intolerant of shade and cannot grow in the shadow of their parents, but the more shade-tolerant hardwoods can. You may have noticed forests with large pine trees comprising the overstory and small hardwoods underneath. Later, as the pines die or are removed, the hardwoods will take over the site.

Most tree species grow best on a moist but well-drained site. Some, such as junipers and pinyon pines, can survive on very dry sites, and these species cover millions of areas in western states. Others, such as willow and baldcypress, can grow in swamps or even in the water.

Some trees are very site specific—that is, they will grow well only on the very best sites. Yellow poplar, found in moist but well-drained cove sites in the Appalachian Mountains, is a good example. By contrast, southern pines often grow on such poor and almost sterile sands that it has been said they will grow in marbles if you water them occasionally.

Trees require less fertilization than agricultural crops. Fertilization of commercial forest lands is not a widespread practice. The nutrient cycle of trees is largely responsible: most of the mineral nutrients used by trees are returned to the soil by falling leaves. Thus, even when a forest is logged, most of the nutrients stay on the site in the leaves and litter left on the forest floor.

Planting and Site Requirements. Here are some specific planting and site requirements of several important tree species.

• *Pines.* Pines are easily planted, and bare-root stock can be bought from state nurseries quite inexpensively. Many species do well on either moist or dry sites, although hardwood competition tends to be more severe on moister soils. Plantings in grass sod often do poorly, and sod should be broken up by plowing or disking before planting.

Most pines need full sunlight to survive and grow, but there are exceptions. Eastern white pine, for instance, can stand light shade. In fact, light shade often discourages the white pine weevil, a pest that often deforms open-grown trees. Pines are generally planted at six- to eight-foot spacing. Growth is rapid, but in early years plantings are vulnerable to competition from hardwoods.

• *Spruces.* Spruces will grow in either shaded or open plantings. Avoid planting them on very dry sites, however. Once spruce crowns close, the shade created is so dense that little or no undergrowth will have a chance. Norway spruce, a handsome tree native to Europe, is widely planted in this country.

   • *Firs*. Like the spruces, firs can grow in either shaded or open situations. Again, they are not generally recommended for dry areas. Growth is usually moderate.

   • *Other conifers*. Douglas fir, a tree of moderate shade tolerance, is widely planted in western North America; growth is rapid. Hemlock is an excellent choice for shaded sites; while easily transplanted from the forest when small, it makes slow growth. Junipers are good choices for dry sites in full sunlight and grow at a moderate rate.

   • *Oaks*. Like most hardwoods, oaks are more difficult to plant successfully than conifers. Most species can endure moderate shade, and some, such as post oak, adapt to dry sites. Oak trees are valuable to wildlife, and many species make fine shade trees, but growth is slow.

   • *Elms*. Like the American chestnut decades ago, large elms are fast disappearing from our landscape. The ravages of Dutch elm disease are so serious that the elm should not be planted.

   • *Maples*. Most maples are tolerant of shade. The hard maples (sugar maple, black maple) grow slowly but make excellent shade trees. Soft maples (red maple, silver maple), on the other hand, grow rapidly but die at a younger age than hard maples.

   • *Other hardwoods*. Poplars and willows grow rapidly on moist sites and can be started by inserting all but a few inches of a two-foot section of limbs from donor trees into the soil. These species require direct sunlight and are not long-lived.

   Black walnut is a valuable tree, with some individual trees selling for several thousands of dollars. The species should be planted only on the best moist but well-drained sites and must be tended carefully. Competition, especially from grass and weeds, must be controlled during the first few years of growth.

   The birches make attractive ornamentals, especially the paper birch. They require full sunlight, are relatively short-lived, and suffer from several insects and diseases.

   The southern magnolia is widely planted as an ornamental in the southern states. It requires full sunlight for best development. Yellow (tulip) poplar is an excellent choice for planting on good sites. It too requires full sunlight. Growth is excellent, and the straight bole is without rival among hardwoods.

   Dogwood should be mentioned as one of our most beautiful

understory trees, capable of growing in shaded areas. However, trees in heavy shade may not bloom as well as those planted in the open. Growth is slow, even in full sunlight, but the landowner is well rewarded for the wait—a single dogwood in full spring flower is a sight to behold.

Range. Several tree species grow completely across the North American continent, others range widely in the eastern or western United States, and some trees are found only in isolated, well-defined pockets. In time, geographic races have developed in these species, races that will respond differently in the same environment; if white pine seedlings grown from seed collected in the southern part of that species' range are planted in Maine, the seedlings will start to grow too early in spring and continue growing too late into fall, resulting in serious frost damage. So, it's best to get native tree seedlings from nearby sources.

You won't have to spend so much time caring for trees if you select those that grow well naturally in your area. Here's a list of trees the USDA recommends by region.

• *Northeast* (Minnesota to Maine, south to Missouri and Virginia): Sugar maple, Norway maple, red maple, white oak, pin oak, northern red oak, scarlet oak, Schumard oak, thornless honey locust, sweet gum, ginkgo, sycamore, London plane tree, common hackberry, green ash, silver linden, littleleaf linden, Kentucky coffeetree, yellow poplar, Japanese pagoda tree, Amur corktree, beech, Canadian hemlock, red pine, eastern white pine, white fir, Nikko fir, oriental spruce, Colorado blue spruce, and white spruce.

• *Southeast* (including eastern Texas): Live oak, southern magnolia, camphor tree, willow oak, red maple, flowering dogwood, sweet gum, American holly, beech, redbud, water oak, mimosa, winged elm, pecan, sugarberry, cabbage palmetto, and Carolina laurel-cherry.

• *Southern Florida:* Oxhorn bucida, horsetail beefwood, coconut, royal poinciana, Benjamin fig, mango, cajeput tree, Cuban royal palm, African tuliptree, and West Indies mahogany.

• *The High Plains* (Texas to Montana): Green ash, white ash, cottonwood, Chinese elm, common hackberry, burr oak, boxelder, northern catalpa, Kentucky coffeetree, sugarberry, black locust, honey locust, silver maple, Russian olive, sycamore, London plane tree, eastern black walnut, weeping willow, eastern red cedar, ponderosa pine, Douglas fir, white fir, Austrian pine, Scotch pine, and most spruces.

• *The Rockies* (including Arizona and New Mexico): Green ash, velvet ash, white ash, boxelder, catalpa, Siberian elm, hackberry, honey locust, linden, black locust, red mulberry, Russian mulberry, oaks (where soil is not too alkaline), London plane tree, lanceleaf poplar, narrowleaf poplar, plains poplar, Russian olive, tamarack, Rocky Mountain juniper, Colorado pinyon pine, Austrian pine, ponderosa pine, Scotch pine, Colorado blue spruce, and Engelmann spruce.

• *California:* Live oak, camphor tree, red ironbark, California peppertree, cape chestnut, ginkgo, Norway maple, London plane tree, sweet gum, velvet ash, Carolina poplar, pin oak, southern red oak, California black walnut, Chinese pistache, pinnacled goldenrain tree, white mulberry, canary pine, Coulter pine, Lawson cypress, California incense cedar, and Deodar cedar.

• *Pacific Northwest:* Common hackberry, yellowwood, sweet gum, yellow poplar, northern red oak, Oregon white oak, pin oak, bigleaf maple, Pacific madrone, Atlas cedar, Lawson cypress, California incense cedar, Himalayan pine, and Douglas fir.

Keep in mind that a list such as the preceding one is a general guide only. It does not mean that trees mentioned for a region will thrive everywhere in that district, nor does it mean that a tree mentioned for one area will not grow in another. A better guide as to what you should plant is to go into the woods near where you live and choose from the trees growing there.

You'll get to know more about all trees as you search for that perfect tree that best fits the purpose you have planned for it. Don't do all your window shopping in the city. Take a look at your neighbor's yard. Take a drive—or a walk—through parks and woods. Talk to local nurserymen, foresters, and county agents—but take their advice as it applies to your planting plan.

As a final word of caution, be careful of nursery bargains advertised. It takes a while to grow a tree or shrub, so make sure you're growing good ones.

TREES FROM THE WILD

You needn't spend a bit of money for lawn trees, not with fine shade trees, nut trees, and fruit trees growing in the wild. Stick to private lands, however, and be sure to get the owner's permission.

Most trees can be transplanted from the wild without too much trouble, as long as they do not have long taproots running deep into the earth. Roots and root hairs are invariably lost in the process, and trees should be pruned up on top to compensate. Or, the roots can be pruned prior to the move. It is best to move the tree with a ball of dirt around the roots.

The less important branches should be removed to allow the sufficient nourishment for the main scaffold branches. Cuts of more than an inch in diameter should be painted over with tree wound paint or wax. For planting instructions, see the section "Planting and young tree care" in the next chapter.

The red maple is a logical choice, starting its display of color in February as its twigs turn red. Soon thereafter, tiny red flowers appear, and it is one of the most spectacular autumn trees. This species does best in moist soils but will do just fine in the typical garden soil. Should you be troubled with poor drainage, this tree is an excellent choice. But before you dig up a red maple for the lawn, observe whether or not it is truly a bright red—not all individual trees are equally colorful. The red maple is superior as an ornamental to the silver maple, a native that has the bad habit of dropping twigs in wind and ice storms.

Another popular native is the sugar maple, known for its sweet sap and spectacular autumn foliage.

The pin oak is a common nursery species, largely because it is a fast grower, but it has nothing on other native oaks, free for the digging. The stately white oak is one species to avoid, however, as it is extremely difficult to transplant from the wild. The red oak is a fast growing tree, quite easy to establish in the lawn. The deep taproot of the black oak and scarlet oak make transplanting tricky, but the scarlet oak with its bright fall color is worth the effort. The shallow-rooted willow oak is easy to transplant, grows rapidly, and its leaves are thin enough that a lawn can grow in the light that filters below.

For a splash of autumn color, consider the sweet gum. You might think it a maple by looking at the star-shaped leaves. But the fragrance of the leaves is a clue that this is a member of the witch-hazel family. You can transplant the tree without much difficulty, but be sure to keep a ball of earth around the roots in the process. Normal garden soil suits it, although in the wild it is most often seen in moist wooded sites.

Hickories are a possibility for the yard, especially hilly sites, but are difficult to transplant because of a deep taproot. The shagbark has been called the best of the hickories for ornamental value, with its handsome form and interesting bark.

The above trees are just a few suggestions. Many other native trees and established imports can be transplanted without very much trouble.

CHAPTER 2 The Home Fruit Orchard

by JOHN VIVIAN

Although rarely a part of the suburban landscape, fruit trees can double as yard trees. In fact, fruit trees may well be the highlight of the home tree planting. From miniatures grown in tubs on city patios to full-sized trees in a semicommercial home orchard, they offer masses of fragrant pink and white blossoms in the spring, cool shade in summer, and baskets of apples, pears, peaches, plums, or cherries later on. And fruit trees stay in service even after they die, yielding valuable wood for carving, furniture making, smoking meats, or burning in the fireplace.

An orchard, with trees laid out neatly in 20-by-20 foot (or 40-by-40 foot) rows, is an appealing landscape in itself, especially when grass carpets the orchard floor. Located to the west of the home, the rows of fruit trees can serve as a windbreak and, with good management, make a fine pasture in which to graze sheep, a steer, or a milk cow.

A home fruit plantation is a paradise for bees, and any

homeowner who plants even a few fruit trees should consider keeping a hive or two. Bees are vital to pollination of apple trees, and many orchardists make it a regular practice to rent colonies of bees for this purpose. This service alone pays well for the bees' care, and you get the bonus of honey.

Fruit trees offer an advantage not generally found in the typical shade tree—you can buy fruit trees according to the desired mature size. Such sized trees are the result of grafting top wood from popular varieties onto roots that allow the tree to grow only so tall. If you only have space for a nine-foot tree, your nurseryman should be able to offer apple, pear, and peach trees to suit your need.

The smallest trees, called dwarfs, mature at a height of six to ten feet, and you can easily pick the fruit just by standing on the ground. Many popular varieties of fruit have been developed as

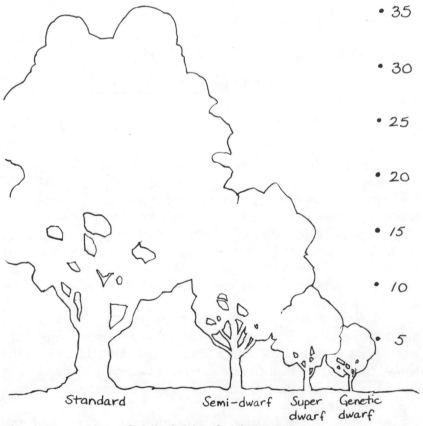

Relative heights of apple tree types.

dwarf trees and, contrary to mistaken opinions of some people, only the tree itself is small. The fruit is in every way the variety named; a Red Delicious apple from a dwarf is identical to one from a full-sized tree.

Semidwarf trees grow to a mature height of from twelve to twenty feet. The illustration shows the relative heights of dwarf, semidwarf, and standard apple trees.

Perhaps one of the more appealing features of a home orchard is the opportunity to grow many choice varieties that today are all but unknown. Discriminating variations of odor, form, color, and eating quality are known only to fruit-garden connoisseurs. Such commercial fruits as Red Delicious and Ben Davis apples, Kieffer pears, and Elberta peaches have done much to deprave the public taste as commercial market ideals have superseded quality: shipability and durability supersede flavor and texture. You should stick with proven varieties adapted to your area, of course, but even the limitation of geography means that you can grow some first-class fruits that have been dropped from the rolls of commercial orchardists.

But enough selling of the idea of a home fruit planting. If your interest has brought you this far, you're ready to learn how to go about it.

LOCATION

By and large, all noncitrus fruit trees need warm, sunny summers of about four months duration, and an equal amount of cold or cool weather (45°F. or cooler) to rest up over winter. They also need plenty of water, well-drained soil, and some protection against disease and insect pests. (We've devoted Chapter 5 to a discussion of insect and disease control.)

Cultural requirements vary among species and between varieties within species. Unless they live in the upper reaches of Alaska or Canada, northerners can grow at least a few Wealthy apples of a super-cold-tolerant variety. Folks in the Deep South or Southwest cannot grow apples with much success, but their Floridasun peaches should thrive, and of course they can enjoy citrus crops and such tropical specials as bananas, mangoes, and avocados. Throughout most of North America—perhaps with some help from irrigation or special soil conditioning—the home orchard can boast a full complement of familiar fruit trees.

Sunlight should fall on trees for at least eight hours each sum-mer day. More is better while very much less will produce insuffi-cient fruit and interfere with healthy tree growth. A normal rainfall supplies the needs of fruit trees in most parts of the country. If you live in an area where farm crops need irrigation, so will your fruit trees. Each mature tree should receive the equivalent of an inch of rain per week during the growing season, while young trees require a constant supply, especially in the first year.

Soil drainage is essential for fruit trees, partiuclarly peaches and other stone fruits. If at any time of the year, except following spring thaw or heavy rainfall, you can dig a foot-deep hole and have water stand in the bottom for more than an hour, you have a drainage problem. The solutions are as varied as the causes. You may be able to plant on a hillside and leave poor-draining flatlands to sycamore, cypress, or willow trees. Perhaps you can install drain tiles or cut drainage channels to let excess water flow away. Some growers plant dwarf fruit trees in planters or raised beds, with the surface a foot or so above ground level and contained by tiers of old railroad ties or concrete blocks. If you use blocks with holes through the centers, you can pack the holes with soil and grow ornamentals or strawberry plants in them for a double-duty planting bed.

Wind and air drainage are often-ignored influences on fruit trees. On a cold day, high winds can increase the chill factor by several degrees below the thermometer reading, so keep frost-

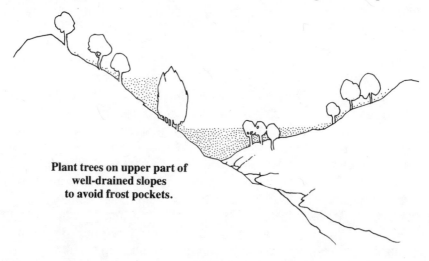

**Plant trees on upper part of
well-drained slopes
to avoid frost pockets.**

tender trees in a relatively sheltered spot if you live in snow country. Blossom-killing frosts tend to gather in low frost pockets, as cold air flows downhill on chilly spring mornings. Keep early blooming varieties out of dips and hollows, and away from tree belts and large buildings.

Peaches are particularly susceptible to blossom-kill by late frosts. If you have a choice of locations, you may want to plant peach trees on northern slopes where soil warms up more slowly. It often helps to apply a heavy mulch in winter after the ground freezes; leave it on until after the last frost date in spring.

In areas of high summer humidity, stagnant air can encourage leaf and fruit mildews and other diseases. Try to avoid areas of dead air, as a modest air flow keeps such problems to a minimum. You don't need a constant gale, but a continual flow of air such as is found in hilly areas and on most flat lands where air currents are not hindered by thick forest growth or large buildings.

Soil types that support native grasses and trees and vegetable gardens should support fruit trees with little or no modification. A mature, standard-sized fruit tree puts its roots deep and draws minerals it needs from the subsoil. Much of its food is produced by the tree itself, via photosynthesis, but of course the richer and more loamy the topsoil, the better life is for fruit trees and most other plants.

Fertility is an important consideration. Before planting an orchard, it's a good idea to grow one or two crops of a green manure, such as rye, clover, or buckwheat, and plow or till it under to add nitrogen to the soil. For best success, you should test the soil and supply organic sources of nitrogen, phosphorus, and potassium as needed, plus a broad-spectrum trace element additive such as rock phosphate or one of the seaweed concentrates. The table shows values of some popular organic materials.

APPROXIMATE POUNDS OF ELEMENT PER TON

Material	Nitrogen	Phosphorus	Potassium
Alfalfa hay	49.0	10.0	42.0
Soybean hay	46.0	14.0	22.0
Clover hay	42.0	10.0	40.0
Bean straw	38.0	7.8	25.6
Poultry manure	32.6	30.8	17.0
Grass hay	25.0	11.0	20.0
Sheep manure	16.6	4.6	13.4

Material	Nitrogen	Phosphorus	Potassium
Tree leaves, mixed	16.0	6.0	6.0
Peat moss	16.0	2.0	3.0
Buckwheat	13.0	7.1	24.2
Oat straw	12.0	4.0	26.0
Horse manure	11.6	5.6	10.6
Hog manure	9.0	3.8	12.0
Cow manure	6.8	3.2	8.0
Sawdust, shavings	4.0	2.0	4.0

Use manures carefully on apple trees, because the nitrogen contained is released slowly and may cause late maturation of trees or of the fruit.

Liming is important, but not critical on most eastern and mid-western soils. Most fruit trees prefer soils that are slightly to moderately on the acid side of the pH scale. A pH reading of 7 is neutral. Higher readings mean the soil tends toward alkaline while lower readings indicate acidity. If the pH is much lower than 6, you'll likely need to sweeten the soil with lime. Five pounds of ground limestone per 100 square feet of soil surface will raise the pH by three-fourths of a point. To lower the pH an equal amount, apply 1½ pounds of sulfur per 100 square feet. The scale shows pH preferences of favorite fruits:

	4	5	6	7	8
pH	Blueberries	Grapes	Apples	Sweet Cherry	Citrus
				Peaches	Plums
				Pears	

Pollinators, whether insects, hummingbirds, or people, are necessary if trees are to bear fruit. The honeybee is the best-known carrier of pollen from flower to flower, although dozens of other creatures help in the job. However, if you fail to notice bees on your roses and other flowers from the minute you first smell the blossom's perfume, you may need to do the pollinating yourself. The increasing use of chemical insecticides is destroying both wild and kept bee colonies all over the world. In fact, there is serious concern that there are already too few bees to pollinate the food crops needed by an ever-expanding world population. Don't expect help from bees if you're growing trees on a patio of a twenty-story apartment building, either. Bees rarely fly that high.

You can hand-pollinate at least a few trees. As soon as the

yellow pollen grains appear in the open flowers, take a soft camel's hair brush and dab it gently into one flower after another. This is *really* learning about the birds and bees—from the viewpoint of the bee. For bigger (but fewer) fruit, skip most of the blossoms. Folks with larger trees and no bees will need a ladder and several hours. But every dab with the brush means an apple or other fruit that you'd pay twenty-five cents or more for in the stores, with a fresh, homegrown taste that can't be found in any store.

Competition should be kept to a minimum; even a thick sod takes plant nutrients that your trees could use. You can keep weeds and small brush at bay with three or four mowings per year. If you till or plow the orchard land and then raise an annual fall-planted cover crop, you'll get rid of many weeds in the process. Or, you may want to run a few sheep in the orchard. They will eat dropped fruit and keep weeds down, while their manure gradually works down to fertilize the trees' roots. You can run cattle in the orchard, too, if you watch the height of the grass and turn animals out before they become hungry enough to start chewing on the trees. Keep the orchard off limits to goats and horses. Both animals eat leaves, twigs, and even bark of fruit trees; a goat can girdle a young tree in just a few seconds. In wet weather, keep all livestock out of the orchard, as their hooves trample and compact the soil, lessening its ability to absorb and release water.

Another source of competition to be avoided is other trees. Never plant a fruit tree so that its dripline—the circle made by its outermost branches—will overlap the dripline of another tree. This is easy to forget when you are planting in spring, before larger trees leaf out. You'll want to keep fruit trees out of the feeding area and shade of other lawn trees, too, if you're making a yard planting.

Which Fruits Do Best Where? The major cultivated fruit types, as well as native fruit trees, have climatic preferences. Find the hardiness zone of your area on the map, below.

Apples thrive in Zone VII and northward and have varying success in the northern part of Zone VIII. Their basic requirement is a good solid winter with temperatures of less than 45°F. for a period of about two months. Like all fruit trees, apples need rain—at least thirty inches per year. An average of an inch a week is the optimum level of moisture during the growing season.

Pears are difficult to grow commercially, even in many parts of

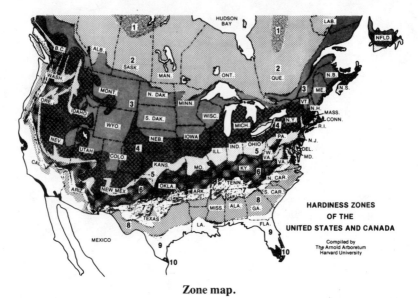

Zone map.

the country having an adequate summer rainfall. The problem is a bacterial disease called fire blight, which seems to thrive during good summer rains. The majority of this country's pear orchards are located in the Pacific Northwest, a fairly safe region. However, home orchardists living east of the Sierras have an advantage— with few large pear orchards to serve as sources of infection, they can grow a few pear trees with little worry about fire blight.

In general, pears are slow to fruit. An old New England saying has it that "you plant pears for your heirs." They need a bit less chilling than do apples—about 1½ months at minimum, although some varieties will produce fruit after but thirty-six days of chill. Pears also are less cold-tolerant, and better sets of fruit are usually made after relatively mild winters in northern regions, when temperatures never get below 20°F.

One pear variety or another should do well in all but Zone X in the South, and but northern Zones II, III, and a few frost pockets in Zone IV. Pears are less bothered than other fruit trees by droughts or lengthy wet periods. They should do well under irrigation in more arid parts of the country.

Quinces are so similar in requirements to pears that you need make few cultural distinctions. In fact, the best rootstock for dwarfing pear trees is a quince bush.

Peaches and their cousins, apricots and nectarines, have similar climate and growing preferences. Depending on variety, they need a month to 1½ months of winter temperatures below

45°F. Except for a few super-hardy varieties, 10°F. is the lowest temperature these fruits can tolerate. That means that peaches will do best from Zone V through Zone VIII, extending into the warmer sections of Zone IV and the cooler parts of Zone IX. Peaches and their relatives need an adequate water supply during the growing season, but they are highly intolerant of poorly drained soil. A peach tree can be killed in a week or two if its feet are wet, even in the spring.

Plums of some kind can be found just about anywhere in the United States except deserts and mountaintops. The native beach plum will even thrive on seaside sand dunes. Other native American plums grow wild in all but the hottest and coldest parts of the country. The more delicately constituted plums found in stores are of two imported types. The European plums are blue for the most part and are as winter-hardy as apples. They need somewhat less chilling, though, and can be grown well into the upper South.

The other import, Japanese plums, includes fruits of all colors *but* blue and need even less chilling than European plums—as little as thirty-three days. They are not frost-tolerant and shouldn't be planted if standard peaches would not easily survive winters in your area.

Commercially, cherries are pretty much a Yankee fruit. From Zone VIII southward, summers are usually too hot and long for these natives of the mild-temperate regions of Europe. They need almost as much winter chill as apples, 1½ to two months for various sweet varieties and about fifty days for sour pie cherries. Cherry blossoms are the first to appear in the spring, thus ranking as the most susceptible to killing frosts. A few super-hardy varieties have been developed, but don't expect much success with sweet cherries from Zone IV northward. Sour cherries are somewhat more hardy and do well in parts of Zone IV, although a well-sheltered location is worth seeking out.

Citrus fruits, including lemons, limes, oranges, grapefruits, and kumquats, are restricted to the semitropical regions of Florida, Texas, California, and spots in between. Citrus trees need plenty of water, a relatively alkaline soil of 7.5 pH, and frost-free winters. Leaves of these evergreens are covered with a heavy wax that prevents undue loss of water during intensely hot weather. The trees require full exposure to the sun, and even partial shade renders them spindly and unproductive. These rules generally ap-

ply to other fruit-bearing tropicals, including guava, mango, avo-
cado, and banana, as well as the somewhat more cold-tolerant
pomegranates, figs, and dates. For growers much beyond Zone X,
the tropicals and subtropicals will be limited to greenhouses or
movable tubs.

PLANTING AND YOUNG TREE CARE

Nursery ads and many books tell you that most trees can be
planted in either spring or fall. And they *can* be. But fall-planted
trees are simply stored dormant in a hole in the ground rather than
in the nursery's properly chilled and humidified warehouse. Their
root structure will not have time to dig down into the soil before
cold weather, and chances of dehydration in winter winds are
considerable. You'll have better success if you buy trees for spring
planting—about February in Zone X and as late as mid-May in the
northern regions.

Citrus trees, most other evergreens, and certain broad-leafed
trees are typically sold with a ball of soil around the roots. Or, you
can purchase bare-root, winter-dormant stock from either local or
mail-order nursery houses. In most areas, the selection is greater
from one of the mail-order firms, but be sure they offer varieites
intended for your planting conditions and climate.

Balled rootstock should be kept in a cool shaded spot until
you're ready to plant. Bare-root trees need a bit more care. They
may have spent a week or more in transit and should be unwrapped
immediately upon arrival and the roots moistened well. Then, close
the package tightly and put it in a cool dark place.

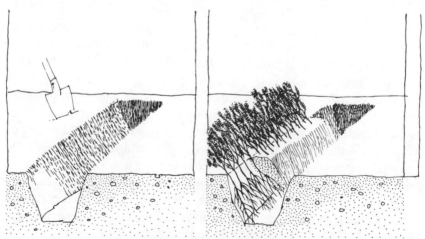

Trenching and heeling-in nursery stock.

If you must delay planting for more than a few days, heel-in the trees as illustrated. Otherwise, rootlets will begin to grow that, lacking contact with the soil, will die and cause the tree to rapidly lose strength and vigor.

Planting young fruit trees requires as much time and care as you can afford. The planting hole and planting medium you prepare will have to sustain the tree through its first several years of growth; do it right and the tree will grow faster and bear a year or two earlier than if you just plug it in and forget it.

First, dig a hole two feet across and two feet deep. This is twice as large as most instruction manuals suggest, but bear with us. Pile the sod in one place, and then dig out the topsoil (the dark upper layer) and put it in another place. Then dig out the lighter colored subsoil, toss out any rocks, and put this soil in still a third pile. Pour a cupful of bone meal into the bottom of the hole. Put the sod back in upside down and tramp it well to squeeze out all pockets of air. (Mix the topsoil with a bit of lime or sulfur if needed to correct the soil pH, and put it into the hole on top of the sod.) Now—here's the essence of fruit tree planting—turn the rest of that soil you've dug into the nearest approximation of a good garden loam that you can. In some areas, the soil will be solid loam down two feet. If you are so blessed, be thankful. Most home-owners are not so fortunate. Heavy clay subsoils that need a lot of treatment should be mixed with two shovels full of peat, another two shovels of good compost, a shovel each of greensand, cot-tonseed meal, and ground rock phosphate (or suitable substitute materials). Toss this mixture until it is well mixed.

Mix a slurry of water, compost, and seaweed concentrate fertilizer in a three-gallon bucket. Remove the tree from its wrap-pings, or from the trench where you heeled it in, and quickly prune away any roots that are broken or more than a foot long, as well as any masses of hair-roots left on main root stems. Plunge the pruned roots into the bucket of slurry and carry the tree to the planting hole you've dug for it.

Decide just how deep the tree should be set in the hole. Nearly all fruit trees are made up of sections from two different plants— the root is one plant, the top another. You will notice a knob where they were grafted together, an irregularity or scar on the lower trunk. If the tree is standard sized, this graft should be planted *below* the ground level. Otherwise, the root part will send up branches, and instead of a pear you will grow a quince; or, rather than Delicious apples, you'll be picking scrawny crab apples. If the tree is a dwarf of any sort (with a normal-bearing top grafted onto a dwarf rootstock), the graft or bud must remain *above* ground. Otherwise, the top part will root, and the dwarfing characteristic will be lost.

With the planting depth decided upon, fill the hole with the proper amount of planting mixture, place the tree's roots as evenly around the bottom as possible, add several more inches of the soil mixture, and pack it all in well around the roots. Make sure each root is surrounded by well-firmed soil. Add more soil to cover the roots to a depth of about six inches, and tramp it well. The rest of the soil goes on loose. Finally, pour on any nutrient-rich slurry left in the bucket.

The top of the planting hole should be shaped into a dish to hold water around the tree bole. Add a six-inch-thick layer of hay or other organic mulch, and then wrap the tree trunk for protection against rabbits, lawn mowers, and other bark-skinning creatures. The wrap also protects the young trunk from sunburn.

Initial pruning is necessary, particularly with bare-root trees. Chapter 4 goes into pruning in more detail, but as the initial pruning should be part of planting, we'll discuss it briefly here.

A bare-root tree has been ripped from the soil, leaving much of its one- to three-year-old root structure behind. You pruned those roots even more before planting, so now you must compensate for root loss by removing most of the tree's top growth. If you don't, the tree will self-prune and may not do as good a job as you would.

If you must err in one direction or the other, it's better to over-prune than underprune at planting time. Try to balance the tree out, leaving as many inches of branch above the ground as there are roots below. If you've ordered one-year-old whip type trees, the pruning is easy; just snip off all branches and prune the small trunk down by half.

Older trees require more thought. Basically, a fruit tree should be pruned and trained into a bowl shape—that is, three to five main branches should be evenly spaced around the trunk and made to grow out rather than up, so that the center of the tree is open to the sun. No tree grows branches spaced as evenly as spokes on a wheel, so you must adjust your pruning to the tree's growth habit. You can leave more branches on larger, more vigorous trees.

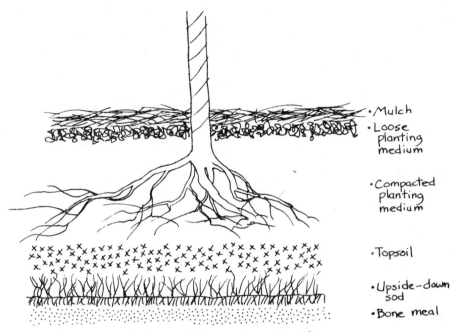

• Mulch
• Loose planting medium

• Compacted planting medium

• Topsoil

• Upside-down sod

• Bone meal

Cross-section of newly planted dwarf tree;
the hole is two feet deep and two feet in diameter.

First-year care of newly planted trees is most concerned with one thing: water. Bare-root stock lacks feeder roots and has to rely on stored-up vigor and water for a time. If the trees dry out, they will die. If trees get less than an inch of rainfall in a week, give them a good soaking—at least two gallons of water apiece. Continue watering the second year, too, whenever the weather turns dry enough to dry out and turn lawn grass brown. Keep a mulch in place for the first two or three years.

In the first tender year, fruit trees seem to attract hordes of such marauders as the rose chafer, Japanese beetle, and all sorts of chewing caterpillars. It may be the bugs realize how weak-kneed the newly transplanted trees are and set out to test them. At any rate, frequent inspections are in order once the trees begin to bud and leaf out. A big June hatch of rose chafers can nearly kill a young tree in just one day. Handpicking of insects is easy on very young trees; just brush beetles and worms into a can of water with a thin film of kerosene or oil on top. For other insect and disease problems, see Chapter 5.

THE FRUITS

Normally, fruit trees will begin to bear soon after they are old enough to blossom freely. You can figure that the tops of nursery-grown fruit trees are probably one to two years old. The length of time from planting to fruit bearing varies with the type of fruit. Trees that grow at a moderate rate usually bear fruit sooner than those that grow either too quickly or too slowly. You can expect your standard-sized trees to bear fruit at about the time (after planting) given in the table.

Fruit	Years to first bearing
Apple	2 – 5
Apricot	2 – 5
Cherry, sour	3 – 5
Cherry, sweet	4 – 7
Citrus	3 – 5
Fig	2 – 3
Peach	2 – 4
Pear	4 – 7
Plum	3 – 6

(Dwarf trees usually bear a year or two earlier than standard trees.)

Apples. Apples are probably the most vigorous fruit trees you can grow. With proper care, pruning, and pest control, a standard-sized apple tree will bear a hundred years or more, though its productivity will be greatest in its prime—the first twenty-five years or so of production. Such a tree may grow as tall as forty-five feet, with branches spread to as wide as a circumference. With good pruning, such an apple tree makes the best of all possible climbing trees for kids, or a treehouse, or swing-hanging tree.

Variety selection depends on whether you want apples for eating or cooking, dessert or keeping, summer or fall bearing, and red or yellow color. In other words, there is an apple for just about every taste and purpose. The amount of space you can devote to the trees is a factor, too. Some apples produce a full crop only every other year, so you would need at least three of any alternate-year variety to have a good chance of seeing at least one tree in full production each year. Of course, there are annual bearers, too, including some of the best varieties grown.

Descriptions of the most popular apple varieties in the United States and Canada follow. They are listed in order of sales by commercial growers, not necessarily by quality ranking. Commercial growers select for even ripening, annual bearing, and ease of shipping—ahead of eating quality.

Red Delicious leads the pack. It is the heart-shaped apple with a knobby base that you see in every store. A favorable result of a freak of nature some years back, the Red Delicious has a mild, sweet flavor that some apple fanciers find too bland. The variety ripens in October. Standard trees bear five to eight years after planting and produce fairly regular annual crops. It is used for dessert and in cooking.

Yellow Delicious begins bearing a year or two earlier than the red variety and has a light yellow skin. There is little difference in taste and texture between Yellow and Red Delicious.

McIntosh ripens its tangy red fruit in September. Trees are large in standard size and bear annually beginning four to six years following planting. Early McIntosh bears in August. Two hybrids ripen later than McIntosh: the relatively mild Cortland and the winelike Macoun. All Mac types are good either raw or cooked. They are not good keepers, however, and last but three months or so at most in home storage.

Rome Beauty and the recent improvement, Red Rome, are annual bearers. A hard-skinned, firm-fleshed apple with relatively low acidity, Rome Beauty is a late-ripening winter variety that will keep up to thirty weeks in good cold storage.

Jonathan is another annual-bearing red apple, for fresh and cooked use. It comes on late and is a good winter keeper. York Imperial, a red cooking apple, also keeps well. It ripens late and bears good crops only every other year.

Winesap and the improved Stayman Winesap are late red apples for dual use. Winesap keeps very well but shows some tendency to biennial bearing. Stayman doesn't keep so well, but it's an annual bearer.

No longer as popular as it once was, the Rhode Island Greening is a semibiennial yellow cooking apple. It has largely replaced the Early or Yellow Transparent, an early-August biennial bearer of yellow pie and applesauce apples.

Among traditional favorite red apples is the Baldwin, considered by many the best eating apple around—at least until the

Macoun came along. It's a popular cooking apple, too. Like most older varieties, Baldwin is a biennial, as is Wealthy, a cold-country favorite.

If you can find the stock, you may want to grow one of the truly old apple varieties. Many produce odd-shaped trees, hard to climb and pick. Others produce fruit that is too soft for shipping or for storing more than a few weeks. But all have superior taste and good, old-time-sounding names such as Tompkins County King, Sheepnose (or Black Gilliflower), Chenango Strawberry, and Smokehouse. There may even be an old-timer near you who has kept up a strictly local variety that never became commercially popular.

Pears. You'll need to plant two or more pear trees of more than one variety, as most pears are self-sterile. That is, they cannot pollinate their own blossoms. Just don't choose one Bartlett and one Seckel—they don't like each other. Aside from this, cultivation, pruning, and pest control are about the same as for apples.

Bartlett is the standard by which pears are judged. Over seventy-five percent of the commercial pear orchards grow Bartlett. The variety needs more winter chilling than others, and therefore is not a good choice for southern states. Seckel is a slow-growing tree that produces smallish fruit which ripen slowly to a honey sweetness. Beurre D'Anjou and Beurre Bosc are two large-fruited varieties, both super-hardy with fruit ripening in late September and keeping well in storage.

New pear varieties are being developed all the time. Moon-Glow, newly released by the USDA, is resistant to fire blight and good for areas where the disease is a problem. Colette and the Max-Red Bartlett are new and subjects of plant patents. Colette bears continuously from August to November. Max-Red has more sugar than standard Bartletts; it's extra hardy, too, down to −20°F.

Peaches, Apricots, and Nectarines. These fruits need annual pruning to bear well. Keep the inside of the tree open, and keep limbs cut well back. Fruit grows on side branches produced the year before, so in your spring pruning you will be cutting away mostly fruiting wood. But there is little choice, as the tree will otherwise grow out too far and limbs will split off under the load of the crop.

The peach tree is a fast grower, and especially adaptable to propagation. New varieties are being developed yearly. Elberta still is the old favorite, however, with firm yellow flesh and a pit that breaks free of the mature fruit. It is quite frost-tender and should not be planted where late frosts are common. Elberta ripens in September.

Red Haven is a hardy peach ripening a month earlier than Elberta. The fruit is red all over and nearly as fuzzless as a nectarine. Sun Haven is even earlier and hardy to $-19°F$. Champion and Belle of Georgia are white-fleshed peaches, juicy and extra sweet. Many offspring have been developed from the old self-sterile variety, J.I. Hale. Hale-Haven is a fine canning peach, freestone and hardy. The hardiest peach developed to date is the Reliance, good to $-25°F$.; it was released by the University of New Hampshire. Nectarines are shiny-skinned peachlike fruits, and some authorities claim they are merely a clean-shaven variety of the peach.

Apricots are neglected by Americans in general, but some homesteaders grow as many trees as they have space for, halving and drying the tangy little fruit for a winter-long supply. You'll need to plant two varieties for pollination. Moorpark is probably the best standard apricot for the eastern states with South Haven a good pollinator companion. Farther west, Early Montgamet does well, and Blenheim (Royal) is a California favorite, with Tilton a good pollinator variety. One two super cold-tolerant varieties will survive winters of New England severity—the dwarfs Sungold and Moongold.

Plums. For easiest plum harvests, order one or more native plums from a reliable nursery, and settle for a plum preserve that takes a bit more sweetening than those made with domestic fruit; beach plum, sand cherry, and Pacific plum take little care and will bear quickly. These natives are also great pollinators for the self-sterile Japanese plums.

Fruit growers in the Northwest will find the greatest variety of Japanese plums in local nurseries, including fruit of every color except purple—green, yellow, and all shades of red—with names like Becky Smith, Red Beaut, Eldorado, Santa Rosa, Beauty, and Elephant Heart. Be sure you plant varieties that bloom at the same time in the season.

Most Easterners will want to stick with the more hardy European plums. Yellow Egg is a yellow-skinned variety. Fallemberg is purple skinned with yellow flesh, much like the Stanley. The Italian Prune plum, Reine Calude, and Lombard are others adapted to eastern culture.

The worst pest of plums is a little weevillike insect called the plum curculio. You may also find it on other stone fruit, as well as apples and, occasionally, pears. Adults appear first at blossomtime, feed on fruit with their long snouts, and lay eggs in fruit under a small crescent-shaped scar. For controls, see Chapter 5.

Cherries. The large Montmorency is a favorite pie cherry, called sour but in reality only semitart. Other varieties include the Duke and Morello types. The recently developed Dwarf North Star is hardy to −25°F. It is a cross between the Morello and Siberian cherries. All sour cherries are self-pollinating.

Neglected Native Fruits. Native fruits provide an interesting variety to home plantings. Although rarely found in orchards and in the suburban landscape, most are commercially available.

One of the saddest cases of neglect in American forests is that of the lowly persimmon. The tree is adapted to a wide range of climates and soil types, and it is one of the first trees Nature sends out to reclaim fields ruined by man's tillage. When fully ripe, the one- to two-inch fruit have a rich, sweet flavor, far superior to the wild plants from which the cultivated oriental persimmon was developed. The fruit are highly nutritious, ranking second only to dates in available sugars.

Persimmons are edible only when dead ripe. Some fanciers believe a frost or two improves the flavor. If eaten green, an excess of tannin gives a terrible mouth-puckering sensation. Individual trees in the wild differ widely in size and sweetness of fruit, time of

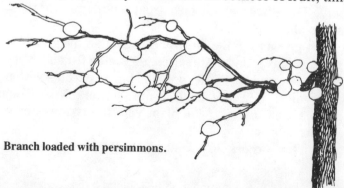

Branch loaded with persimmons.

ripening, and time of fruit drop. Varieties with desirable traits have been developed and named, including Early Golden, Penland, Killen, and Garretson.

Early settlers found the Indians made good use of this wild fruit, often setting up camps by a productive persimmon grove. Indian women removed the seeds and dried persimmons for winter use. The dried pulp, mixed with water and cornmeal, was baked into a delicious cake. See Chapter 6 for two persimmon recipes.

Persimmons are nourishing swine feed, too. And it's not unusual for a thirty-foot-tall tree to bear five bushels or more. If you multiply that times even one hundred trees per acre, the yield outpaces the best corn crops by at least two-to-one, while rivaling the best-producing apples.

The pawpaw is also called the Arkansas banana, the Michigan banana, and the Missouri banana; it seems that this wild fruit is held in high enough regard that the states wanted to attach their monikers to the tree. The pawpaw looks like a jungle tree, and in fact its close relatives are tropical trees; it is the only hardy member of the custard-apple family. In late summer, the pawpaw bears large, four-inch-long curved fruit resembling short, stubby bananas. The fruit is nutritious, offering about 450 calories per pound. The large seeds, resembling black lima beans, are high in protein but contain a strong alkaloid that is mildly poisonous to some people.

Most people find that the flavor of the pawpaw takes getting used to, and some write it off as not worth the effort. Somewhere out there, along fertile hillside benches or on alluvial bottomlands, grows a pawpaw tree that bears superior fruit. But until it is found, a few commercial varieites offer a sweet yellow pulp; they are available as young trees and seedlings.

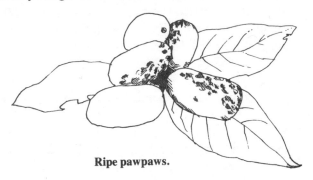

Ripe pawpaws.

The red mulberry is an excellent—and convenient—feed for hogs and poultry. Animals harvest the crop themselves. The tree is easy to transplant, grows fast, and bears faithfully. In the Cotton Belt and southern Corn Belt states, farmers used to plant a row of mulberry trees along the south side of their hog lots. The berries, falling from the trees into the hog lot, were gobbled up by the pigs. Then, as pork producers turned to more intensive production systems and abandoned open-lot hog raising, the mulberry trees they once used as animal feed have become a nuisance. The heavy crops of berries attract flocks of birds, and the birds bomb cars and drying laundry with their inky droppings.

Mulberry wood makes good, long-lasting fence posts, and because the tree is easy to plant and grows fast, it has been grown for that purpose on many farms.

The beach plum *(Prunus maritima)* grows naturally along the East Coast from southern Maine to Virginia and along the shores of the Great Lakes. This plum is also occasionally found on dry sandy soils inland. Improved varieties have recently been developed and are commercially available as plants. While the tree can also be propagated from seed, you'll have to put up with the great variability of the resulting plants. Vegetative and soft-wood cuttings will keep the desirable qualities of a productive type. The fruits are purple and measure from a half to one inch in diameter. They can be eaten as are, or made into jams and jellies.

A hot growing season is necessary to allow the Chinese jujube *(Ziziphus jujuba)* to fruit successfully. You can buy either seeds or grafted trees, or propagate the tree from stratified seed (seed exposed to a period of moist, cold treatment), root cuttings, grafting, budding, or by layering.

The highbush cranberry *(Viburnum trilobum)* offers large red berries high in pectin, making them an ideal fruit for jellies. The berries hang on all winter and have a large flat stone. White flowers appear in clusters in May or June, and the foliage turns a brilliant scarlet in fall, so it is easy to see why this tall shrub has a reputation as a fine ornamental. It will grow from northern New England south to New Jersey and Pennsylvania, and west through the Great Lake states into Iowa.

Clones with superior fruiting characteristics are available: Wentworth ripens early, Hahs in mid-season, and Andrews late. *V. opulus* is a bitter-fruited species often stocked by nurseries. The

Seviceberry.　　　　　　　High-bush cranberry.

highbush cranberry can be propagated from stratified seed and hardwood cuttings or by layering and tip layering.

The serviceberry *(Amelanchier arborea)*, also known as Juneberry and shadbush, is a shrub or small tree found from Maine west to Minnesota and south into Georgia. As a tree, the Juneberry may reach a height of forty feet, measuring up to 1½ feet around at the base. The showy white flowers, small size, and attractive form make this an ideal planting for the front of a low-profile house. And the berries are very edible either raw or cooked. They have a cherrylike flavor when raw and lend a hint of almond to pancakes and muffins. Juneberries are also fine for jams and jellies, wine, and, when dried, in any recipe calling for currants. Trees, dwarfs, and seed are sold at nurseries. You can grow the plant from suckers and stratified seed or by grafting and budding.

Sweet cherries include over a thousand different varieties, including the Black Tartarian, a dark purple variety, Napoleon, a yellow cherry, and the dark red Bigarreau types. Plant two or more varieties for pollination. Remember that sweet cherries will not stand temperatures much under 30°F. either when buds are swelling or when trees are in bloom.

CONTAINER ORCHARDING

You *can* grow apples in Florida, peaches in Alaska, and cherries in Manhattan, simply by growing dwarfs in containers. Plant genetic or super dwarf trees in washtubs, large redwood planters, or garden carts full of pure compost or topsoil. Punch or drill holes in the bottom, put a layer of pebbles or broken crockery in the bottom, and you have yourself a portable orchard. In cold regions, keep dwarf peach trees in a cool cellar or basement over winter. Small citrus trees make good winter house plants, too. In the South, give trees the required winter chill by leaving them with a northern friend or relative, or stable them in a packinghouse cooler.

For trees on a city patio, keep leaves washed clear of smog. You'll need to hand-pollinate many varieties. In-town homeowners can grow miniature citrus trees, dwarf bananas, or fig trees for both home decoration and a limited, but much-appreciated, source of fruit. Citrus trees will produce lovely, fragrant blossoms and a surprising number of fruit. Figs begin with three or four fruit the second year after planting. Just let the fruit ripen fully, and taste a treat you cannot buy in any store.

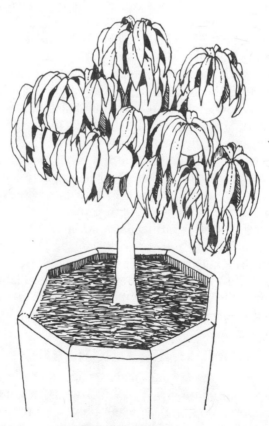

Potted peach tree.

CHAPTER 3 Rediscovering Nut Trees

by RICHARD A. JAYNES

It's not hard to find a good reason for growing nut trees. Besides providing shade and improving the appearance of your property, they produce food for man and wildlife and the finest wood for either building or fuel. And it shouldn't be hard to select a variety that is suited to your land, since nut trees come in many shapes and sizes. Black walnut, hickory, and pecan grow to over ninety feet when mature, while others are low and spreading, such as Chinese chestnut, butternut, Persian and Japanese walnut, and macadamia. In outline, these smaller varieties look like old-fashioned apple trees. Almonds are smaller still, and filberts and chinkapins are little more than shrubs. If you prefer the appearance of an evergreen, select a nut pine—a slow-growing tree that bears good-tasting seed.

Nuts can contribute rich flavor and crunchy texture to food— baked goods, confections, main dishes, salads, and sauces. You don't need a recipe book, just a little imagination. For instance, try serving sour cream with nuts on meat or baked potatoes. For muffins, waffles, or breads, stir chopped nuts into the dry ingredients before adding liquid. Try sliced nuts in tossed vegetable salads. Use toasted chopped nuts as a quick topping for pie or ice cream.

The excellent nutritive value of nuts is widely known. Most are high in oil and protein, although some—like chestnuts—are mostly carbohydrate.

FOOD VALUE OF NUTS

	Calories (1 oz.)	% protein	% fat	% carbohydrate
Almond, unblanched	170	21	55	14
Beechnut	200	22	57	13
Butternut	215	28	61	3
Chestnut, fresh	55	6	6	41
Filbert (hazelnut)	180	13	64	5
Hickory	220	15	67	11
Pecan	225	12	71	8
Walnut, black	195	30	58	6
Walnut, English	205	18	61	14

In addition to their food value, nut trees are a good choice for the yard because of their sturdiness; whereas most lawn trees are shallow rooted and difficult to mow or even grow grass around, the roots of nut trees grow deep, and this explains why nut trees seldom blow down in strong winds. In general, nut trees require less maintenance than most fruit trees. And enough hardy nut varieties are available so that growers in even the coldest regions have a good selection.

Commercial growing of nut trees in the United States is limited to certain geographical areas, but these have tended to expand in recent years. Pecan, our most important native nut, is grown in the South and as far west as Arizona and north into Illinois. In the Midwest, native black walnut trees are grown for the nuts, but a growing demand for walnut wood has increased the number of dual-purpose plantings. English or Persian walnuts are confined largely to California and Oregon. Commercial almond production is also located in California as are recent large plantings of pistachio and macadamia. A few Chinese chestnut orchards grow in the Southeast.

These geographic areas do not confine the hobbyist, however, and the locales where these various varieties will grow are a good deal more extensive than this list suggests. In fact, small-scale growers take much satisfaction from successfully growing a tree in a new area. Although much has been written about the range of nut trees, you should evaluate book information with an open mind. Take for example the pecan: it has been reported that hundreds of so-called hardy pecans planted in the northeastern United States have demonstrated that filled nuts will not be produced, even though the plants survive. But don't conclude that planting pecans in the Northeast is a waste of time. Perhaps some of the natural pecan-hickory hybrids would bear well, and seedlings from some unusual pecan trees that grow and fruit in northern Illinois and Ohio might be worth considering. Trying such untested sources is often worthwhile for the experimentally inclined. Although a great deal is known about nut trees, there is always room for discoveries by the hobbyist or homesteader.

When it is suggested that a nut tree be planted, the reply is frequently along the lines of, "Why bother? By the time the tree bears, I'll be gone." This is an unfortunate response for two reasons. First, the planter of a nut tree leaves behind a valuable legacy. If Johnny Appleseed and so many others had thought this way, the world would be the poorer for it. Second, many of today's varieties bear easily, and growing nut trees can earn you a profit in a couple of ways. You can sell surplus nuts either in the shell or as cleaned meats. A For Sale sign at the end of the driveway should bring a steady stream of customers; other markets include farm outlets, garden centers, and neighborhood grocery stores. Some of the more industrious hobbyists sell gift packages to local businessmen, who give them out at Christmastime to favored customers. Clean, shelled, or cracked nuts, when attractively displayed, always seem to be in demand.

Another way in which the nut hobby can be profitable is by propagating nut trees. You can grow them for seed or propagate them vegetatively by grafting or rooting cuttings. The demand for named nut tree cultivars far exceeds the supply, and grafting, budding, and rooting cuttings are challenging and highly gratifying when successful. (A *cultivar* is a plant selected for propagation and increase because it shows better qualities or advantages than other plants of the same species.)

Increasing food prices and the demand for foods high in protein should make nuts more popular than ever. The constantly increasing pressure for greater world food production assures that the multipurpose nut trees will be considered for the food they can supply. Trees can do more for man than shade him from the sun—instead of planting an ordinary shade tree, why not plant a shade tree that also produces an abundant supply of nuts?

The experimenter will find unlimited possibilities for crossing or hybridizing, not only of the best cultivars within a species but between related species as well. Exciting hybrids can be created by crossing and recrossing butternut, Siebold walnut, heartnut, Persian walnut, and black walnut. Pecans and the hickories also hybridize readily. Hybrid seedlings are often vigorous, but their nuts are usually inferior to those of either parent. Still, there is always the chance that you may come up with a new nut with much better characteristics: large nut size, thin shell, free kernel, fine flavor, improved resistance to disease, and high productivity. And you can bring about early fruiting by grafting scions from small seedlings to outer branches of mature trees.

PROFILES OF SOME AMERICAN NUT TREES

Pecan. The pecan, *Carya illinoensis,* is a hickory and without a doubt rates as our most valuable native nut tree. There are still extensive natural stands on the rich river bottom soils of the south central United States that are harvested annually for their bountiful crops, but the trend is rapidly changing to nut production on planted, managed trees of selected cultivars. If you live where pecans thrive, you may want at least one of these handsome American hickories in the yard. It is an outstanding shade tree.

The pecan is native to the south central United States from Texas to Oklahoma and north to Iowa and Illinois, but the area where it is successfully cultivated for nut production is larger and expanding. The tree is grown in the Carolinas, Georgia, and Florida, and extensive plantings have recently been made in western Texas and New Mexico. In these drier areas, irrigation is a regular practice.

Will pecans grow satisfactorily in your area? You must first consider many climatic factors. Pecan trees require a long frost-free period during the growing season, the actual number of days varying from 150 to 210, depending on the cultivar. The so-called northern cultivars are adapted to the shorter season. The pecan grows best where the average summer temperatures are between

Pecan.

Shagbark hickory.

75° and 85°F. and without too wide a fluctuation between day and night. New growth in the spring is quite susceptible to frost damage, and an early freeze in the fall will ruin immature pecans. If nights are cool during the growing season, the nuts do not mature and will not fill properly. Although the pecan is a warm-climate plant, it does go through a period of winter rest during which it has to be exposed to some cold weather to break dormancy properly in the spring.

Pecan trees are native to areas where the relative humidity is often high; however, excessive humidity during flowering may lessen fruit set and allow the maturing nuts to sprout in the fall. Leaf and nut diseases also become more severe if the humidity is high, and this is one good reason for planting the trees in areas of low rainfall and low humidity. On the other hand, an abundance of soil moisture is necessary for good tree growth and nut set; unless forty inches of rain or more fall per year, irrigation will likely be necessary.

As with other valuable crops, there are always new cultivars of nut trees to be tested. The oldest cultivars propagated from outstanding trees found in the wild. Most of the newer ones are either selections from seedlings of these earlier cultivars or selections from among populations of seedlings that result from controlled crosses. The USDA at Brownwood, Texas, has conducted a pecan breeding program for years and recently released many good cultivars, naming them for Indian tribes; examples are Choctaw, Mohawk, Sioux, and Shawnee.

Newer selections replace older ones for numerous reasons. Most of the newer cultivars will bear at a younger age, producing fair crops in five or six years, whereas some of the old standby cultivars like Stuart may take between nine to twelve years. Improved varieties are constantly being found, and the local branch of the state extension service can often provide up-to-date information on cultivars suitable for your area. In general, the varieties are grouped according to the region where they have performed best. The following is an abbreviated list of some popular cultivars: in the West, Apache, Comanche, Ideal, Sioux, and Western; in the East, Choctaw, Desirable, Mohawk, Shawnee, and Stuart; and in the northern states, Major, Peruque, and Posey.

Shagbark and Shellbark Hickory. The kernels of the shagbark hickory have the finest flavor of all nuts. The trick is how to find or grow them, and then to crack enough for use.

There are some twenty species of hickory and all but four are native to the Americas. Other than the pecan, already discussed, only two of these are worth growing for the nuts. One is the shagbark hickory, *Carya ovata,* the leaves of which commonly have five leaflets. It is found in the eastern half of North America from Quebec and Ontario to Florida and Texas, usually on upland soils. The other is the shellbark hickory, *C. laciniosa,* occurring mostly on river bottom soils that are occasionally flooded. Its natural range is confined largely to the drainage basin of the Mississippi and Arkansas Rivers. Shellbark leaves usually have seven leaflets.

Both species are characterized by shaggy bark, the outer layers of which split in long, vertical strips. Shellbark hickory nuts are large, often bigger than a large pecan, and hence have earned another common name, kingnut. Unfortunately, the largest portion of the nut is shell. Shagbark hickories have smaller nuts, but a higher proportion of kernel to shell, and they are often easier to crack open.

The shagbark and shellbark grow into columnar, tall, stately trees. The wood is dense and heavy and is noted for its strength and toughness. Hickory veneer, including that of the pecan, makes beautiful paneling. Hickory wood has long been used for the flavor it imparts in smoking hams and bacons, and bourbon is cured in charred hickory barrels. These native shellbark and shagbark hickories should be prized wherever they grow. Even if the nuts are not of high quality, the enterprising gardener who knows how to graft can topwork the trees to named cultivars bearing good, easily cracked nuts with large meats.

Hickories are not to be planted or tended by the impatient, and even experienced tree growers are occasionally frustrated by the slow growth of young seedlings or transplants. But in old fields and developing forests these slow-growing seedlings somehow avoid being crowded out by other vegetation. Sprouts that grow from the roots of a felled hickory grow much faster than seedlings. While a young pecan transplant can be brought into bearing in only five years, a shagbark hickory on upland soil might take from fifteen to twenty years, and a shellbark hickory would take somewhere between five and fifteen.

The challenge to nut growers and amateur gardeners is to find hickories for the colder climates that regularly bear good nuts, even when the trees are young. Trees with exceptionally fine nuts have been noted among the native hickories, and the best of them have been named and propagated by grafting. They have been selected not so much for absolute size or even thinness of shell as for their ability to give up the kernel when cracked. While the kernels of the better cultivars can be extracted in whole halves, it is often difficult to extract more than an occasional quarter from many of the native seedlings; this is because of the way the kernel is bound by the convolutions of the shell. However, shagbark hickory trees vary greatly in the size, shape, and shell thickness of their nuts. In hickory groves of the Midwest, no two trees may have nuts shaped exactly the same. Seasoned hickory nut hunters examine all the trees to find the ones from which they can crack out kernels in whole halves.

Some of the better nut-bearing shagbark hickory cultivars are Davis, Fox, Porter, and Wilcox. Shellbark cultivars of note include Keystone, Nieman, Ross, and Stephens. Although these are not available through the usual nursery, specialized nut tree nurseries may have what you want. For sources of graft wood, you can turn to members of one of the many state nut grower groups or members of the Northern Nut Growers Association.

Shagbark, shellbark, and pecan can all be intergrafted—that is, any one can be used as a stock for the others. Also, bitternut hickory, *C. cordiformis,* can be used as stock for pecan. If any of these hickory species are growing on your property, then all you have to do is topwork them with graft wood of a selected cultivar. This is by far a faster way to get good hickory nuts than planting a small, grafted seedling. An alternative method is to plant a young seedling and, once it is established, graft it to one or more select-ed cultivars. The pignut hickory, *C. glabra* and *C. ovalis,* and mockernut hickory, *C. tomentosa,* have nuts of little value and are unsatisfactory stock plants for the other hickory species.

Black Walnut. Black walnuts *(Juglans nigra)* were valued by Indians for food long before the white man arrived in North America. Colonists soon came to appreciate not just the nuts but the handsome wood as well. Antique walnut furniture is prized today, and old barns in Ohio and Indiana show walnut beams thirty feet long and a foot thick. Nonetheless, until a few years ago, some farmers were still stapling fence wire to the trunks of these superior trees, and nuts often went ungathered.

Times change swiftly, however, and today the black walnut is truly a money tree in the eastern half of the United States. Choice veneer logs sell for several dollars per foot, on the stump—boosting the price to several hundred dollars for a single tree. In fact, rustlers armed with power saws and knowledge of the demand for top-grade walnut are a growing menace.

The once-neglected fruit of the black walnut gets a lot of attention, too. Processors cannot keep pace with demand, even though they set up hulling and buying stations each fall in walnut country and collect sixty million pounds or more of this black gold.

The black walnut has a natural range from Connecticut through southern Minnesota, southward to Florida and Texas. It grows best on fertile, limestone-derived soils that are nearly neutral in pH. The commercial range for wood production is smaller than the natural range, while nut production extends somewhat beyond the natural range. Black walnuts can be found in virtually all of the forty-eight contiguous states.

Commercial shelling is centered in the southern Midwest and relies almost entirely on nuts collected from wild trees. However, selected cultivars that produce larger, better-quality nuts are being planted on thousands of acres. These trees will produce nuts for from twenty-five to fifty years and then be harvested for the wood. During early stages of such plantings, the space between trees is used for other crops, such as hay, pasture, or berries.

Even the shells are used, coarsely ground for use in sandblasters and other polishing equipment, and finely ground for fillers in plastics and glues. Other major uses of walnut shells include cleaning compounds for jet aircraft engines and drilling-mud for oil field operations.

Black walnut.   **Butternut.**   **Chestnut.**

Selected cultivars for planting cost more than seedling trees, but nuts are superior. There are over one hundred named varieties, although many are no longer being propagated because better selections have made them obsolete. As with other plants of wide geographic range, it's usually best to grow rootings, cuttings, and grafts in about the same climatic area from which they originally came. For instance, black walnuts originating south of a planting site start growth earlier in the spring and grow more during the year, but this early growth makes them vulnerable to frost damage. Generally, it is best to use trees that originate within 150 miles north or south of where you will plant them. Some walnuts selected for nut production, and their state of origin are: Michigan (Michigan); Mintle (Iowa); Ohio (Ohio); Sparrow (Illinois); Stabler (Maryland); and Thomas (Pennsylvania). The present selection emphasis is on trees with upright growth that will produce good nut crops, even when grown for timber.

While most of us are familiar with newspaper accounts of black walnut trees worth several hundred or even a few thousand dollars, don't slip into thinking that growing these trees is an easy way for you or your children to get rich. A good site for walnut and good planting stock are only the first of many requirements. Growing the trees into good specimens requires constant attention to weed and brush control, pruning, and thinning. Many a potentially valuable walnut log has been spoiled because of a crook, unpruned branch, damage from grazing animals, or marks of nails or staples driven into the trunk.

For the homeowner, however, the black walnut does make a lovely, large shade tree. The nuts are without equal as a condiment in baked goods because, unlike most other nuts, they do not lose their flavor in the cooking process.

The black walnut and some other walnuts can have an effect

on nearby plants. Kentucky bluegrass is apparently improved in quality and quantity under black walnut trees, and this is a good reason to use the tree for shade pastures. However, the black walnut doesn't get along with some plants: apples, tomatoes, potatoes, alfalfa, and members of the heath family may be killed if they come in contact with the roots. A toxic substance called juglone is responsible, and it has been found in walnut roots and nut hulls.

No other native American tree has wood as valuable as that of the black walnut. If you also consider the value of the nuts as food and the tree's ornamental value, this native could be called a diamond in the rough. And like a diamond, the black walnut becomes truly valuable only after it has been tended and cared for.

Persian (English) Walnut. Persian or English? The proper common name of *Juglans regia* is often a point of confusion. The tree came to be known as English because the nuts were carried on English ships, but was never extensively grown in Great Britain; it has come to be called Persian because of its supposed place of origin.

Hardy strains grown in southeastern Canada and the eastern United States are referred to as Carpathians. The popularity and wide distribution of these hardy Persian walnuts in eastern North America can be traced directly to the seed collected by the Reverend Paul C. Crath from the Carpathian Mountains of Poland in the 1930s. Actually, hardy walnuts had been introduced to the United States as early as the 1700s in the pockets of German emigrants, and trees raised from these seeds and their offspring can still be found near old homesites in Pennsylvania and neighboring states. The term Carpathian is now extended to include all hardy Persian walnuts, including those from the Ukraine, Russia, Czechoslovakia, and Germany.

This cold-hardy race of Persian walnuts is adapted to the northern latitudes ranging from approximately 35 to 45 degrees north latitude, or from Ottawa, Ontario, to Chattanooga, Tennessee. Early fall freezes, late spring frosts, and extreme winter cold can discourage the species to the north, and fluctuating warm and cold spells in winter limit its range in the South. When fully dormant, Carpathian trees can withstand −35°F., but these same trees can be injured by −10°F. if the cold has followed a warm winter spell.

Persian walnuts start growth early in the spring. To avoid injury from frosts they must be planted on slopes with good air drainage, rather than in low areas where cold air collects on still nights. New growth and developing blossoms are commonly injured in such frost pockets.

The Carpathian walnut tree is of medium height, is rounded in form, and has smooth, light gray bark and ample foliage. The leaves have a pleasing fragrance. This tree looks fine on a lawn, along fence lines, or along a street.

The trees are usually grown from seedlings, since that is all that is offered by nurseries. This is unfortunate, considering that each seedling is at least slightly different from every other. Ideally, nut growers select trees for hardiness, nut quality, and nut production, and many named cultivars have resulted. Their wider distribution is limited only by the difficulties of grafting and budding or rooting cuttings. The preferred rootstock is the eastern black walnut, *J. nigra*. Of the many selections that have been named, only a few can be mentioned here. One of the most highly thought of is Hansen. Assumed to be of German origin, it produces a surprisingly small nut, but the shell is thin and full of kernel and the tree bears annually. While most named cultivars consist of about fifty percent shell and fifty percent nut meat by weight, the Hansen has sixty percent kernel. Other named cultivars of merit include Metcalfe, Fickes, Somers, Broadview, and Lake.

As with the other trees discussed, it is safe to assume that newer and better selections of Carpathian will be made and propagated. Also, as improved selections are widely tested, individual cultivars will prove to be best adapted for certain areas. There are good reasons based on differences in soil and climate to assume, for instance, that the best cultivars for Illinois will not necessarily thrive in Connecticut.

Persian walnuts are an important commercial crop in the West, particularly in California, but in Oregon, Washington, Idaho, and southwestern Arizona as well. The trees are not tolerant of extremely low temperatures, but when fully dormant they will generally withstand from 12° to 15°F. without serious injury. Persian walnut production in the West is close to 100,000 tons a year with a return to the growers approaching fifty million dollars.

In areas where Persian walnuts do so well commercially, it seems that backyard gardeners often see no novelty or merit in growing their own trees. This is unfortunate, because Persians are handsome shade trees and bear an abundance of tasty, easy-to-crack nuts. Unlike the black walnut and butternut, which have a persistent husk, the Persian walnut drops free with little work.

In contrast to the Carpathian seedlings grown in the East, virtually all the plantings in the West are of named cultivars. You should be able to purchase some of the better named cultivars through contacts with growers, nursery people, and state extension agents. Among those looked on favorably are Ashley, Eureka, Franquette, Hartley, Nugget, and Payne.

For over sixty years the common rootstock for grafted Persian walnuts was the northern California black walnut, *J. hindsii.* But in recent years a disease (actually a graft incompatibility) called black line has limited the use of this species for a stock. Black line failure may be due to a virus or viruslike agent; it is an insidious disease in that the tree may be healthy for twenty years and in the peak of production when, over a period of two or three years, it will decline due to a failure at the graft union and then die. The preferred rootstocks are generally seedlings of the Manchurian walnut, another race of Persian walnut. These make good rootstocks and, like the Carpathians, are apparently adapted to a colder climate. In California, natural hybrids between the northern Californian black walnut and the Persian walnut, called Paradox hybrids by Luther Burbank, are common rootstocks.

All tests show that Persian walnuts are self- and cross-compatible. A common problem that prevents fruit set is that the pollen and pistils on any one tree mature at different times. To ensure cross-pollination, at least two different cultivars need to be planted; because young trees produce little pollen, three or more trees would be even better. If there are other Persian walnuts flowering within a few hundred feet, you should have no problem in planting a single tree.

Butternut. The butternut, *Juglans cinerea,* is one of our most neglected native nut trees. It is found in approximately the same area as the eastern black walnut but its range extends farther north and often to less favorable sites. Butternut can thrive on upland soils, especially if plenty of moisture is present, and the tree has proved to be hardy in areas where the temperature drops as low as −50°F. in the winter.

The nuts hang in clusters of up to nine in number. The nut shell is rough and convoluted. The fruit within have a fleshy husk similar to that of the black walnut and can be a nuisance to remove; however, the husk can be left on and allowed to thoroughly air-dry so that it becomes papery and will crumble if abraded in the hands (use gloves) or underfoot. Unfortunately, nuts of many seedling trees do not readily give up the nut meat when the shell is cracked because the inner convolutions of the shell may bind the kernel. Selections of butternut have been made, however, which yield large nuts and kernels that can be extracted in whole halves. Chamberlin, Craxeasy, Kinneyglen, and Love are four such varieties. For the present, you will find it almost impossible to locate a supplier of grafted butternut trees, and until such propagators are found or come forward, the rest of us shall either have to be content with seedling trees and the variation inherent in them or else do our own grafting.

In addition to its hardiness, the butternut is easily transplanted and bears at an early age—just four years from transplanting. When grown in the open, the tree spreads out into a low, massive form with sturdy limbs. It has an attractive, smooth, light-colored bark, and grows rapidly to a mature height of up to thirty-five feet and twice as broad. The wood is light colored, strong, warpless, and durable, and is a favorite of wood-carvers. One problem with older trees on poor sites is that they may suffer from a disease called juglans dieback. This affliction begins as a twig dieback and eventually spreads to larger branches, killing the tree. Dropping leaves monitor the progress of the disease. The only way to check it is to prune affected branches back to sound wood.

Japanese or Siebold Walnut and Heartnut. The Siebold walnut, *J. sieboldiana,* was introduced to this country around 1870. It is closely related to the butternut and is often referred to as the Japanese walnut. The heartnut is merely a particular kind of Siebold walnut characterized by a smooth-shelled, heart-shaped nut. An outstanding attribute of most heartnuts is that, if set on edge and tapped on the suture with a hammer, they will cleave into two halves and the kernel may be easily removed. Luther Burbank noted that the two nut forms came rather haphazardly from seed. Included among seedlings raised from heartnuts would be some bearing the small, round, butternutlike nuts. If these were then planted, some of the seedlings would bear heartnuts. There is no difference in the leaves or tree growth of the two kinds.

Like the butternut, the Siebold grows rapidly as a young tree and becomes low and wide branching. The trees have an exotic appearance with their large compound leaves and unique, long strings of nuts (up to twenty per cluster).

Although the Siebold walnut was introduced in the Southwest, it is now grown more extensively in the northeastern United States and southern Ontario. It is not worth planting in the pecan territory and is not valued where the Persian walnut thrives. Bunch disease, perhaps caused by a virus, has been a problem in some plantings. Affected plants have bushy growth and undersized leaves, causing the branches to somewhat resemble feather dusters. Nuts of seedlings are often small, but the named cultivars (virtually all of them heartnut types) have been selected for size as well as easy cracking. Fodermaier, Marvel, Mitchell, and Wright are selections that have been propagated to some extent.

When grown near each other, the butternut and Siebold walnuts will often cross-pollinate, resulting in vigorous hybrids that usually have the tree shape of the Siebold walnut and the nut characteristics of the butternut. The hybrids retain their leaves much later in the season than the butternut and, like the Japanese walnut, are resistant to juglans dieback. Thus they make better shade trees than either parent and bear fairly good nuts. The Grietz and Helmick are two such named, selected hybrids.

The Persian walnut is closely related to the Siebold and butternut, and in mixed plantings it may hybridize with these two species. This could produce trees with some outstanding attributes; in time, perhaps a low, spreading tree like the Siebold walnut might reward the experimenter, having the hardiness of the butternut and the nut size, flavor, and cracking quality of a Persian walnut. Such mixed plantings are not likely to result in a tree with the wood quality of the eastern black walnut, however. Black walnut is more distantly related and more discreet in its cross-pollination behavior.

Chestnut. Do you remember the American chestnut, *Castanea dentata*? Unless you are over sixty the chances are that you do not. Perhaps the first image to come to mind is of vendors in the city peddling hot roasted chestnuts, but most of those chestnuts are actually imported from southern Europe. Few recall that this stately tree was at the turn of the century the most important hardwood in the deciduous forests of the eastern United States. The American chestnut went into utility poles, railroad ties, mine timbers, fence posts, and tannin for leather. Today, this giant of the forest is gone, reduced to a shrub by a fungus disease introduced from Asia in the late 1800s. The disease was discovered in New York City in 1904 and by 1940 had completed its march through the eastern forests to the Smokey Mountains. Only a few large trees, isolated escapees, still grow in the Midwest and West, but the nostalgia for this magnificent tree, its timber, nuts, and shade continues on. This is true not only of the older generation, but surprisingly of younger Americans as well—people who never chanced to see a chestnut forest or perhaps even a large tree.

Part of the reason for the popularity of the chestnut, aside from the attributes of the American chestnut, is the blight-resistant quality of varieties introduced from the Orient, especially the Chinese chestnut, *C. mollissima*. The USDA made large importations of nuts of this species in the 1920s and the trees have been widely distributed and tested. They are not impressive forest trees but have a spreading habit similar to an apple tree, growing to a mature height of thirty-five to fifty feet. The better seed sources produce fine seedlings that bear annual crops of high quality nuts, and the trees are generally resistant to the chestnut blight fungus.

A few large plantings of Chinese chestnuts have been established in the southeastern United States. Whether chestnut orchards will ever be highly successful commercial ventures will depend not so much on the demand for the nuts as on the ability of growers to rapidly mechanize harvesting and other operations. In the climatic areas favorable to peaches, Chinese chestnut is one of the most popular backyard nut trees. A survey made in 1963 reported that chestnut trees were growing in virtually every state in the Union excepting a few of the dry Rocky Mountain states. With irrigation, the chestnut could probably be grown even in these dry areas. The Chinese chestnut can grow in a wide area if the soil is acidic and well drained, and if the trees are not located in a frost pocket. Hardiness varies; in general the Chinese variety is fully hardy from $-15°$ to $-20°$F. when dormant.

Several varieties of Chinese chestnut trees have been selected for their outstanding production of large, high-quality nuts. Among those most widely distributed are the USDA cultivars Crane, Nanking, and Orrin. (Eaton, a hybrid with predominantly Chinese chestnut characteristics, is a recent Connecticut selection that is best suited to the Northeast and areas with a short growing season.)

Unlike most other tree nuts grown for human consumption, chestnuts are high in starch and comparatively low in protein and oil. The nuts are borne in a very spiny burr that contains between one and three nuts. The burr opens and releases the nuts to the ground in the fall. The nuts have a high moisture content when harvested and are susceptible to drying, unlike nuts high in oil. Their somewhat perishable nature has to be recognized, but when handled properly they have a long shelf life.

After harvest they should be allowed to air-dry for two or three days and then refrigerated at 32° to 40°F. in closed plastic bags containing paper toweling or other moisture-absorbing material. Molding can be a problem if the nuts are too moist; if free moisture collects in the bags, there is a good chance that mold will form. On the other hand, nuts stored in open containers will rapidly dry and become very hard. This is not all bad because they can then be peeled and made usable for cooking by boiling in water. When dried, nuts can be stored for a long time. Another convenient way to preserve the nuts is to boil them for three to five minutes in water (to make peeling easier) and then freeze the kernels for later use. There are literally hundreds of uses for chestnuts in soups, vegetables, and desserts. They are great roasted or fried in butter and salt and taste great in turkey dressing.

Besides the American and Chinese chestnut, there are eleven different species of chestnut, and several are worth noting. The European chestnut, *C. sativa,* is cultivated in southern Europe and unfortunately is susceptible to the chestnut blight fungus as well as a root rot called ink disease. The Japanese chestnut, *C. crenata,* is usually as blight resistant as the Chinese chestnut but it is often not as vigorous a tree and the nuts are of inferior quality. (The sweetest nuts were certainly those of the American chestnut. They were tasty eaten fresh, but were very small compared to the more bland European chestnut.)

Several species bearing small nuts and just one per burr are collectively called chinkapins. They are native to the southeastern United States and are usually shrublike. Although the nuts are tasty, their small size (3/8 inch diameter) limits their value as a food crop for man. They are appreciated by wildlife and the nuts seldom go to waste.

A great deal of effort has been spent developing hybrid chestnut trees that would have many of the fine attributes of the American chestnut with the blight resistance of the Chinese or Japanese chestnut. Progress has been slow but recent advances indicate that cuttings of selected chestnut trees can be rooted (this was not previously feasible) so that it should be possible to test more adequately some of the new hybrids. In addition to hybrids that have good form and vigor there are others selected for ornamental use and food-producing value for wildlife. Some of the more intriguing of these are dwarfs that bear large nuts at an early age— ideal trees for the small yard.

Filbert. The filbert (also known as hazel) is an easily grown and desirable nut tree that is suitable for home cultivation. The trees are smaller than those of other hardy nuts and may be easily established; coming into bearing in four to five years, they yield fair crops annually under favorable conditions. Filberts are useful for odd bits of fertile ground around farm buildings and look good on lawns. They can even be used as a tall hedge if grown as shrubs. However, closely planted trees are less productive and hedges are not likely to bear heavily.

Fifteen species of filbert are now recognized. Some are small or large shrubs, and others are trees. The two most widely grown in the United States for their nuts are the native American filbert or hazel, *Corylus americana,* and the European filbert, *C. avellana.* The American filbert is native from New England to Saskatchewan, and south to Georgia and Oklahoma. The nuts are relatively small, and the tree is valuable for nut production only where the European filbert is not handy. Rush and Winkler are two of the better American filbert selections.

The European filbert is the only species extensively cultivated for its nuts. Commercial production in the United States is limited to an area west of the Cascade Mountains in Oregon and Washington. The important cultivars are Barcelona, Nooksack, and DuChilly. In the East the success of European filberts has been limited by the lack of catkin (flower) hardiness in the winter and by the eastern filbert blight. The cultivars Italian Red, Medium Long,

Hazelnut.

and Cosford have been the three most reliably productive and winter-hardy.

Fortunately, hybrids between the two species combine some of the best traits of the parent species; Bixby and Buchanan are two such selected hybrids. Additional selection and hybridization hold forth the promise of even better hybrids that will be adapted for particular areas of the country.

Filberts sucker freely and grow naturally as shrubs. In commercial orchards of the Northeast, the suckers are generally removed and the plants are grown with a single stem as a tree. In the East this is not generally practical; the suckers are left but are usually thinned to five or six in number to encourage vigorous growth and fruiting. Growers take advantage of the suckering habit in propagating the filbert. Stool beds are formed in which the suckers are layered into the soil, wounded, and rooted to develop new plants.

Thievery of nuts by wildlife, especially squirrels and chipmunks, is a threat to the crop of any nut grower, and filberts have to be among the most susceptible to predator damage. While a chipmunk will not go up into a tall tree, the shrubby filbert is just to his liking. The only way to keep the squirrels out is to completely screen the plants, but this is a costly and impractical method. Trunks of tall, isolated trees can be covered with metal flashing to prevent squirrels from climbing. While walnut husks have bitter tannin and chestnut husks have spines to inhibit squirrels at least a little, there seems to be no such natural safeguards to protect the filbert. Indeed, these trees apparently spread naturally because the busy rodents take so many of the nuts that they forget where they buried them all.

Almond. The almond, *Prunus amygdalus,* originated in southwest Asia and is adapted to hot, dry, and even poor soils. It differs greatly from the other nut trees in that it is in the rose family and is a close relative to other stone fruits such as the peach. It is about as hardy as the peach but other requirements limit the area in which it can be successfully grown. After a relatively brief chilling period in the winter, followed by a few warm days, the flowers will open. In many climates this trait of early flowering exposes the trees to killing frosts. For proper maturation of the fruit, almonds need a long, hot growing season with low prevailing humidity to discourage hull rot. The best growing conditions have been found in the Sacramento and San Joaquin Valleys of California and, to a limited extent, in other southwestern states.

The almond fruit has a thin, leathery, inedible hull which splits open when mature to expose the seed (nut) that contains the edible kernel. The fruit differs from the peach in that it has no thick fleshy pulp surrounding the seed. The most important cultivars grown in California are Nonpareil, Texas Prolific (Mission), Ne Plus Ultra, and Peerless. New cultivars are continually being introduced.

One selection, Hall's Hardy (also called Ridenhower), has been promoted by mail-order nurseries in the East, but to some the flavor is bitter and unpleasant. This quality discourages growers in the eastern and central states who would otherwise take advantage of its relatively late bloom and lack of the need for cross-pollination. Unless you live in an area with a climate like that of the San Joaquin Valley, it is probably best to try some other variety of nut tree.

Apricot. The apricot kernel can be more than just something to spit out: the idea of harvesting a good fruit crop of apricots, *Prunus armeniaca,* and then being able to crack the seeds for the edible kernels is appealing to many growers. Although most apricots have bitter kernels, those of some cultivars are sweet and reportedly much better flavored than the Hall's Hardy almond. In the commercial apricot growing areas of California, the kernels are recovered for use as an almond substitute. Unfortunately, not many kinds of apricots have been tested and developed for their sweet kernels. The Vineland Horticultural Research Institute, Ontario, has identified four selections with sweet kernels: Reliable, Montgamet, 510915, and 60031; the latter two will presumably be named and released for propagation.

Site requirements for apricots are similar to those for peaches, although apricots must also have good air drainage to avoid late spring frosts. They flower early in the spring and ripen a week or two before peaches.

Macadamia. The macadamia, *Macadamia integrifolia* and *M. tetraphylla,* is native to the subtropical regions of Australia, particularly the state of Queensland, and is sometimes called the Queensland nut. It was first introduced to Hawaii in 1878 and has become the third most important crop on the islands, following pineapple and sugarcane. It is not adapted to a large area of the United States, but where it will grow it is the preferred nut tree.

The macadamia grows on fairly heavy clay soils and can handle temperatures ranging from 115° down to 26°F., and in a dormant state may withstand temperatures as low as 20°F. for brief periods. In its native habitat the rainfall is between 60 and 90 inches a year, but the macadamia can survive on as little as 40 inches, and some productive orchards in Hawaii have a natural rainfall of up to 200 inches a year.

The trees do well in southwestern California, within fifty miles of the coast and ranging from San Luis Obispo to Mexico. They can also be grown in southern Florida. In addition to the value of the nuts (it tends to be everbearing), the macadamia is widely used as an ornamental in landscaping homes, parks, and highways. The bright evergreen foliage is attractive and the flowers are very showy. Nuts are borne in clusters of from ten to twenty. Beaumont, a pink-flowered cultivar, is recommended as a dual-purpose ornamental nut tree.

Pistachio. The pistachio, *Pistacia vera,* has been cultivated since before recorded history and is apparently native to south central Asia. It is grown from Pakistan westward through Syria and the island of Cyprus. In the United States, the pistachio succeeds where almonds thrive; they do best in the southwestern United States, especially the Sacramento and San Joaquin Valleys of California, since the summer temperatures are high, the humidity low, and there is a minimum of danger from late spring frosts. Unlike the early flowering almond, the pistachio blooms immediately after most peaches and cherries.

The pistachio is a relatively new crop to the United States. Much of the recent work with new cultivars and cultural practices had been done at the USDA Plant Introduction Station, Chico, California, which was closed down in 1973 for reasons of economy. However, an industry has been started and hopefully it will continue to thrive. Homeowners and small landowners who live in the right areas can take advantage of several popular cultivars: Kermen, Bronte, Trabonella, and Red Aleppo are among the best.

When nuts are ripe they are commonly shaken or knocked from the trees onto sheets with poles. Commercial processors dehull the freshly harvested nuts in abrasive tumble machines similar to electric potato peelers and then dry them on trays in the sun. It's interesting to note that relatives of the pistachio include such diverse plants as cashew, mango, sumac, and poison ivy.

Pistachio plants are like hollies in that they have the sexes on separate plants. They are wind-pollinated, and male trees (the pollinators) must be spaced to take advantage of the prevailing winds. One male tree is usually adequate for up to a dozen female pistachio trees.

Oak. The most common and abundantly produced nuts in North America are generally ignored by man—the acorns of our many oak species, *Quercus*. They contain a bitter substance called tannin that makes them unpalatable, but some of the white oaks are relatively sweet.

The Indians made considerable use of acorns, crushing the kernels and boiling them in several changes of water to remove the tannin and to produce an acorn flour. A few sweet-tasting white oaks have been named, but the best are most notable not for flavor but merely their lack of bitterness. The real value of oaks is in the food they supply to wildlife and to domestic animals such as swine.

Beech. The American beech, *Fagus grandifolia*, is the only beech native to North America; it grows in the eastern states and west to Texas and Wisconsin. In general appearance and requirements it is similar to the commonly planted European beech, *F. sylvatica*. The small, triangular nuts are borne in pairs in prickly burrs. Regrettably, these tasty nuts are not often plentiful, and most trees bear irregularly with several years between crops. With a few exceptions, little effort has been made to select superior nut-bearing types, and none has been widely distributed. (In 1926 Williard Bixby located two trees with relatively large nuts and named the trees Abrams and Abundance. More recently, Fred Ashworth named a tree that bears large nuts annually, the Jenner beech).

Pine. Several pines produce a large seed containing an oily, edible kernel that tastes somewhat like a sunflower seed. In the Southwest there are four closely related edible pines collectively called pinyon pines. These were an important food source for the native Indians, and their nuts are still valuable as a cash crop. Today, the real value of these nut pines is not in the quantity of nuts produced (the annual yield per tree is not great), but in their novelty and value in the landscape. While the trees are not usually cultivated, they are the favored nut of the region.

The digger pine, *Pinus sabiniana,* is another nut pine. This one is native to the foothills and high valleys of coastal California where it exists on very dry and gravelly soils through the nearly rainless summer. The Italian stone pine, *P. pinea,* from the Mediterranean, is another with tasty seed kernels and has adapted to warmer parts of the country where temperatures do not go much below 20°F. For colder climates, with winter temperatures as low as −40°F., there is the Korean pine, *P. koraiensis.*

PROPAGATING NUT TREES

A number of small landowners and homesteaders have found an interesting hobby in growing nut tree seedlings and grafting onto them the best-known cultivars. Some growers have space for all these seedlings, and others give them away to friends. The grafting techniques are easily learned and scions are available at low cost from nurseries and other hobbyists. Grafting is not limited to within species: for example, black walnut is a desirable rootstock for not only black walnut but Persian walnut, Siebold walnut, heartnut, and butternut as well.

The easiest means of propagating nut trees is to start from seed. However, because of genetic variation within the parents, seedlings will not give rise to trees that are identical to the parents. If you want either a Chinese chestnut or a black walnut without special characteristics, a seedling will do. But if you want a proven, good-bearing tree, it must be vegetatively propagated by the grafting, budding, layering, or rooting of cuttings; also, vegetatively propagated trees are required whenever a particular selection (a named cultivar) is needed.

Seed Propagation. Chestnuts, walnuts, hickories, filberts, and most other nuts of our temperate climate trees are incapable of germinating at the time of harvest. A period of moist, cold treatment (stratification) overcomes this built-in dormancy, and they are then capable of germinating. Moist seeds are subjected to temperatures just above freezing for two to four months before planting. Seed planted outdoors in the fall receives this treatment naturally in all but the warmest parts of the country. Seed stored for spring planting should be kept cold (32° to 40°F.) and moist (mixed in with barely damp peat moss) in plastic bags.

Grafting, Budding, and Layering. These techniques are covered in Chapter 4. Generally, hardy nut trees are more difficult to graft and bud than fruit trees. Layering or stooling is used commonly only for filbert.

Rooting. The rooting of cuttings of walnut, hickory, filbert, and chestnut has been almost impossible. Recently, however, experiments by Dr. Loy Shreve of Kansas State University indicate that rooting is possible by wounding the parent tree to force adventitious shoots or suckers from the tree's base. Cuttings from these shoots are then treated with high concentrations of auxin (plant hormone) and placed under mist. Hopefully, the method will be adapted by commercial growers so that many presently unavailable cultivars will come on the market.

Spacing. In the past it was common practice to plant fruit and nut trees at wide spacing. But, as new cultivars are selected for precocious bearing and as it becomes apparent that pruning and spraying are more easily done on small trees, many growers now plant trees at closer spacings. While trees at forty-foot centers were once common, many Persian walnut plantings are now going in at twenty-five- and thirty-foot centers.

The number of trees per acre can readily be computed by dividing 43,560 (the number of square feet in an acre) by the product of the planting distance between trees. Thus, with trees spaced 25 feet by 25 feet, the product is 625, and this number divided into

43,560 equals 70 plants per acre. The chart gives the number of plants per acre for a few spacings.

PLANTS PER ACRE

$4 \times 16 = 681$	$16 \times 16 = 170$	$25 \times 25 = 70$
$8 \times 8 = 681$	$20 \times 20 = 109$	$30 \times 30 = 48$
$10 \times 20 = 218$	$20 \times 40 = 54$	$40 \times 40 = 16$

WILDLIFE PLANTINGS

Although growers often wish it weren't so, the main consumers of nuts are wildlife. Animals use this high value food to fatten up in the fall, and the long storage life of nuts ensures that this food can be used during the winter and spring months.

The ubiquitous squirrels are the most obvious gatherers and consumers of nuts. Each requires approximately a hundred pounds of food a year, and this diet may be composed of as high as seventy-five percent nuts. Where oaks are common, most of these nuts will be acorns; interestingly, the sweeter white oak fruit are taken first, and the nuts of the black oaks, bitter with tannin, are left for leaner days.

In an oak forest, deer may actually consume more acorns than the squirrels. Game birds—such as turkey, pheasants, quail, and ducks—and some song birds also eat large quantities. Fluctuations of squirrel and game animal populations is often correlated with the availability of nuts. It appears that the demise of the native chestnut was in part responsible for the decline of the wild turkey.

Attracting wildlife to nut trees is seldom a problem, but to lure the wilder species, try to locate the plantings near wooded areas. Although wild animals will cross open fields to find food, they prefer to have access with cover. Wooded areas such as lanes along fencerows are ideal. (It is not a good idea to plant nut trees along busy streets and highways—dropping fruit can be a nuisance, and it attracts wildlife and children to a dangerous place.) On the other hand, if plantings are to be protected from squirrels and other game, it is best that they be isolated from forested areas, with no easy access through dense ground vegetation or by aerial routes. Squirrels can gain access to nut trees by traveling from tree to tree and even along utility lines. To prevent squirrels from climbing isolated trees, you can wrap the trunks about five feet from the ground with a two- or three-foot strip of aluminum.

Local site conditions will determine the best kind of nut to plant to attract wildlife. You should choose trees that are abundant, annual producers of food. Annual production is important to avoid a feast or famine situation, and in this respect the Chinese chestnut is one of the best game food plants available.

HARVESTTIME: NUTS, SHELLS, AND WOOD

It is strange but true that there are people who have patiently waited five to ten years for their nut trees to bear and then, when the first big harvest came, they didn't know what to do with the nuts. And others often purchase property with nut trees and don't appreciate what they've got. Some people try chestnuts once, uncooked, and decide they don't care for them. What they fail to realize is that there are literally hundreds of ways to serve chestnuts, from hors d'oeuvres through soups and stews to dessert. We shall not go into recipes here but the uses of the energy- and vitamin-rich nuts are limited only by your imagination.

To be sure, black walnuts are a bit of a nuisance for the average homeowner to dehull and crack. You might try putting on an old pair of work shoes and abrading the husks off by rolling the nuts under foot on a cement walk. Or, you could use an old corn sheller or even a small cement mixer to do the job; throw in a few stones and some water so that the husks are worn off the nuts as they tumble. Another way to husk walnuts is to dump them on a lane or driveway and drive over them with a car. In the course of a few days, the walnuts should be almost completely dehulled.

A hammer and anvil are adequate tools to crack most of the hard-shelled nuts, but for an investment of about ten dollars you can get a sturdy nut cracker. For cracking pecans there is a relatively new gadget called an inertia cracker that is fast and efficient for home use, in addition to being a real conversation piece.

When first harvested most nuts are "green," and the flavor improves by air-drying over a period of a month. Walnuts and hickories keep well when hung in coarse mesh bags in a cool garage or basement.

In time even good nut trees have to be cut down. While you may not be able to interest a sawmill in purchasing just a few logs, amateur carvers and cabinetmakers will come running if they get the word that there is some good nut tree wood available.

CHAPTER 4 Propagating, Grafting, and Pruning *by* JIM RITCHIE

A handcar squealed to a stop on a long railroad grade in central Missouri. In the woods below, a man sat on a stump, aiming a scope-mounted .22-caliber rifle at the top of a tall, straight cottonwood. The eyes of the railroad crew went first to the rifleman, then to the bare branches of the tree, then back again to the man aiming from the stump.

Zing! The rifle spat, and a long, straight twig toppled from high up on the tree.

The railroad crew looked at each other, then started their handcar and putt-putted out of sight around the bend of the tracks. They likely thought the man with the rifle had gone around the bend in a different way. But he was completely sane and knew exactly what he was doing. Gene Brunk is a tree improvement specialist with the Missouri Conservation Department's forestry division and uses a rifle to collect limbs from superior trees. His objective is to find varieties (or clones) of different tree species that can be multiplied in state nurseries for replanting by foresters and landowners. But such professional foresters have no corner on tree propagation—many small landowners and homesteaders have developed interesting hobbies (and even well-paying businesses) by growing tree seedlings and grafting onto them the best-known cultivars. Others grow rootstock for nurseries and seedlings for forest tree plantings or Christmas trees.

Tree propagation is an exacting but not overly difficult skill. You can learn the techniques and with practice become a specialist in your own right.

PROPAGATING FROM SEED

Growing tree seedlings in a home nursery is much like growing garden plants for transplanting. It's the easiest means of propagating nut trees and many other tree species. You don't need a lot of space. For instance, you can grow 3,500 Scotch pine Christmas tree seedlings to their one-year size in a 3-by-10 foot seedbed.

The big drawback to growing trees from seed is the genetic variation that results—seedlings do not produce trees that are identical to the parent tree. If you want a Chinese chestnut, a black walnut, or an apple tree without any special characteristics, a seedling will do. But if you want a proven, good-bearing tree, it must be vegetatively propagated by grafting, budding, layering, or rooting of cuttings—techniques discussed later in this chapter.

Growing Nut Trees from Seed. Most nut trees of our temperate climate are incapable of germinating from seed at the time the nuts are harvested. A period of moist, cold treatment overcomes this built-in dormancy, and the seed then are capable of germinating when planted.

Nature takes care of stratification in the wild, but you also can gather, store, and plant nuts. We'll discuss black walnuts, but the same methods apply to chestnuts, hickories (including pecans), filberts, and most other native United States nut trees.

Collect seed in the fall, selecting nuts from tall, straight, thrifty trees. Crack a few nuts before storing them to make sure they're good. Nuts may be either hulled before storage or left unhulled. Store them in a cool, moist environment where they will be subject to the variations of winter temperature. Be sure to protect them from rodents. The stratifying bin shown here provides ideal storage

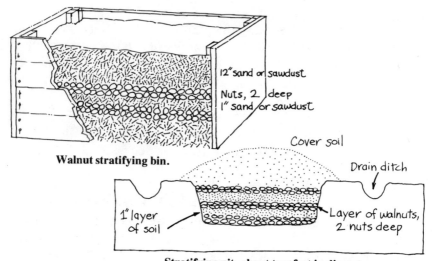

Walnut stratifying bin.

Stratifying pit, about two feet in diameter.

for walnuts. Alternate layers of sand or sawdust and walnuts in the box, and then cover with a foot of sawdust.

Nuts may also be planted as they fall from the tree, usually in autumn. Acorns often start sprouting vigorously soon after they hit the damp ground, and they should be planted immediately, covered with a thin layer of soil and mulch. A disadvantage to planting in fall is that the nuts are vulnerable to rodent appetites. One method of protection is to place the nut an inch or two from the bottom of a soil-filled tin can. Cut an **X** in the bottom, and bend the four sharp points outward. The resulting hole should be large enough for the emerging sprout. The can is then planted bottom up so that the sharp points will ward off mice, chipmunks, and squirrels. Or, unhulled nuts can be rolled around in a can of creosote, available in tarry form from hardware stores.

Plant nuts two or more per hill, as you would melons or squash. Inferior seedlings can be pulled out to leave a single good tree. If the planting site is covered with sod or dense weed growth, you may want to till or disk the area. If you are planting the nuts in a seedling bed, prepare the soil as you would for spring vegetable plantings. In soft ground—soil that has been tilled—you can merely drop a nut on the ground and use your heel to press it about two inches into the soil; kick dirt over the nut and tamp it firm with your foot. Or, you can use a sharp stick or iron bar to jab two-inch holes in the ground.

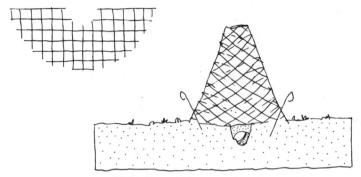

**Protective screen covers can
greatly reduce nut loss to rodents.**

For heavy sod, use a hoe or mattock to strip the sod from an area three feet square and dig holes two inches deep. Plant one nut to each hole and tamp the dirt over the nut. Use wire hardware cloth to form a cone-shaped shield against rodents, as illustrated, holding it in place with a wire rod. Remove the cone when seedlings are four to six inches tall.

Growing Evergreens from Seed. Raising coniferous trees (forest seedlings, lawn trees, or Christmas trees) from seed is more exacting, but you can master the technique with practice. One advantage to growing your own evergreen seedlings is that you can raise species not commonly offered for sale by commercial or state and federal nurseries. Also, you can use your homegrown trees for any purpose. State laws generally forbid the use of state or federal nursery seedlings for anything but reforestation, Christmas tree plantations, windbreaks, and other conservation uses; these seedlings cannot be planted within incorporated city limits and cannot be resold with roots intact.

As with nut trees, the recommended planting time for conifers is spring, as soon as the soil can be worked and the danger of killing frosts is past. Most viable seed will germinate within sixty days, and some push through the soil in only two weeks.

You can either collect your own seed cones and thresh out the seed, or order cleaned seed from a dealer. Your county extension agent or farm forester should have a list of seed dealers. Most dealers will send a price list on request; seed prices vary from year to year, depending on the supply.

If you can find good specimens of the desired trees growing in

Open cone has lost its seed

Closed cone still has seed

Collect closed cones only, preferably by picking them from trees.

your area, you may be better off collecting your own seed—particularly if there are no nearby seed dealers. Professional forest managers like to get seed from about the same elevation (within five hundred feet or so) and from locations near the area to be planted. Collect seed only from healthy trees having the form you desire in your own planting. It's important to note that open cones have lost their seed.

Even if you're planning a reforestation project, you may want to plant coniferous seed in a bed and transplant the seedlings at one or two years of age. Locate the growing bed in a deep, loose, sandy loam. Loosen heavy soils by adding and tilling in compost, peat moss, rotted sawdust, or other organic material; work the soil to spade depth, removing rocks, sticks, roots, and clods. Soil should be on the acid side, about 5.5 pH.

How large should beds be? Make yours any convenient size. For most small plantings 3-by-10 feet or 4-by-12 feet are adequate dimensions. Figure on forty to fifty seedlings per square foot of bed, unless you plan to leave the trees in the bed over two years.

As with other temperate-climate trees, coniferous seed needs to be treated to break dormancy. You can do this by the same method outlined earlier for stratifying nuts, or you can use the so-called naked stratification treatment:

1. Put the seed in a polyethylene bag with enough clean water to cover the seed. Close the bag and let the seed soak overnight, in a cool place but where the water will not freeze.

2. The next day, pour off the water and arrange the bag so that it will drain. Partly close the bag, leaving an opening about one-half inch in diameter, and place it in a cold place (35° to 40°F.). A home refrigerator works well.

3. At intervals, inspect the seed and remix them. If the seed begin to dry out, moisten them, making sure they don't freeze. You'll need to keep seed in this cold storage for at least two weeks before planting, and longer if possible.

4. When you're ready to plant, take the seed out and dry them slowly. Avoid direct sunlight and strong winds. When the outer surface of the seed is dry enough so that they will not stick together, plant them.

Protection from hot sun is vital to evergreen seedlings. Any dry soil with organic matter can get hot enough to kill first-year seedlings in one-half hour of direct hot sunlight. Place snow fence, slats, or other screening that lets fifty percent of the light through when set about twelve inches above the surface of the seedbed.

Growing Other Trees from Seed. Many attractive and useful species can be easily grown from seed. This takes a bit more patience than starting them from seedlings or small trees—but you can collect seed yourself, at no expense.

To help get you started collecting and growing seed, instructions for a number of trees follow. The information is taken from *Seeds of Woody Plants in the United States,* published in 1974 by the Forest Service, USDA, Washington, DC. This book details how to collect and propagate 187 genera of shrubs and trees; the trees that follow are only a sample.

Basic similarities run through the instructions for most species. The first step is accurately identifying the desired species in the field. A good key or illustrated guide is indispensable here. Timing is important in collecting seed or fruit, as the period between maturation and dispersal is often brief. Another complication is that fruit may take two or three years to develop.

Seed must often be treated before they will germinate in the seedbeds. One method is scarification, which involves working on impenetrable seedcoats with sulfuric acid or hot water, or mechanically scratching the surface. A second method is stratification, inducing changes within the seed to overcome dormancy. Typically, this is done by chilling the seed in a moist place. Temperatures usually run from 34° to 40°F. Aeration is needed to allow heat to escape from the seed.

Presowing treatments can often be avoided by sowing seed in the fall, thereby stratifying them naturally. In northern areas, fall-sown seed should be mulched over the winter and often must be covered with screens to ward off birds and rodents.

• *Acer* (maple). Winged maple seed spinning to the ground are a familiar sight. Plant them in fall in a mulched bed. It is possible, but less satisfactory, to sow stratified seed in spring. Exceptions are the red maple and silver maple, which should be sown soon after collection in late spring. Set the seed ¼ to one inch deep.

• *Aesculus* (buckeye, horsechestnut). To collect the fruit in number, shake the tree in fall, as soon as the capsules turn yellowish and begin to split open. The fruit can also be left to drop on their own and then gathered from the ground. Then, dry the fruit for a time at room temperature, without leaving them so long that the seed coats turn dull and wrinkled. Germination is hastened by stratifying the seed in moist sand, or a mixture of sand and peat, at 41°F. for 120 days. Exceptions to this treatment are the California buckeye *(A. californica)* and the red buckeye *(A. pavia)*, which need no stratification. Seed can be sown either after the drying period, in fall, or in spring after being stratified. Cover the seed with one to two inches of soil. Again, the California buckeye is an exception, germinating in November. Take care to avoid overwatering seedbeds, as the seed rot quite readily.

• *Alnus* (alder). Collect the cones from trees in late summer or fall, at the time the scales begin to open. Dry the seed indoors at room temperature in order to make them fall from their cones. Sow in spring at a depth of approximately ⅛ to ¼ inch. If seed have dried out greatly over the winter, it may be necessary to stratify them. Dormant seed have been successfully treated for thirty to sixty days at between 34° and 41°F.

• *Amelanchier* (serviceberry). The berrylike fruit turn dark purple to black when ripe, each containing four to ten seed. Pick the fruit soon after they ripen and before the birds get to them. Spread out the fruit to dry. Store the dry seed in sealed containers of 41°F. Either sow the seed in fall or stratify them and sow in spring. The seed may not come to life until the second spring. Cover the seed with ¼ inch of soil, and protect them over the winter with a mulch. Most species respond to a moist stratification period of two to six months at between 33° and 43°F.

• *Aronia* (chokecherry). Pick the fruit of this attractive ornamental soon after they ripen, or birds are likely to beat you to them. Whirl the fruit in a blender to separate the seed. Sow the seed in spring after two- to four-month's stratification at between 23° and 41°F. Seed should be set ⅜-inch deep.

• *Asimina* (pawpaw). Just as the fruit flesh turns soft, pick or shake the fruit from the tree. Seed can be either separated or planted in the fruit. Sow seed in fall, or stratify them (sixty days at 41°F.) and sow in spring at a depth of ¾ inches.

• *Betula* (birch). Pick the ripe, brown, woody catkins and put them into a bag to prevent loss of seed. Spread out the seed to dry for several weeks. Sow birch seed in late summer or fall, soon after they are collected (or in spring after stratifying four to eight weeks). Scatter the seed or cover with just a thin layer of soil. Give seedlings light shade through the first two or three months of their first summer.

• *Carpinus* (hornbeam). Pick the ripe, light greenish brown to brown fruit in late summer or fall, before they dry out. Dry them indoors, and then free the seed by beating the fruit in bags. Sow seed that fall, or stratify and plant in spring. The ideal soil is a moist, rich loam. Cover with ¼ to ½ inch of soil. Seed sown in fall should be mulched with burlap or other material until after spring's last frost. The soil should be moist until after germination, and the beds shaded lightly on the first year.

• *Maclura pomifera* (Osage orange). Pick up the fruit soon after they hit the ground. Extracting the seed is easier if the fruit are left outside over the winter in a pile; they will become soft and mushy. Seed can be planted in fall without treatment, or in spring if left out over the winter. Cover with ¼ to ½ inch of firmed soil. Mulch fall-sown beds.

• *Ostrya virginiana* (eastern hophornbeam). When the hoplike strobiles have turned a pale greenish brown in color, they are ready to be picked from the tree. Stratification is rather involved, but seed can be sown without treatment in fall. Cover with ¼ inch of firmed soil, and protect the beds with mulch over the winter. The mulch can be removed when germination begins.

• *Paulownia tomentosa* (royal paulownia). Pick the dried fruit anytime before they drop their seed. Propagate by surface sowing on moist, shaded nursery beds.

• *Photinia arbutifolia* (Christmas berry). Snip the pomes from the tree in fall, and soak them in water to ferment. The seed can then be separated from the resulting mash. Soak them in a warm place, no longer than necessary as they may be damaged by being in water for a long period. Germinate the fresh seed in sand or soil flats. There is no need to stratify seed if they are sown soon after collection. Christmas berry can also be propagated by grafting or taking cuttings.

• *Platanus* (sycamore). Collect the fruiting heads at anytime after they turn brown, but preferably after the leaves have fallen. No pregermination treatment is needed for the American sycamore and oriental plane tree, but the California sycamore benefits from moist stratification for two to three months at 40°F. in sand, peat, or sandy loam. While it is possible to plant in fall or late winter, spring is the best planting time. Cover seed with ¼ inch of soil or mulch. Seed sown in fall should be protected from birds by a screen.

• *Populus* (poplar). Cut catkins just as a few are beginning to open, and lay them on a pan or screen inside. Pick aspen catkins when the seed have turned a light straw color. Growing the seed successfully takes some doing, and you should read the detailed instructions given in *Seeds of Woody Plants in the United States*.

• *Prosopis juliflora* (mesquite). Either pick ripe pods from the tree or gather them from the ground. The pods should be set out to dry for several days at room temperature. Fresh seed do not need treatment to germinate successfully. Dried seed can be readied for germination by nicking the hard seed coat with a knife.

• *Pyrus* (pear). The common pear makes an attractive ornamental, although trees grown from seed will not normally produce outstanding fruit. The pears usually measure less than two inches long. Once fruit have started to fall, they are ready to yield seed for sowing. A period of stratification is needed to break the internal dormancy of the seed; use a temperature of from 32° to 36°F. for two to three months. First soak the seed for twenty-four hours in water, and place them in moist vermiculite in polyethylene bags. Unstratified seed can be sown in fall, stratified seed in spring. Cover with ½ to one inch of soil.

• *Quercus* (oak). All you need to prepare seed is to pluck off the acorn caps. The exception is that black oaks must be stratified before spring planting; use moist, well-drained soil, sand, and peat for thirty to ninety days at a temperature of from 32° to 41°F. Generally, planting in fall is recommended. The acorns of the white oak group will begin to germinate immediately, while those of the black oak group undergo a natural stratification over the winter.

Cover acorns with ¼ to one inch of firmed soil. Mulch fall beds with leaves or straw held down securely with screen to protect against both cold weather and rodents. Remove the mulch after the danger of frost has passed. Germination of acorns is favored by partial shade.

• *Rhododendron* (rhododendron). Once capsules have started to change from green to brown, they are ready to collect. Spread out the capsules to dry at room temperature. Germinate the seed in flats of sandy peat or sand and half-decayed oak leaves, covered with shredded or sifted sphagnum moss. The seed are sown on the surface and covered with a light sprinkling of sphagnum; this can be done in April in a cold frame, or in winter in a cool greenhouse.

• *Salix* (willow). Collect the seed as soon as the fruit capsules turn from green to yellowish; sow the seed immediately thereafter, broadcasting the seed on beds and going over the soil with a roller. Keep the seedbeds moist until the seedlings have got a good start.

• *Sassafras albidum* (sassafras). When the fruit turn from green to dark blue, they are ready to be picked for seed extraction. Seed can be stored over the winter by cleaning and putting them in sealed containers at a temperature of between 35° and 41°F. If seed are to be sown the same season they are collected, wait until late in fall so that they will not germinate prematurely. Cover seed with ¼ to ½ inch of firmed soil, and mulch and cover with screens until after the danger of frost passes.

• *Sorbus* (mountain ash). These attractive ornamentals may be propagated from seed of fruit picked as soon as they are ripe. Seed sown in fall needn't be stratified; just cover them with a very thin layer of soil.

• *Syringa* (lilac). Pick ripe capsules in the fall, and lay them out to ·dry in a room having good ventilation. Dry seed can be stored in a dry, well-aerated place for up to two years. Stratification some-times is an aid to seed planted in spring. Subject seed to 34° to 41°F. for one to three months. Fall-sown seed don't require treatment. Cover seed with ¼ to ⅜ inch of soil, and give the beds half-shade. Keep the seedbeds moist.

• *Ulmus* (elm). Sweep elm seed from the ground soon after they fall, or strip them directly from the branches. Most elm species do not require treatment prior to sowing, but the slippery elm and American elm are benefited by stratification at 41°F. for two to three months before spring sowing. Seed ripening in the spring are usually sown immediately after collection, while fall-ripening or stratified seed are planted the following spring. So, species to be sown in summer are winged Russian and Siberian elms; sow American, cedar, Chinese, slippery, September, and rock elms in spring.

• *Ziziphus* (jujube). Take the stones from seed picked in fall. The stones can be sowed in fall without treatment, or stratified in moist sand at 41°F. for two to three months prior to spring planting.

GRAFTING, BUDDING, LAYERING, AND ROOTING

Vegetative propagation by grafting, budding, or layering produces trees with the same characteristics as the parent from which the material is collected.

Grafting. Fruit and nut varieties, with rare exceptions, do not come true from seed. Seed from a Johnathan apple, for example, may give rise to apples that are red, green, or striped, sweet or sour, and large or small. At times, this deviation in seedlings is a blessing in disguise. The Red Delicious apple, for instance, was propagated from a chance discovery of a seedling—a freak of nature growing wild in an Iowa fencerow.

But the odds are about a thousand to one that a seedling will be a duplicate of its parent, and many thousands to one that a seedling will be an improvement over its parent. For this reason, nurserymen and growers increase plants of a given variety by transferring vegetative parts of that variety to a stock upon which these parts may be grown. Grafting is such a process. It's easily learned, and scions (plant parts to be grafted) are available at low cost from nurseries and fellow growers.

Tree growth takes place in the cambium cells beneath the inner bark, and grafting places the cambium tissue of the stock in contact with that of the parts being grafted. Grafting of all kinds should be done in the spring, just as new growth is starting.

Cleft grafting involves grafting a new top onto a tree that is several years old. Even mature trees can be grafted, but success is surer with younger, smaller trees. Substituting an entire new top of a different variety is called topworking.

Cleft grafting is the most common form of topworking. As the name implies, the process involves making a cleft, or split, in the stock into which the scion is inserted (see illustration). On smaller trees, the scions usually are set in the trunk of the rootstock; on larger trees, they are placed in the branches.

On larger trees, allow two or three years to complete the work. All the grafts may be set in one year, but part of the original top should be left another year or two. The reasoning is that danger of winterkill and other damage is increased if the tree is cut back to much at one time. As top wood is cut back, nature prunes the roots accordingly, weakening the entire tree.

Apple and pear trees can be cleft grafted easily. Mature grape vines also may be worked by cleft grafts. Plum and cherry trees are more difficult. Wood of peach and apricot trees is too soft for cleft grafting, and these trees can be better propagated by budding, discussed later.

Nut trees, particularly the hickories and pecans, can be topworked by cleft grafting. In fact, one species can be placed on another. For example, black walnut is excellent rootstock not only for black walnut, but Persian walnut, Siebold walnut, heartnut, and butternut as well. Pecan scions can be grafted onto several of the other hickories with good success.

To perform cleft grafting you'll need a sharp knife with a straight blade, a grafting chisel, a mallet for driving the chisel, a fine-toothed pruning saw, and grafting wax. Select a smooth area on the branch or trunk of the stock that is straight grained and free from knots, and saw off the stock just above this point. Use a chisel to make the cleft. If you're grafting onto a limb, cut the cleft in the horizontal (rather than vertical) plane so that the scions don't interfere with one another when they start to grow. The cleft should be made two to four inches deep, carefully splitting the bark with the knife ahead of the chisel. Reverse the chisel and drive the wedge-shaped part into the split to open the cleft.

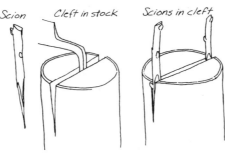

Cleft graft.

Take scions from wood of the previous season's growth, preferably from bearing trees so that you're sure of the variety, and use only sound wood with well-developed buds. Store the scions in a cool, moist place so that they will remain dormant until used. Keep them moist (but not wet) in sawdust, sand, moss, or burlap. If you're grafting while trees are dormant, the scions may be cut as needed. Use a scion with three buds, and cut off the twig just above the top bud. Beginning at the base of the lower bud, use the knife to form an inch-long wedge with even sides that is slightly thicker on the outside than on the side to be placed toward the center of the stock. The wedge should be blunt on the lower end. With a bit of experience and a sharp knife, two strokes will prepare a scion for grafting.

Use this chisel to open the cleft, and slip in the scion at the outer edge so that the cambium tissue of the scion is in contact with the cambium of the stock. Slip the scion down until the lower bud is close to the cut surface of the stock. If the stock is two inches or more in diameter, insert another scion into the cleft on the opposite side. Remove the chisel and the pressure of the stock will clamp the scions in place. Wax all cut and exposed areas carefully to prevent drying and to keep out disease and parasite organisms.

Whip grafting, or tongue grafting, is used to attach parts too small to be cleft grafted. This technique is useful in establishing cultivars on seedling roots.

A sharp knife, some waxed cord, and grafting wax are all you need to make whip grafts. Selecting a smooth, clear place on the trunk or branch of the stock, draw the knife at an angle to expose a sloping surface an inch or two in length. Make a 1½-inch cut (downward, to prevent splitting) in preparation for the tongue.

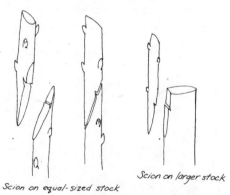

Scion on equal-sized stock

Scion on larger stock

Whip graft.

Select and handle scions as for cleft grafting. Cut a four- to six-inch piece having several firm buds. Make a long, even sloping cut at the base of the scion, just as you did in the stock, and make the tongue in the same way. Slip the tongue of the scion inside the tongue of the stock until the scion is firmly in place. Make sure the cambium tissue of at least one side is in contact with the cambium of the stock (it's doubtful that both scion and stock will be of equal diameter). Wind the graft with a length of waxed string, and then wax all cut surfaces thoroughly.

You'll have some grafting failures, no doubt—even experienced nurserymen do occasionally. But once you've mastered the technique, the ways in which you can combine varieties or even species is limited only by your imagination and the fact that distantly related trees do not get along well together. Conceivably, if you have the time, patience, and interest, you could even develop your own nursery business.

MAKING YOUR OWN GRAFTING WAX

Although commercial grafting wax is available, many growers prefer to make their own. A simple formula you may want to use involves finely broken resin, 4 parts; beeswax, 2 parts; and tallow, 1 part. Melt the tallow, and then add beeswax. When this is melted, add the resin. Boil slowly for thirty minutes, stirring occasionally, and then pour the mixture into cold water. Grease your hands, remove the cooled wax and work it by pulling and twisting until it becomes smooth grained and straw colored. Twist the wax into skeins and wrap it in waxed paper. It will keep almost indefinitely and should be applied with greased hands. The wax hardens in storage but will soften again with heat—usually with just the heat from your hands.

With side grafting, the scion is placed in the side of the stock. One variety of the method, *side-tongue grafting,* is used for branches of trees that are too large for a whip graft. It works best when the scion's diameter is just less than that of the stock but also finds application when the scion is much smaller than the stock. A long cut is made into the stock at a thirty-degree angle, with a tongue made into the cut surface. Make a long cut on the scion, with a small tongue and short cut on the opposite side, as illustrated. The *slotted side graft* is another method used if the stock is greatly larger than the scion. First cut a half-moon shape

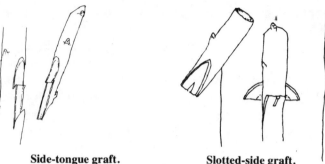

Side-tongue graft.   **Slotted-side graft.**

by making a downward and then a horizontal cut into the bark. Then, cut the scion into a wedge on two sides, one cut made longer. To prepare the stock, make two parallel vertical cuts, just a shade closer together than the scion is wide. The cuts are as long as the longer wedge. Insert the scion with the longer wedge facing the stock. A thin nail will keep the graft in place.

When the cambium is injured by rodents or winter storms, *bridge grafting* is often used to carry the living wood over the damaged area. (If the tree is very young and completely girdled, a better solution might be to saw it off at the damaged point and above the nursery graft, giving rise to shoots.) Scions are cut from new growth on the tree, or from another of the same variety; they should measure at least an inch or two longer than the damaged area is wide—longer scions are easier to handle. Cut four or more scions for each grafting job. They should be spaced every two or three inches.

Bridge grafting is best performed just as the buds are unfolding, for it is at this time that the bark slips free easily. Clear the damaged area of bark, and cover with wax.

Remove the buds from the scions, cut bevels on each end, and fit them into two-inch slits in the bark, as illustrated. The flaps of bark are nailed down. A stick can be placed under young scions to give them the proper bow. Cover all exposed areas with wax. Remove buds as they appear on the scion.

A simple method, *bark grafting* involves splitting the bark at the top of the stock and nailing or tieing on the scion to keep it secure. One splice suffices for most stocks, while those with thick bark may need two parallel splits cut the width of the scion. Cover the area with wax. Bark grafting is often used on stubs that are too big for cleft grafting.

Bridge graft.   Bark graft.

If you want to change the variety of older trees, *top grafting* (topworking) may be the answer. Limbs are sawed off, and each receive two scions, by bark, whip, or side grafting. Select branches at a forty-five-degree angle that receive good sun; they should be well spaced around the tree. Take care that sunscald will not result from removing branches. You can avoid trouble by working when the trees are still dormant or by leaving on water sprouts to provide shade. When top grafting apples, see to it that the two varieties are fairly similar in level of vigor.

Budding. T-budding, or shield-budding, is an easy method of tree propagation. It can be used on most fruit trees and many ornamentals. While peaches and apricots are difficult to graft, they are easily propagated by budding during the seedling stage of growth.

For the stock, young seedlings of at least pencil thickness are best. If seedlings are this large in June, they can be budded with the desired variety and forced into growth in a short time. If seedlings are smaller, budding usually is done in August or September, and buds are not forced into growth until the following spring.

Collect budding wood from desired varieties at the time budding is to be done. Select strong, vigorous new shoots. Bud wood is big enough to use when a reddish color develops on the twig and the buds show brownish spots. Remove leaves from the bud wood with a knife, clipping all but a short stub of a petiole of the leaf below the bud. This stub protects the bud adjacent to it and also is a handle to hold the bud while it is being cut from the stick and inserted into the **T**. Immature wood at the terminal end of the bud wood should be removed. Keep bud sticks moist by wrapping them in moist burlap or other material.

Remove all growth on the lower six to ten inches of the seed-

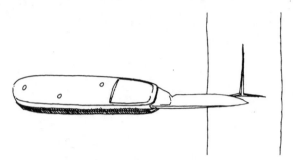

Cutting a T for budding.

ling rootstock. On the north side of the seedling's trunk, make a vertical cut in the stem near the ground line. At the top of this cut, make a cross cut with a rolling motion of the knife to form a **T**. Next, cut the bud from the budding stick by making a cut upwards, just beneath bud and bark. This cut should be about an inch in length, extending below and above the bud. Remove the bud from the wood by making a cut across the top, through the bark and into the wood. Peel the bark and bud from the stick, leaving the wood attached. If the bark does not slip readily, take the wood with it.

Insert the bud into the **T** and push it down until it is firmly in place. If part of the tissue extends above the top of the cut, remove it. Wrap the bud securely with ⅛-inch rubber budding strips, making at least two wraps below the bud and two above. Rubber strips maintain constant pressure, expanding as the tree grows.

When budding in June, force the bud to grow by breaking over the top of the stock at about one-half the distance from the ground to the top of the seedling, leaving this top attached to shade the bud. When budding in late summer, force the bud into growth the following spring. Once forced buds start to grow you should remove the top of the seedling (rootstock) just above the new shoot. Keep all new growth removed from the base of the tree below the bud. After a year of growth, the tree is ready to be transplanted to its permanent location.

Layering. Some trees that do not propagate readily by grafting can be increased by layering. Layering involves the formation of roots from a portion of the stem, but differs from rooting in that roots and stems of the new layered plant are formed while it is still attached to the parent. Layering is used frequently with cane fruit and with certain trees, including quince and filbert.

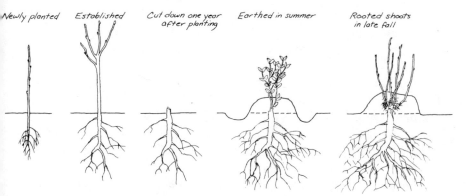

Newly planted   Established   Cut down one year   Earthed in summer   Rooted shoots
                                after planting   in late fall

Mound layering yields severed rooted shoots.

Mound layering is often used to propagate rootstocks. By cutting back plants close to the ground in the spring and leaving a few buds on each stem, vigorous new shoots are produced. In June these shoots are mounded up with earth high enough to cover the lower buds. The soil is worked in well around the buds, and roots develop. If enough growth has been made by the following fall, the dirt can be removed and new plants cut off and stored until spring for transplanting; in southern areas, they may be planted at once.

Rooting. Many plants can be propagated by rooting cuttings which are eight- to ten-inch pieces of wood cut from the parent. Rooting of grapes and many cane fruit is fairly simple, but true trees are more difficult.

Cuttings from walnut, hickory, filbert, and chestnut have been rooted, but success is limited. Recent experiments indicate that it is possible to root by wounding the tree to force shoots or suckers from the parent tree's base. Cuttings from these shoots are then treated with high concentrations of a plant hormone and placed under mist. The process is too complex for most home growers, however.

PRUNING

From time to time you hear people say that pruning, even of fruit trees, is a waste of time. That's true, if you want to grow brush. But if you plant trees for a purpose—fruit, nuts, shade, beauty, or timber—you'll find they often need help. Letting nature take its course will not produce the largest, reddest, tastiest fruit;

Christmas trees do not grow naturally into perfectly symmetrical cones; and hedges do not grow into natural fences by themselves. It takes pruning—training a tree by cutting away branches.

Pruning Fruit Trees. Fruit trees need annual maintenance prunings after the first year to keep them in bounds. The degree of pruning depends largely on the type of dwarfing and variety of the tree. Many superdwarfs need only an occasional leggy twig snipped off, while rank-growing trees demand annual pruning of masses of new growth. Pruning results in larger fruit, as there are fewer fruit to make use of the tree's resources. Also, the fruit have a better color because of improved sunlight distribution.

All cuts made in the pruning operation should be flush with and parallel to the branch structure, as close cuts heal more quickly than stubbed-off limbs. You'll need a sturdy pair of lopping shears and a pruning saw for work on mature trees. Hand shears come in handy for smaller trees, grapes, and bramble fruit. It is best to prune in late winter, when trees are fully dormant. Remove all dead and dying wood, as well as the upright-growing suckers that would soon clog up a tree's interior. All wounds larger than one inch in diameter should be treated with a good tree wound dressing.

Apple trees should be trained to a modified leader (or main stem), with lower scaffold branches located from twenty to thirty inches above the ground. As the tree grows taller, leave eight to ten other branches at about eight-inch intervals, arranged spirally around the tree. It normally takes three to five years to decide which branches to keep for scaffold branches, but it is important to select them, as trees trained in this manner form strong branches that will support a heavy fruit load. Branches that are to form the skeletal structure should, if possible, form approximate forty-five-degree angles to the central leader of the tree.

Apples trees tend to grow bushy, and thick areas occur in the tops and on northeast sides, due to south winds. Some of this growth should be cut away as an annual pruning chore. When inspecting trees, remember that the lower scaffold branch, especially on the south side of the tree, will grow fast if left unpruned and will soon unbalance the tree by shading out desirable branch development along the central leader.

As important as pruning is, don't overdo it. Vegetative growth and water sprouts can result from too much pruning. Multiple-variety trees (such as five-apples-in-one) should be pruned carefully to maintain each variety. The top branch variety will grow fastest and must be contained.

Pear trees tend to grow upright. They should be pruned lightly each year, with cuts made inside to divert growth to the outside. A central leader should be selected to form the structure of the tree. When pruning away pear branches affected with fire blight, disinfect the shears between cuts with household bleach to avoid spreading the disease.

Peach trees grow rapidly and pruning begins soon after transplanting. About a third of the growth can be removed each year if the tree is in good growing condition. Branches should be thinned yearly to shape the tree, either to an open-center or a modified leader type.

In the open-center pruning system, you should select three or four scaffold branches that form wide angles to the tree, located one to two feet above the ground and distributed evenly around the trunk. Lateral branches are allowed to grow, forming the fruit-producing area of the tree. These branches should be cut back to a side branch to keep the tree open in the center and low in height.

The modified leader system is similar to apple tree pruning. Scaffold branches should be shortened each year to control the tree's size.

In years when fruit fails to set (because of late frost or whatever), peach trees grow rapidly. This makes pruning more difficult the next year, but severe pruning will encourage formation of more new lateral limbs.

Plum and *cherry trees* require less pruning than other fruit trees. The scaffold-branch structure of plums resembles that of peaches. About all the pruning that is required is removal of branches that are tangled, crossed, or otherwise interfering with each other.

Pruning Landscape Trees and Shrubs. More has been written about pruning fruit trees than shade trees and shrubs, and people generally think that pruning yard trees is unnecessary. True, you don't *have* to prune lawn trees and ornamentals. But you may well take satisfaction in doing some pruning to promote the tree's health and encourage a pleasing shape. That means, first of all, that you should literally heed the old dictum: As the twig is bent, so shall the

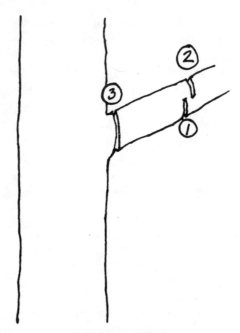

Pruning large limbs.

tree grow. Prune trees when they are young and you won't have to risk your neck when they (and you) are older.

Before you begin cutting, though, research the tree to determine its natural form, habit of growth, rate of growth, and height and time of flowering. You want to use pruning and thinning to help the tree fulfill your purpose for planting it. The most common pruning tasks involve removing dead, diseased, or insect-infested parts; changing the density of the tree, either opening up the center to allow more air and light to enter or making a leggy tree look denser and fuller; rejuvenating old, declining trees by pruning older wood on trees and shrubs to stimulate the growth of new wood, better flowers, and better shape; and developing a special shape or form, as in hedges (but not to be confused with shearing, which is the clipping of all new shoots to create an unnatural form of the plant).

Pruning mistakes may last a season, or for the life of a tree. Here are several important cautions.

• Don't leave short stubs when you make a cut, but trim twigs and branches flush with the main stem. Stubs do not heal quickly. To prune larger limbs, see illustration.

• Don't prune flowering trees and shrubs before they blossom. Flower buds form the season before, and you'll cut them off before they have a chance to open.

• Don't shear hedges so they are narrower at the bottom than at the top. A wider bottom exposes more of the plant to light and eliminates the twiggy base often seen on "upside-down" hedges.

• Don't cut all stems or shoots of a tree or shrub to the same height. This gives the plant an unnatural crew-cut look and stimulates excess growth in the top of the plant.

• Don't leave a clipped-off branch without a bud at the end to continue growing. It is best to slant the end cut slightly so that a small portion of the twig remains above the bud.

Light Tree Surgery. A few basic steps in tree surgery stand the homeowner in good stead, although professionals should be called in to work on large trees—especially those near buildings and power lines.

When a tree limb dies and is not pruned off properly, decay will work back from the base of the dead limb into the tree trunk like a cancer. Cut out the punky, decayed wood with a good

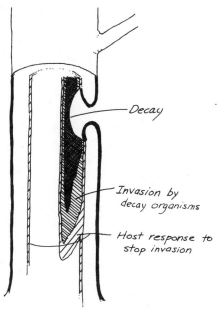

Cut-away view showing decay.

pocketknife. Cut back to hard wood and to healthy green cambium on the inner bark. The trick is to form a cavity that is more or less oval in shape, with the ends of the oval pointed up and down. The tree can heal the wound with new callus tissue over an oval more quickly than over a squarish, round, or horizontal wound.

Once you have cleaned out the dead wood, paint the wound with tree wound dressing. Don't fill the hole with cement or other such material; that practice is outdated, except in special cases. If water will lie in the cavity, dig a very small channel at the bottom for a drain.

If you have a weak-forked tree that must be saved, it is bad practice to tie the two limbs together by running a cable through them. Instead, put eye screws into the limbs about halfway up their lengths and run a cable through the eyes. To make sure the cable is stretched tight, tie a rope around the limbs and pull them together, closer than they should be, before installing the cable. Then, when you release the rope, the cable will be tight. Do the job in summer when there's a full load of leaves on the tree so you know what kind of weight you're working with.

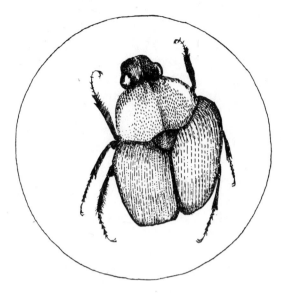

Japanese beetle.

CHAPTER 5 When Trees Ail

by ROGER B. YEPSEN, JR.

Big trees symbolize, to medium-size man, the qualities of passive strength and immutability. But even massive oaks can be killed by a small wound.

Being passive, a tree can do little to ward off or avoid potential threats. Lawn mowers, insects, lightning, fire, heavy winds, and pollution are all common causes of damage and may lead the way for disease.

PREVENTING TROUBLE

Planting. The first danger a tree meets in life is planting. Transplanting is usually best done in spring or fall, although recommended times vary with species and location. If in doubt, check with your local nursery.

Planting holes should be wide and deep enough to accommodate bare-root trees without cramping the roots. For balled-root trees, make the holes at least a foot wider than the diameter of the ball. If planted too deeply, the tree's collar may rot; if the hole is too shallow, the collar is apt to dry out.

Burlap wraps should be untied and rolled back from the trunk after planting. Completely remove plastic wraps, as they won't decompose in the soil. Fill in the hole with topsoil to the level at which soil originally surrounded the tree. Water immediately after planting, and continue to water periodically for two seasons thereafter. (Some experts suggest adding vitamin B_1 to the water to minimize the effects of transplant shock.) Saturate the soil, but don't waterlog it. Evergreens will need more water than deciduous trees and shrubs.

If the tree is more than three feet tall, you may want to support it with hose-wrapped guide wires. Leave these wires in place for one to two years, at which time they should be removed to keep from girdling the trunk. You can prevent sunscald and ward off minor injuries by wrapping the trunk with burlap, creped kraft paper, or a couple of thicknesses of aluminum foil. To keep deer, mice, and rabbits from nibbling the young, vulnerable tree, set up a perimeter of wire mesh, held up by stakes set several inches from the trunk. The aluminum mesh sold to keep leaves from gutters should work well.

Mulching and Fertilizing. A tree makes use of the branches and leaves it drops to the earth. In time, the layer of vegetation weathers down into a rich, humusy mulch that conserves soil moisture, prevents the soil from cracking, and discourages competition from weeds and upstart trees.

Should you suspect that the leaves harbor disease or insect eggs, remove them to the compost pile. A properly made pile should kill the pests and render the diseases harmless. In spring, return the material to the trees. If trees are prone to mildew and fungus diseases, it may be wise to rake back the mulch and let the sun shine on the bare soil for a time. A sunbath should be scheduled for each spring in damp climates. After a few weeks of baking, the material can be returned to the tree, leaving a narrow open space around the trunk to prevent rotting.

A good all-around fertilizer is made from equal quantities (by weight) of cottonseed meal (or dried blood); phosphate rock (or bone meal); wood ashes, granite dust, or greensand; and dolomitic limestone. The mixture can simply be spread around smaller trees.

Large trees are best fed by punching eighteen-inch-deep holes in the soil with a pipe or crowbar. Place the holes two inches apart, covering the entire area out as far as the dripline, and slant them toward the trunk. Fill each hole with six to eight ounces of the fertilizer mix, and then cap the hole with peat moss or topsoil.

Pruning. A tree transplanted from the wild will fare a lot better if about a third of its foliage is pruned after the move. Aside from this, pruning is also done to spruce up ornamental or yard trees, to improve the production of fruit trees, and to permit valuable woodlot trees to grow unhindered. Generally, removing crowded growth will ensure adequate sunlight and air circulation.

Most pruning chores can be done at any time of the season, but maples and birches bleed profusely in spring and should be trimmed in summer. Those evergreens that are pruned to induce bushiness or extra foliage, such as white pines, Norway spruce, and Colorado blue spruce, should be pruned back to a lateral bud in spring. Summer is a good time to observe which branches are diseased or dying, and they can be pruned in late fall. It's best not to prune in very hot or very cold weather. See Chapter 4 for detailed information on pruning.

Treating Wounds. The tough bark that encases most trees is tough for a reason—trees are very susceptible to decay by various pathogens, and these bacteria, fungi, and viruses gain entry through holes in the bark. So, it is important to patch up these holes as they occur.

Decay organisms are usually encouraged by moisture, and the first step in treating a wound is to carve away at it so that water will not collect. If the injury is a scrape or a wound on the trunk or on a major branch, use a jackknife to trace an elongated pointed ellipse around the whole wound—in the shape of a football standing on end. The knife should cut through firm bark all along its path. If the bark is loose, make a bigger football. Then, clean the area within the ellipse, removing all the bark, fibers, and shreds. You can use a broad stroke of the jackknife, a broad chisel, paint scraper, or file to get the area within the ellipse down to smooth, bare wood. Don't leave islands of bark within the ellipse, no matter how good the bark looks. Next, use the knife to bevel the edges of the ellipse.

Between the bark and the sapwood you'll notice a thin juicy

layer. This is the cambium, the part of the tree that grows, and out of it forms the callus or scar tissue that will gradually creep over the wound, protecting the tree from rot.

As a final step you can apply a dressing, although it's not essential. Cover the edge of the ellipse with orange shellac to prevent the cambium from drying out. (Shellac is a tree's very own dressing, made by pine trees specifically to seal their own wounds.) Then swab on the tree paint—unpleasant, sticky, asphalty stuff available in most garden shops.

If a wound has been neglected for a long time, rot may have already set in. Should the wood seem soft or punky, it's too late for first aid, and you'll have to perform a bit of tree surgery. First, make a few test holes into the rotten area with a brace-and-bit drill to determine how extensive the damage is. If you hit solid wood within a foot, go to work; however, if the rot is much more extensive about all you can do is wish the tree good luck.

Surgery is best done with a woodcarving gouge. Dig in as far as you can using the palm of your hand as a hammer to drive the gouge. Then smooth the inside to eliminate shreds and pockets where water can collect. You still must provide a means of drainage. If the hole is shallow you can simply slope it outwards so that the water drains through the mouth of the hole.

If the cavity is deep, however, you will have to drill a hole from the outside of the tree, angling it up toward the bottom of the cavity. Make sure the drainage hole hits the cavity at its lowest point. It is considered good practice to insert a length of pipe or copper tubing into the drainage hole to prevent the tree from sealing itself up within a few years.

Finally you can, if you want, apply a dressing. First disinfect the cavity and the tools with alcohol. You might then smear a layer of tree paint throughout the cavity, being careful not to seal the drainage hole. But as long as the sides of the cavity are smooth and the hole is well drained, tree paint isn't absolutely necessary.

Tree troubles can be grouped under three rubrics: environmental troubles, insects, and diseases.

ENVIRONMENTAL TROUBLES

Increasingly, man has made it tougher for trees to make it in a world dominated by his hand. Dr. Alex Shigo, plant pathologist at the USDA's Northeast Forest Experiment Station in Durham, New Hampshire, has lumped these man-made maladies under the term People-Pressure Diseases. Common symptoms include small and discolored leaves, premature fall coloration, loss of leaves, reduced twig growth, dying twigs in the upper crown, and the decline of parts or all of the tree.

What's behind the symptoms? Air pollution, building and road construction, improper use of home and garden equipment, deicing salt from highways, soil compaction by the tramping of feet or roll of tires, flooding, agricultural chemicals, and improper wound treatment. Michael A. Weiner's *Plant A Tree* (Macmillan, 1975) is a good source of environmental precautions, some of which follow.

Pollution. *Air pollution* affects trees as well as people, whether it be from factories, cars, or leaking gas mains. Generally, hardwood species fare better. Factory pollution causes discoloration, mottling, and browning of foliage, especially on evergreens. Dust may smother leaves. A leaking gas main is evidenced by yellowed foliage, slow growth, brown or blue streaks in the wood of the roots and trunk, and may even result in death of the tree. If you have reason to suspect a gas leak, call the utility company. Once the leak is mended, revive the tree by digging a trench on the side of the leak or around the entire tree, and then aerate the soil with compressed air. Finally, water heavily.

As an individual, you can cut down on pollutants by keeping your car tuned up, by not burning trash, and by working in a community-level effort to persuade industrial polluters to take prompt remedial action.

Pesticides or *herbicides* may wash or blow in from neighboring areas to make your trees sick. Should the problem persist and claim a few trees, check to see if you have legal recourse under the state law. Domestic pollutants cause other consequences. Strong detergents poured into a nearby septic system can kill a tree having roots in the drainage field. Oil leaking from an oil burner intake pipe may soak the root area. Trees along highways deiced with salt often suffer damage to their roots and irrigation systems. Evergreens are sometimes killed by being sprayed with salty slush from passing cars. One way out is to plant salt-tolerant trees, including Austrian pine, bigtooth aspen, birches, black cherry, black locust, Japanese black pine, pitch pine, quaking aspen, red cedar, red oak, white ash, white oak, white spruce, and yews. Among the trees known to be vulnerable to salt are American elm, basswood, eastern white pine, hemlock, ironwood, red maple, red pine, shagbark hickory, speckled alder, and sugar maple.

Weather. The *sun* may make trees sick. A condition known as sunscald hits when bark accustomed to shade or protection from the weather is suddenly exposed to heat and drying from the sun or wind. This is apt to happen when trees are thinned out or when young trees are planted in open areas. Injury shows as cracking or curling bark on limbs and trunks that were previously smooth. To protect trees from sunscald, either wrap burlap or wrapping tape around the trunk or set up a vertical board on the tree's south side. Another condition, known as sun scorch, appears as yellowed, browned, or withered foliage on either one side or all of a tree. The condition is first seen on leaf tips and edges. Trouble starts when high temperature and drought injure roots so that part or all of a tree is unable to pick up sufficient water. To compensate for the reduced root system, you can prune the branches above. Avoid such a problem by keeping trees well watered in dry spells and conserve soil moisture with a mulch.

Just as too much sun is potentially damaging, too little sun often results in spindly growth and the death of lower limbs or inner twigs. Light-loving trees, especially evergreens, should be spaced well apart when transplanted. Shade-tolerant trees can be set in areas shaded by larger trees.

A more dramatic change wrought by nature is *lightning*. Damage may either be done directly to the limbs and trunk or indirectly through ground discharges. If the lightning burns a ring all the way around the cambium layer of the trunk, the tree may die. Lesser symptoms include wilting of foliage, abrasions on the bark, and dieback. A characteristic sign is death of the superficial layers of bark between the nodes of twigs, while bark at the base of the petioles and thorns stays a healthy green. Injured bark is greenish yellow at first and later turns a brownish color that is very visible against the healthy sections. Lightning rods may help prevent trouble but are a bother to install. For some reason, well-watered trees are not struck as often. A tree can be helped to recover from its wounds by fertilizing and watering.

In another dramatic act of nature, *flooding* can kill tree roots by suffocating them. You shouldn't plant certain species in low-lying areas apt to be flooded, including eastern white pine, hemlock, paper birch, red cedar, red pine, sugar maple, and white spruce. Ash, black gum, cottonwood, elm, overcup oak, red maple, river birch, silver maple, sweet gum, sycamore, white cedar, and willows will put up with an occasional flooding and can be planted in damp sites.

Frost and unseasonably *cold weather* may kill parts of trees in the fall and new growth in spring. To prevent fall damage, avoid fertilizing the tree late in the season, as new growth cannot stand up to the cold snaps. Plant trees native to the region or those known to be hardy. Small and valuable exotic trees and bushes can be sheltered with wooden A-frames or tarps. A coat of ice or sudden change in temperature may cause bark to split along the trunk. The wounds often form successive layers of callus until large frost ribs protrude from the trunk. Excessive moisture about the base of the tree is thought to encourage this problem, so provide good drainage and avoid saturating the ground late in the season. To fix up damaged trees, you might cut away the dead bark and apply a tree paint.

In addition to frost damage, trees may show a browning and withering of foliage and twigs late in the winter season. This condition, known simply as winter injury or winterkill, commonly strikes evergreens. The problem is that dry winds remove the moisture from the above-ground part of the plant, while the frozen roots are unable to replenish the moisture. A moisture-conserving mulch, applied in early fall, should help. Burlap screens and wax emulsions also give some protection.

It takes trees a while to register the effects of *drought*. Leaves appear scorched or drop off, usually because of a dry spell the summer before. A tree cannot live without functioning leaves to make food, so keep your charges well watered in dry times.

Wires and Lighting. *Electrical wires* can wound trees both by chafing the bark and by short circuiting in wet weather to cause high, lethal temperatures. Entire limbs and trees may die, so prune as necessary or prevent trouble by having wires strung up where they will do no harm.

A seemingly unlikely threat to a tree's well-being is high-intensity *street lighting*. The bright, blue white lights can keep trees growing well into autumn, rendering them susceptible to frost damage. London plane trees have been found to be particularly susceptible, while ginkgoes, often chosen as street trees, are somewhat resistant. As young trees are most apt to be injured, you should plant trees in the fall when they are dormant.

COMMON INSECT PESTS

Fortunately, it usually takes bugs a long time to finish off a tree. And a few insect attacks rarely result in death. If you decide to take action, the first steps are water sprays (to wash off insects on foliage), pruning of infested branches, and organic fertilizing. If trouble persists, check to see if you could be enlisting the services of a biological agent, such as the bacterium *Bacillus thuringiensis,* ladybugs, and trichogramma wasps. The three are commercially available. If all else has failed, you may elect to resort to dormant-oil or repellent sprays. Keep in mind that the less you interrupt the natural scheme of things, the better your trees will like it.

In identifying and dealing with tree pests, it helps to think of them as falling in to one of four groups—chewers or foliage-feeders; gnawers or wood-feeders; suckers or sap-feeders; and gall insects.

Chewers or Foliage-Feeders. This first of the four groups is comprised of such enemies as caterpillars, beetles and their larvae, and leaf miners.

Cankerworms (commonly called inchworms) grow to one inch long, may be pale yellow green, brown, or black, and are typically marked with several pale stripes running their length. They appear in two generations a year, one in spring and the other in fall. The female moths lay their eggs on the tree but are wingless and must climb the trunk. You can therefore thwart them by placing bands of sticky goop around the trunk. Tree Tanglefoot is a commercial preparation made for such things, but roofing cement out of the can ought to do the job. You might also stir up your own preparation from pine tar and molasses or from resin mixed with oil. To keep the sticky substance from harming the bark, it's best to first put down a layer of paper. Apply the bands in February to trap the spring species and in mid-October to trap the fall cankerworms. The larvae may still get to protected trees by blowing through the air at the end of long, silky strings. A spray of *Bacillus thur-*

Wingless cankerworm moth (female).

ingiensis, sold by mail and at garden supply centers, will take care of these worms. The powder is suspended in water and sprayed in April or May.

The larva of the *codling moth* is distinguished from other caterpillars by its color (white tinged with pink), its habit of tunnelling directly to the core of fruit, and its considerable appetite—the worm is considered the most serious of apple and pear pests. Fortunately, there are a number of effective ways of saving the crop without resorting to the poisons that many growers have unfortunately accepted as a necessary part of fruit growing.

Larvae develop from eggs laid in the blossom end of the apples in June, work their way into the core, and then tunnel out to the skin again. After leaving their trail through the apples, they spin cocoons in bark crevices to spend the winter. The gray brown moths, showing fringed hind wings, make their appearance in June. One of the best organic controls involves banding tree trunks in spring with corrugated paper to draw larvae looking for a place to spin their cocoons. The bands should be wrapped in several thicknesses and can be wired on. Keep the bands on at least until September when the second generation of worms crawls across the bark to find a place to winter. Remove the bands later on in fall and burn them.

The codling moth larvae, like many other fruit tree pests, are reduced in number by a careful scraping of rough bark each spring. If a water faucet is handy, a high-pressure spray from a short distance will dislodge some larvae from their hiding places in the bark. Codling moths have been found to be vulnerable to several sprays. Soapy-water and fish-oil sprays seem to work best, causing caterpillars on the prowl to drop to the ground. Dormant-oil sprays will take care of many of the eggs. Nasturtiums can be planted around the trunks as a repellent barrier.

Perhaps the most promising means of control is the tiny trichogramma wasp, available through the mail as eggs. Making successful use of this helper depends on timing—the eggs should hatch just about the time the moths are laying their eggs, as this wasp is an egg parasite. If the number of wasp eggs seems paltry in comparison with the task at hand, keep in mind that the trichogramma can have fifty or more generations in a favorable season. Woodpeckers are able helpers and can be drawn to the orchard by setting out hunks of suet in winter.

In 1868, a strong wind knocked open some cages kept by a Medford, Massachusetts, scientist. The monster that escaped is known to us all—the *gypsy moth*. Over the years this pest has spread from New England through the Middle Atlantic states to Michigan. The larva is brown and hairy and grows to two inches in length. Look for them on alder, apple, basswood, birch, elm, hawthorn, hickory, hornbeam, larch, maple, oak, poplar, and willow. As the larvae grow older their tastes change, and you may also see them on cedar, hemlock, pine, and spruce. Evergreens may die after one season's defoliation, while broad-leaf trees typically must be hit hard two or three years in a row. Broad-leaf trees that are stripped in early summer sometimes put out a second set of leaves, and this overtaxes and may kill them. The caterpillars feed nocturnally through June and July and appear later as brown, yellow-marked moths (male) or low-flying beige moths (female). Larvae hatch in early May.

To trap the pests, wrap several lengths of burlap around the tree trunk and fold the top over to form a shelter. Worms will be attracted to the burlap when they instinctively feel that it is time to pupate. Crush the caterpillars inside the band or remove the band

Gypsy moth larva.

and shake them into a container of water topped with kerosene. The tan egg clusters, shaped in one-inch ovals, can be scraped off the hard surfaces—cars, houses, tree trunks, or stones—on which they are usually laid. A *Bacillus thuringiensis* spray is effective. Be sure to observe federal quarantine regulations. If you leave an infested area, for an area that is not, check your car and trailer for their eggs.

The hairy black *eastern tent caterpillar* (also known as the appletree tent caterpillar) attacks foliage by day and spends rainy days and nights in its communal nest. There is one generation a year. Serious infestations usually come in cycles of from seven to ten years (the result of the effects of effects of parasitism and disease), and the extent of damage ranges from none at all to complete defoliation. Wild cherry and apple trees are most often attacked; peach, pear, plum, hawthorn, and various shade and forest trees are occasionally infested. In spring, you can gauge the scale of trouble by the numbers of tents along the side of the road and in orchards. The pests mature in early summer and do not pose a threat for the remainder of the season.

A generation of the eastern tent caterpillar develops over the course of a year. Larvae are present in late spring, cocoons and

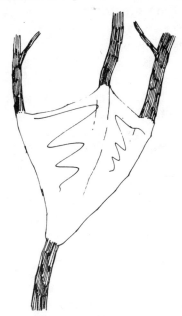

Tent caterpillars' tent.

moths in early summer, and eggs for the remainder of the time. The larvae, or caterpillars, hatch in spring from egg masses about the time the first leaves are opening. After feeding for two days or so, they begin to weave their tent in a nearby tree crotch, sometimes joining with caterpillars from other egg masses. Upon reaching maturity they spin cocoons on tree bark, fences, brush, weeds, or buildings, or among dead leaves and debris on the ground. When fully grown (about six weeks after hatching), the caterpillar is almost two inches long and sparsely hairy. It is black, has white and blue markings, and shows a white stripe along the middle of its back. The pupal cocoon is about one inch long and white or yellowish white. In early summer, reddish brown moths emerge, and the females deposit masses of eggs in bands around twigs. The eggs are covered with a foamy secretion that dries to a firm brown covering which looks like an enlargement of the twig.

You can control the tent caterpillar by hand if you have only a few infested trees. Since many insects are concentrated in a few groups, they are easily destroyed. When you first see the nests, tear them out by hand or with a brush or pole, and either crush any surviving caterpillars on the ground or burn them with a torch made from oily rags tied to a pole. In winter, you can destroy the egg masses by cutting off the infested twigs and burning them. Remove wild cherry trees growing in the vicinity of orchards, if possible, as they are often hosts.

The caterpillar eggs are vulnerable to a red-and-orange digger wasp that puts the larva to sleep with a sting and lays its eggs on the victim's skin. And a fly that looks much like an ordinary housefly, only larger, helps man by inserting its living maggots beneath the skin of tent caterpillars. These maggots later emerge full grown from the caterpillar pupae. Baltimore orioles have been known to clean up entire infestations, and the bird's hanging sacklike nests are a sign that your trees are insured against tent caterpillar trouble. *Bacillus thuringiensis* is potent when sprayed on trees.

Gnawers or Wood-Feeders. The second group of tree-damaging insects is made up of beetles, borers, and ants that tunnel through trunks, limbs, and twigs.

Carpenterworms excavate large tunnels of up to an inch in diameter in the wood of a number of shade trees. They measure about 2½ inches long and are colored pinkish with a brown head

Flat-headed apple tree borer.

and brown spots (or tubercles) down the back. Remove and destroy infested branches. Dress and paint wounds to discourage the female moth from laying her greenish white eggs in them. A light trap can be set out when the moths emerge in early summer.

Flat-headed borers are among the worst enemies of deciduous trees and shrubs. Borer holes lower the value of lumber. Young transplants are especially prone to damage. The larvae burrow underneath the bark, girdling the tree in the process, and metallic gray or brown beetles appear in early summer to lay eggs in wounds in the bark. When infested trees are cut, the borers may be seen in their frass-filled tunnels; in winter, they often are found in a curled-up posture. Look for a wide, flat enlargement just behind the head of this yellow white worm.

Thwart egg-laying adults by wrapping the trunks of young trees with paper or place a board vertically on the south side of the tree to shade the trunk. Some borers can be killed by snaking a wire into the tunnels. Paint over any wounds that you can find. Pruning young trees to a low profile seems to help, and organic fertilizing and watering offer long-term benefits.

A variety of *twig girdlers,* gray beetles with long antennae, break off twigs and small branches, and you may notice girdled sections from the trees in late summer through winter. The girdlers may hollow the twigs and branches from the inside, in which case the neatly trimmed pieces are found on the ground. Young trees are especially vulnerable. Rake up and burn girdled branches late in fall, when the larvae and eggs are stashed within. Birds can clean up an infestation and should be attracted to your area with plantings, supplementary food, and shelter.

Suckers or Sap-Feeders. Making up the third group of insects, suckers or sap-feeders feed by piercing the tissues and sucking out

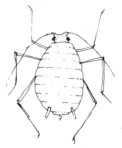

Aphid.

the juices to cause retarded growth and death of twigs and limbs.

Aphids are well-known pests, attacking just about every crop, ornamental, and tree. They are small, soft bodied, and come in a variety of colors. While healthy trees shouldn't be endangered by an infestation, the so-called honeydew that aphids secrete can support a dark mold that blocks the light from leaves, thereby cutting down the trees' ability to make food. You may find spots on cars and lawn furniture below infested trees.

Aphids can give weak trees a hard time, and the best cure is to revitalize such trees with regular watering and organic fertilizer. Water sprays will knock aphids from leaves, but even this moderate treatment should not be resorted to lightly—ladybugs will be washed away too, setting the scene for a rapid pest buildup. A more potent spray is made of two gallons of kerosene, a half-pound of hard soap, and one gallon of water. Heat the water and soap solution, and add it boiling hot to the kerosene. Churn the mixture with a force pump and spray nozzle for five to ten minutes. The resulting emulsion forms a cream that thickens on cooling and should adhere without oiliness to a glass surface. Just before using, dilute one part of the emulsion with nine parts of cold water. This formula yields about three gallons of emulsion which will make, when diluted, thirty gallons of wash.

The gossamer wings of the *lacebug* belie the fact that this is a common pest on basswood, cherry, hawthorn, white oak, and many broad-leafed evergreens. The small, flat insect sucks sap from leaves to cause white or yellow spotting. Molasseslike bits of excrement are left behind on the underside of leaves. While deciduous trees are seldom harmed, evergreens may lose leaves and twigs and smaller branches may die back. If control is necessary, you can resort to spraying or dusting the foliage with pyrethrum.

Individually, *scale* insects don't seem much of a threat—

Gall of gall wasp.

they're small, inconspicuous, and for a good part of their lives, immobile. But infestations suck the life from foliage, twigs, and branches, and their honeydew secretions support a black, unsightly fungus. This fungus may block out the light needed by chlorophyll to produce food. On some trees, a dormant-oil spray can be applied to smother scales. Apple, boxelder, burr oak, dogwood, elm, linden, pin oak, post oak, and white oak are relatively tolerant to oil sprays; on the other hand, some trees cannot tolerate the sprays, including species of beech and maple, butternut, hickory, mountain ash, red and black oak, walnut, and yew.

Gall Insects. These insects irritate trees as they feed, and the trees respond by swelling locally. Galls may occur on leaves, stems, and twigs. There are about two thousand insects in the United States that can instigate galls, most of them wasps and midges. Luckily, the growths shouldn't be serious, and at any rate there is little you can do to control the responsible insects.

COMMON DISEASES

Trees are susceptible to various kinds of diseases: wilts, rusts, cankers, mildews, root rots, and wood decay. Many of these can be avoided by taking care not to injure the tree or by dressing the wounds it does receive. Once a disease gets a start, pruning and burning the affected branches will often halt its spread. Pruning tools should be disinfected afterwards to prevent spreading the disease-causing fungus or bacteria. If only the leaves are affected, rake and burn them when they fall.

Decay. Before decay begins in a tree's wood, a series of events takes place. The first is an injury, whether from fire, birds, animals, breaking branches, lightning, or jarring from mechanical equipment. The tree reacts to its injury: chemical changes take place in the wood and the wood discolors, either darkening or bleaching. Next, bacteria and certain nondecay fungi become active; a growth ring forms, the cells of which act as a barrier and help seal off the injury. The wood discolors further; decay fungi infect, and decay begins. The process is irreversible and cannot be short cut. Decay begins only after the other events in the sequence, after the wood has become discolored. Of course, the process may stop at any stage: an injury to a tree does not inevitably mean decay. The tree often heals its wounds or other microorganisms may come into play that compete with the decay-causing fungi.

In northern hardwood trees, the discoloration and decay take a definite pattern, forming a column in the tree related to the location of the injury. This column spreads outward. Because the tree will grow healthy new wood around the defect, the column of discoloration and decay is no larger in diameter than the tree was at the time it was injured. If there have been repeated injuries, as is often the case with forest trees, several columns may be present in various stages of development at the same time and place. These multiple columns can sometimes be seen on the ends of logs, where they take on a concentric or a cloudlike pattern.

The defects that form in a tree under cankers (dead areas in the bark) produce a somewhat different pattern. A canker tends to form a localized defect rather than a column of discoloration and decay. Of northern hardwoods, red maple and yellow birch are highly susceptible to this decay process, and sugar maple ranks as the most resistant.

Total prevention of decay is not possible, since trees are subject to injury from many different sources. All decay is not serious—some wounds that look very bad actually do little damage to the wood. In estimating the extent of decay, remember that a process is involved; time is important. If the wound was recent, this process will not be far advanced. Many poorly healed branch stubs usually indicate a good-sized central column of moist wood and decay. Multiple wounds on a tree frequently result in severe defect. Healed wounds and vigorous calluses are good signs that the decay is limited.

Common Diseases. *Anthracnose* is a fungus disease most evident as spotted, blotched, distorted leaves that often fall prematurely. On twigs and branches, anthracnose causes disfigurement. Buds and small twigs may be blighted early in the season, appearing to be frost injured. Cankers (dead areas in the bark) often form at the juncture of buds and twigs. Anthracnose fungi overwinter in leaves on the ground or are carried over to the next year in infected buds and twigs. The spores develop under cool, moist conditions.

Gather and destroy the diseased leaves when they fall, or compost them under several inches of soil. Prune out infected twigs and branches. When planting new trees or shrubs, consider using anthracnose-resistant species. The London plane tree is more resistant than the American sycamore, and black oaks are much more resistant than white oaks.

Leaf scorch causes a browning between the veins or along margins of leaves of ash, beech, dogwood, elm, horsechestnut, linden, maple, and oak. A noninfectious disease, scorch usually develops during July or August and is especially severe following periods of drying winds and high temperatures, when the roots are unable to supply enough water to keep up with the large amount of water lost through the leaves. The condition may also result from, or be made worse by, shallow soils, roots that girdle the crown of the tree, a diseased root system, drought, and other diseases that weaken the tree. Fir, pine, and spruce often show leaf scorch as a brown discoloration of the needle tips. The more severe the scorch, the farther down the needle the browning is found. Scorch on needles may result either from hot, dry weather or from high winds during cold weather.

Trees should be fertilized to prevent new growth from becoming easily susceptible. Watering is very helpful, particularly to recently planted trees. Apply water to the ground around the trees, not to the limbs or foliage.

The several *leaf spot* diseases are characterized by yellow, brown, or black dead blotches in leaves; heavily infected leaves turn yellow or brown and fall prematurely. The leaf spots of deciduous trees and shrubs are caused by fungi that overwinter in dead leaves on the ground. Under the warmer, moist conditions of spring, the spores germinate and the fungus grows into the leaf. Some leaf spot fungi produce summer spores that splash about in rainy weather and intensify the disease. On conifers and broad-leafed evergreens, the fungi pass the year on the host plant. All leaf spot diseases caused by fungi are favored by cool, moist weather, especially early in the growing season as the tender new leaves are developing.

To prevent leaf spot, gather and compost fallen leaves in autumn. If only a few leaves are infected, they may be removed by hand. A strong stream of water often helps remove dead foliage from dense evergreen shrubs such as boxwood or arborvitae. For evergreens, spacing the plants well and keeping down weeds and grass under the lower branches will provide better ventilation and reduce the moist conditions that favor infection.

Nectaria canker appears on birch, black walnut, elm, linden, and other hardwoods in the Northeast. Water-soaked areas, darker in color than the adjacent healthy bark, are formed on the trunk and large limbs. The edge of the diseased areas cracks, and callus tissue that forms under the cracked bark becomes infected and dies. The annual repetition of this process forms concentric circles of dead callus tissue. When a canker completely girdles the trunk or branch, the portion above the canker dies.

Where the cankers are not too large, it is important to cut out the diseased areas and treat the wounds with a wound dressing.

Fungi of the *powdery mildew* group infect the leaves of various trees, producing powdery patches of white or gray on leaf surfaces. Tiny black fruiting bodies of the powdery mildew fungus are often found on the white patches. Trees commonly affected with powdery mildew in the Northeast are catalpa, dogwood, horse-chestnut, linden, magnolia, and sycamore.

In most cases mildew is more unsightly than harmful. Sanitary measures, as described above under leaf spot, are usually sufficient to control the trouble.

Shoestring root rot (also known as mushroom or armillaria root rot) infects many trees, including birch, black locust, chestnut, larch, maple, mountain ash, oak, pine, poplar, spruce, sycamore, and yew. Affected trees show a decline in vigor of all or part of the top of the tree. Foliage becomes scant, withers, turns yellow, and drops prematurely. Fan-shaped white fungus growths are found between bark and wood close to and below the ground line. Rootlike dark brown or black "shoestrings" of the causal fungus grow beneath bark and in soil near affected roots. These strands are rather brittle, and they fuse or grow together where they cross. When one of them is opened, the inside appears to be a mass of white compressed cotton. The strands may cause infection of roots of nearby trees, especially if these trees are in poor vigor. In late fall, clusters of honey-colored mushrooms are often found growing around the base of affected trees. Prevent trouble by avoiding injuries to the roots of healthy trees.

Sooty mold fungi grow as saprophytes on honeydew secretions of such insects as aphids and scales. The heavy sooty growth covers needles of various evergreens and leaves of elm, linden, magnolia, maple, and tulip tree. Although the heavy coating of mold on leaves is unsightly, it does not often interfere seriously with food manufacture in the leaf.

Control the insects responsible for secreting the honeydew on which the mold exists. Aphids are usually at the root of the trouble. Ladybugs can be depended upon to keep their numbers down; you can help by applying a sticky band around the trunk to keep aphid-carrying ants on the ground.

Verticillium wilt is a fungus disease that attacks many trees, causing a wilting and yellowing of foliage that is followed by premature defoliation. One limb or the entire tree may be affected. Some trees wilt and die suddenly, while others gradually fade over a period of years. Yellowish brown streaks are present in the outer rings of the wood of infected branches.

Prune all dead branches and fertilize affected trees to stimulate vigorous growth. Remove badly infected trees, together with as many roots as possible. Do not replant ailanthus or other wilt-susceptible trees in the same location: black locust, catalpa, elm, Kentucky coffeetree, linden, maple, redbud, smoke tree, tulip tree, and yellowwood.

A powdery mildew fungus and gall mites are usually associated with broomlike growths on branches known as *witch's brooms*. Several hundred galls may be found on a single tree, causing an unsightly appearance in winter. Affected branches are weakened and break easily during wind storms, and the broken wood is exposed to wood-decaying fungi. Affected buds are larger and more open and hairy than normal. Mites may be found inside the buds along with small black fruiting bodies of the mildew. Threadlike strands of mildew are found on the outside of the bud. Branches that develop from these buds are dwarfed and clustered, giving the witch's broom effect. There is no practical control for this disease. If the brooms are unsightly, prune them off.

SPECIFIC TROUBLES

The above are general pests and diseases, those harming a wide variety of tree species. But there are many important problems that have a limited number of hosts, and such troubles are best discussed under the tree they are most apt to bother. Fruit trees will be discussed first; as a group, they are the source of most serious problems—indeed, to grow fruit is to confront bugs and diseases.

Fruit Trees. Fruit trees will have a far better chance of producing a good crop if you spray—sanely and safely, with dormant oil—and if you enlist the services of biological control. The oil spray will help take care of aphids, scales, the red apple bug, the buffalo treehopper, red mites, fruit tree leaf rollers, and others. Mix up two gallons of oil to one hundred gallons of water and spray at the delayed dormant, or silver-tip, stage. When the trees are too far into the season for oil, you can switch to microfine wettable sulfur or diatomaceous earth. Many worm pests can be killed with a spray of *Bacillus thuringiensis* powder, mixed 1½ pints to a hundred gallons of water. It also helps to keep plenty of praying mantises, ladybugs, lacewings, and trichogramma wasps on hand. All are commercially available.

Dormant-oil sprays should be applied in still air. Stir or otherwise agitate the emulsion frequently to keep it well mixed. It's wise to start a dormant-oil spraying program as a regular precautionary practice, tapering off after several years of observing its effects; don't expect one spraying to cure a heavy infestation.

Rough, loose bark can harbor overwintering eggs and pupae, so in spring you should go over the tree with a paint scraper, old hoe, or piece of saw blade, scraping carefully so that the blade doesn't lay open living wood. Put a sheet or piece of canvas beneath the scene of activity to catch all the scrapings.

A variety of plant-based insecticides and repellents are available to the organic orchardist. Rotenone is extracted from a South American plant and acts as both a stomach and contact poison. (It is poisonous to fish and baby birds, so apply it with extra care.) The ground-up heads of several kinds of chrysanthemum yield pyrethrum, a valuable poison that's safe to mammals. Ryania and sabadilla are also popular.

For a schedule of tree protection, try the following spraying times:

1. Just as the buds begin to look as though they are going to pop open at any minute.

2. When the swelling blossom buds show a trace of pink where the green covering is beginning to part.

3. When the blossoms have nearly all fallen off. (Don't ever spray—even with these mild products—during blossomtime. You may kill or chase off the bees.) These first sprays keep bugs away from the fruit buds, an apple's most vulnerable place.

4. Two to four times during the year when the major apple pest populations hatch. These times vary from area to area and from year to year. The agricultural extension service of your state university or a federal farm agent can give you precise dates. (They will also tell you to spray with legions of broad-spectrum pesticides. Do it and you'll be destroying some of your best allies, the ladybugs, lacewings, mantises, small wasps, and other predators that keep most pests under natural control.)

The *apple maggot* is a prime cause of wormy apples. The adult fly (which looks much like a housefly) can be shared by hanging up wide-mouthed jars baited with one part blackstrap molasses or malt extract to nine parts water. You may need to add a little yeast to get the mixture working. Collect and destroy drops through the season. (Cankerworm, codling moth, eastern tent caterpillar, flatheaded borer, and gypsy moth are discussed in the general section; see above.)

Wounds are favorite hiding places for *codling moth* larvae and other destructive pests and should be cleaned out to healthy wood and then dressed with a good tree wound paint. You can make your own dressing from roofing tar thinned as necessary with gasoline.

Curculio beetles play possum when frightened, and you can turn this trait to your advantage by jarring trees with a padded board. The beetles pull up their legs and drop to the ground, where they can be anticipated with a tarp or sheet. The pupal stage rests within the two inches of the soil, sometimes deeper in dry periods, and disking during the pupal period will lower the population. First collect any drops, and then start to cultivate about three weeks after the infested peaches began to drop. Repeat this practice at weekly intervals for several weeks.

Several species of *fruit fly* can be lured to their deaths by a

Plum curculio.

simple device—just a plastic orange rendered sticky with Tangle-foot or Strikem, two commercial preparations. It may take a season before any real improvement is noticed. An infestation can be further reduced by picking up and burning drop fruit twice a week. Light traps help many organic orchardists produce a cleaner crop. Blacklight is usually used, as it attracts the most species. It's best to set the traps in operation early in spring, just as soon as moths begin to appear.

The *oriental fruit moth* is an important pest of peach and apple. It starts its life of destruction as a worm, tunnelling in tender spring peach shoots. It later goes to the fruit, eating itself into a half-inch-long pink worm. If a larva enters the fruit through the stem, there may be no external sign of trouble within. To manage these pests, cultivate the soil to a depth of four inches, one to three weeks prior to blooming. Collect and destroy culls. A potentially important wasp parasite can be lured to the orchard by planting strawberries about the orchard. This beneficial seeks out both the oriental fruit moth and the strawberry leaf roller. Above all, don't intrude upon the orchard ecology with chemical pesticides—you'll only succeed in wiping out any beneficial parasites and predators you have at work.

Peach trees may host small, dark green *pear psylla* nymphs that feed on the topside of the leaves until only veins remain. The nymphs become orangish brown, winged adults. Much of the sap they suck is secreted as honeydew, a sweet substance that supports a dark fungus. A dormant-oil spray in spring should take care of psylla. If they are already established, try syringing the tree with soapsuds or dust limestone over them.

The *plum curculio* is an important threat to peaches and plums. The larvae are yellowish white, legless grubs with bow-shaped bodies; the only other larvae commonly found in peaches are those of the oriental fruit moth, which have true legs. Sanitation is important. At harvest, remove rotted fruit to the compost heap. Take off mummies left hanging on the tree before spring.

As for diseases, prudent orchardists use the cloverleaf method of pruning in late fall. This opens up a tree to allow air to circulate through the foliage, and dry foliage is less prone to fungi that get their start on wet surfaces. Prune off all dead, split, or broken branches and stubs cleanly, and paint the pruning cuts. The danger of bacterial diseases such as fire blight can be minimized by cutting cankers and diseased limbs during winter. Rub off suckers and water sprouts as they appear.

Apple scab, appearing on leaves and fruit as darkening spots, will result in premature dropping of fruit, reduction of quality, and reduced vigor because of damage to the foliage. The fungus overwinters on fallen leaves, so thoroughly rake them up or plow them under in fall or early spring. Prune twigs that appear scabbed.

Both peaches and plums may be damaged by *bacterial spot.* The disease first appears on leaves as small, round, pale green spots that later turn light brown. The spots may drop out, causing a condition called shot hole. Leaves are often shed, and sticky droplets on the underside of leaves serve to identify the disease from other leaf troubles. On fruit, look for sunken spots that later crack. To avoid bacterial spot, use only healthy, vigorous nursery stock. There is a growing number of good cultivars highly tolerant to the disease. Enrich the soil with a natural source of nitrogen, such as composted manure.

Brown corky flecks in the flesh of apples is a sign of *Baldwin spot,* or *bitter pit.* While the cause of this malady is not known, you can reduce the chances of spotting both by following practices that encourage heavy cropping and by delaying thinning as long as possible. Use nitrogen and potassium fertilizers moderately, and try to maintain a uniform level of soil moisture throughout the growing season.

East of the Rockies, cherry growers are often confronted with *brown rot.* Fruit is particularly prone to damage after being damaged by curculios, the oriental fruit moth, hail, or too much rain. The rot first appears as a small round brown spot that quickly spreads to cover the cherry. Grayish tufts on the fruit are spores. There are a variety of cultural controls. Briefly: collect and destroy mummified fruit that stay on the tree; turn under dropped fruit to interrupt the fungus life cycle; prune to allow proper air circulation and better evaporation of rainwater; avoid damaging fruit at harvest; and pick cherries before or after the hottest time of day.

Cherry leaf spot causes shot holes, yellowed foliage, and early defoliation. As a result, fruit is dwarfed and unevenly ripened. After the leaves drop in fall, mow the orchard grass, and apply a nitrogenous fertilizer to hasten the decay of the leaves so that the fungus will not be able to overwinter in the immediate area. You might also disk around the trees just before bloom.

Fire blight, serious to apple, pear, and quince, is evidenced by a variety of symptoms. Blossoms and leaves wilt and collapse; pear leaves turn black and apple leaves turn brown. Inner bark is at first water soaked and then turns reddish. The surface of smooth-barked branches darkens, and cracks typically appear at the periphery of the affected area. To discourage this bacterial disease, prune every year so that the size of cuts is minimized. Cut out all infected areas in winter or as soon as sighted on young trees (remembering to disinfect tools in the growing season). Several varieties of pear and apple show some resistance; check with a nursery or agricultural experiment station.

Soon after leaves unfold, they may show symptoms of *peach leaf curl,* appearing crinkled or puckered, thicker than normal, and discolored yellow, red, or purple. They feel leathery to the touch. As spring turns to summer, the upper surface turns grayish and takes on a powdery appearance due to the production of spores. Dry, warm weather will cause the leaves to turn brown or black and then fall from the tree. The fruit may be misshapen, fuzzless, discolored red, and bear one or more wartlike growths. A three percent dormant-oil spray should do the trick. One grower found that the onion spray he was using on his aphids also worked for leaf curl. As soon as new leaves show signs of curling, snip them and cart them away.

Pear blight (or *fire blight*) often rates as the most destructive disease of pear and is nearly as injurious to certain varieties of apple. The responsible bacterium enters at the blossom and causes blossoms to turn black and shrivelled. Leaves on the spur are darkened. Affected leaves tend to persist and serve to call attention to cankers on the supporting branches. As the infection spreads to the supporting branches, smooth patches of bark become darker.

Affected tissues are at first water soaked, later develop reddish streaks, and finally die and turn brown. Fruit becomes sunken and discolored, often showing necrotic cankers.

To avoid pear blight, don't overdo nitrogenous fertilizers. Mulch trees late in fall or in very early spring. Avoid late cultivation; in young orchards, it is best to abandon cultivation altogether in favor of a sod-mulch system of culture, using either alfalfa or grass as a cover crop. Then mow the grass or alfalfa sod early in the season and let it grow through midsummer in order to discourage late-season growth of the trees. Dormant sprays will help keep down the number of insect carriers, especially aphids and leafhoppers. A single site of infection can destroy an entire tree, so it is important to cut off infested twigs at the end of small branches, along with at least twelve inches of healthy-looking wood. You can tell how far the disease has spread by checking to see if smooth areas of bark have turned darker than normal and by making small cuts with a knife to see if the affected inner bark tissue is water soaked. Be sure to disinfect the knife between each cut. Check with your agricultural experiment station to find which varieties do best against blight.

When *X-disease* strikes cherries, you are apt to see pale or partly white fruit on red-fruited trees, while black sweet cherries appear red in color, and light-colored fruit, as on Napoleon, are dull white. On all varieties, the fruit is worthless. Growth is retarded, bloom is delayed, and some of the fruit may never mature. Late in the season, look for a bronze discoloration along the midveins of leaves. The disease may eventually cause dieback. Even with all these symptoms, X-disease is hard to detect in its early stages. If you suspect it, however, eliminate all doubt by destroying any chokecherry bushes for a distance of at least five hundred feet. Continue to check the orchard for sprouts; cultivation will help to control these.

Chestnut. The most serious disease affecting chestnut is *blight*. Within fifteen years after it was first noticed, blight had spread across the country. Few native chestnuts remain today. Even sprouts that arise from old stumps are hit, as the disease is still very much with us. On young wood, cankers appear as swollen, yellowish brown, oval or irregular areas. On older wood they are brownish, circular or irregular areas with slightly raised or depressed edges. Partial or complete girdling of stems by cankers causes leaves to yellow and eventually turn brown. Dead leaves and burrs cling to diseased branches long after normal leaf fall. The surface of older cankers is covered with minute pinpoint fruiting bodies of the blight fungus. During wet weather, yellowish spore masses ooze from fruiting bodies. These spores are carried by rain, birds, and insects. New infection develops following the entry of spores through wounds.

As soon as the disease is definitely identified, cut down the tree and burn the branches and the trunk. Debark the stump to prevent sprout growth, and replace the tree with resistant hybrid chestnuts. Breeding of resistant varieties is in progress. Chinese varieties, such as Crane and Orrin, and some Japanese varieties are known to be resistant.

Dogwood. The most serious pest of dogwood is the *dogwood borer,* a white worm with a pale brown head. A very young tree may be killed, while older dogwoods show reduced vitality and dead or dying branches. Look for swollen, knotty, gall-like areas on the trunk, either just below the ground or on the lower trunk. Young trees are most often attacked at the crown. Once the borers enter a tree, they are difficult to control. So, keep them from causing trouble by wrapping the tree with kraft paper, especially if it is a new transplant, for two years or until it is well established. Tree wounds should be painted over with shellac. Maintain the tree's vigor by fertilizing organically, watering, mulching, and pruning out dead wood. Trees planted more than three hundred yards away from an established infestation should not become seriously affected.

Elm. The worst pests of elms are the *bark beetles* that transmit *Dutch elm disease.* Since being introduced to the eastern United States around 1930, the disease has spread over most of this country and Canada. There are several wilt diseases that attack elms, all of which produce symptoms that look very much alike, but if you see oval-shaped, depressed feeding holes at the crotches of one- and two-year-old twigs, you can be fairly sure of Dutch elm disease. The first noticeable symptom is the wilting and yellowing of one or more branches. Internally, a brownish staining appears in the annual rings, showing as discontinuous streaks when the bark is peeled away from the wood or as small, shiny black or brown dots (or a partial to complete ring) when the branch is viewed in cross section. However, the only way to be sure a tree has this disease is to send twig samples to a laboratory for examination by plant pathologists. Cut six twigs or small stems about seven inches long and a half to one inch in diameter from the diseased branches of each tree. Carefully mark the twigs or stems from each tree, and wrap them securely in a cardboard box for mailing. Do not send material that has been dead for some time or is without the discolored ring under the bark. Send the samples to the laboratory of your state's agricultural extension service. It is very important that you mail the samples immediately after collecting, as the longer you delay in getting the twigs to the laboratory, the harder it is to identify the disease. Remember that a letter giving the tree's location, city, county, and date of collection should accompany each sample you send.

The only known control for Dutch elm disease is to prevent the fungus from moving through root grafts and to keep the bark beetles from carrying the fungus from diseased to healthy trees. Keep all old and dying branches pruned, and promptly remove elms that are diseased, dead, or in low vigor from injuries. Any elm wood that might harbor bark beetles is a potential breeding place for the disease fungus. Destroy elm debris by burning dead elm wood, peeling tight bark from elm wood and stumps, or by using mechanical branch chippers. Elm wood that has been cut and stacked should either be burned or buried at least six inches deep. Or, if you are using it for firewood, you should first remove and burn the bark from all logs. Pruning healthy branches may increase the incidence of Dutch elm disease if carried out from July through September, as the cuts attract the smaller European bark beetle that introduces the fungus.

Fir. Fir trees are apt to be damaged by the *spruce budworm*. This is a dark brown caterpillar with cream-colored tubercles that grows to a length of ¾ inch. Look for budworm webs holding the needles together. If you plan on setting out many seedlings, it would be best to plant stands mixed with a reduced percentage of balsam fir in order to cut down on chances of infestation. In case of a budworm infestation, cut off and destroy infested tips. If this insect has a bad record in your area, encourage birds to help out by providing birdhouses and alternate sources of food.

The small brown or black *hickory bark beetle* and its larval grubs tunnel in wood to girdle branches, and the adults eat the base of leaf stems, causing foliage to turn brown. As this pest does most damage to weak trees, fertilizing and watering may help to prevent infestation. For hopeless cases, cut and burn the seriously affected trees between fall and spring.

Juniper. *Rust* diseases of juniper are generally more unsightly than destructive, but consecutive severe infections may seriously damage trees. The three common rust diseases—cedar-apple, cedar-hawthorn, and cedar-quince—require two hosts to complete their development. The cedar-rust variety causes chocolate brown, globular or irregularly shaped corky galls that are often called cedar apples. Orange spore horns form on these galls, and the spores cause bright orange spots on apple foliage. Spores formed by these leaf infections in turn infect leaves and twigs of juniper in late summer.

Cedar-hawthorn rust results in galls on juniper and leaf rust on both hawthorn and cultivated apple. The galls are formed each year, rather than taking two years for their development as in cedar-apple rust disease. Cedar-quince rust is responsible for slightly swollen, elongate cankers that appear on the branches of red cedar and other junipers.

Because the rust diseases of red cedar and other junipers require an alternate host for the completion of their life cycles, the logical control is to avoid growing susceptible junipers within a mile of the alternate hosts—apple, hawthorn, and quince. Also, avoid planting varieties of juniper that are highly susceptible to cedar rusts. The eastern red cedar and all its horticultural varieties are very susceptible to cedar-rust diseases. The western and Colorado red cedar are much less susceptible. The columnar Chinese juniper, pfizer juniper, prostrate juniper, and andorra juniper are rarely seriously troubled. If you have time and can go to the trouble, prune out galls during the first week in April before the spore horns develop.

Maple. Maples shouldn't cause you much worry, although aphids may make a mess with their falling honeydew. See the discussion of general tree troubles, above.

Oak. Oaks may benefit from a dormant-oil spraying to manage *scale* populations. A number of foliage-eating *caterpillars* are vulnerable to a *Bacillus thuringiensis* spray.

Oak wilt is a serious disease of black and red oaks. The first symptom to keep an eye out for on these species is a slight curling of the leaves near the top of the tree or toward the tips of lateral branches. Affected leaves turn to bronze and then to brown, and finally tan progressively from the tip to the base. The first really obvious symptom then occurs—a premature defoliation that even the least observant homeowner would have trouble ignoring. On white and burr oaks, and others of the white oak group, symptoms are more localized.

In either case, control depends on preventing the spread of the causal fungus. Infected trees should be cut and either burned or hauled away as soon as possible after you spot trouble. Fortunately, trees that wilt in July usually do not produce spores until September or October. As an additional precaution, do not prune oaks in fall or spring, since the fungus can gain entrance through pruning wounds. The fungus also travels underground by way of natural root grafts, so it is best that all oaks within fifty feet of an infected tree be killed and disposed of. However, an especially valuable oak neighbor can be saved by digging a trench between the diseased and healthy trees to sever any root connections that might transmit the fungus. The trench should be thirty-six to forty inches deep and can be filled up immediately. Once infected, white oaks are slow to die, and their lives can be extended by removing infected and dead branches.

Pecan. The *hickory shuck worm* and the *case-bearer worm* can be controlled by setting out trichogramma wasp eggs two or three times during the growing season. The first release should be some time in mid-April, the second about two weeks later, and the third (if it is not an off-year and the pecans are setting), after another two weeks. One package should handle three or four trees unless the trees are widely separated, in which case you should use one package for each.

Pines. Ornamental pines are apt to be damaged by larvae of the *European pine shoot moth*. Look for short, yellowed dead needles near the tips of new shoots, with partially developed or hollowed-out buds. Young pines are most seriously affected and may become stunted and bushy from heavy infestation. Early in the year, before spring growth starts, prune the infested tips and destroy the overwintering larvae within. In Christmas tree plantations, infestations can be controlled by delaying summer pruning until the larvae are either on the twigs or inside the buds. Again, you must destroy the clippings.

A variety of stout, short-legged *pine beetles* bore into trees, especially weakened ones, about the time dogwood flowers in spring. Before you become aware of the crisscrossing tunnels through the inner bark, you'll likely notice white, yellow, or reddish brown pitch tubes (about the size of a wad of gum) scattered over the outer bark. About two weeks after attack, trees show yellowish green foliage. By the time a tree crown has turned red, the beetles have usually already left. To prevent trouble, keep pine stands properly thinned, removing damaged, old, or unhealthy trees. Take out infested trees before the weather warms up, if possible; in winter, check your trees for yellowed or reddish crowns, as these are the best indicators of attack.

When *white pine weevil* larvae girdle terminal shoots (leaders), the shoots wither, bend over, and die. The attacks rarely kill young trees, but the insect attacks provide forked and crooked trunks. Control by removing and burning tips well below the dead part to prevent emergence of the beetles. Trees planted in a shady area will be less bothered, according to tests conducted by the Canadian Department of Agriculture. Also, varieties having a thicker bark and wider trunk diameter are less susceptible to attack.

The principal disease of pines that you'll have to worry about is *white pine blister rust*. This is a fungal disease that must have an alternate native host plant on which to complete its life cycle—it can't spread directly from tree to tree. In spring, windborne spores blow to alternate hosts, including currant and gooseberry. The fungus enters trees through the needles and grows into the bark to produce cankers. Branches and stems may be girdled by these cankers. Control by removing gooseberry and currant within nine hundred feet of white pines and by keeping the area free of these alternate hosts.

Poplar. Little *European shot-hole borers* may tunnel into poplars. They make their entrances about bud scars or some other roughened place. The blackening of the so-called shot holes is due to fungi. Tunnels contribute to wind breakage and are excellent places for pathogenic fungi to get a start. The only means of control is to keep trees in a thrifty growing condition. Prune out and destroy any affected plant parts early in spring.

Spruce. Spruce, as well as pine, hemlock, and arborvitae, are occasionally beset with a serious infestation of *spruce mites*. These are tiny, dull green to nearly black bugs with a pale stripe on the back. They spin webs and cause a graying or browning of the needles. Thorough dormant-oil spraying usually will kill their brownish, flattened eggs. (An early oil spray will also take care of the gall aphid, another important pest.)

Norway and Colorado spruce are vulnerable to *cytospora canker,* a fungus disease. The lowest branches die first, followed by branches higher on the trees. The cankers are inconspicuous and may be covered by dripping resin. Control involves pruning all diseased branches back to the trunk or to the nearest healthy lateral branch. Prune only when the trees are dry. Avoid nicking the bark as you mow the lawn.

Walnut. The most important insect pest of walnut is the walnut caterpillar. Damage is signalled in midsummer by trees partially stripped of foliage. The worms' habit of congregating at the base of branches each night makes them easy to eradicate on small trees. Just rub them out with a rolled-up burlap bag late in the evening.

Willow. The *poplar-and-willow curculio* infests and destroys pussy willows and several types of poplar. The adults, black inch-long beetles, emerge in midsummer and lay their eggs in punctures in the bark. Infested tree parts should be cut and burned before the beetles emerge. In early spring, an oil emulsion can be sprayed or brushed on infested parts to kill the white, legless larvae within.

Weak poplars may be hit with *cytospora canker,* a disease that enters through wounds or weakened twigs. Twigs are killed back to larger branches, and round brownish cankers with sunken bark are formed. In moist weather, the yellow to reddish threads of the fungus spores appear from fruiting bodies on the diseased bark. To avoid trouble, keep trees growing vigorously by using organic fertilizer and watering. Prune affected limbs and cut out cankers, disinfecting the cut surfaces with tree paint.

Witch's brooms.

CHAPTER 6 Woodslore

by NEVYLE SHACKELFORD

To the settlers of rural America, a good portion of one's day-to-day living came from the woods. A young married man chopped, hewed, hauled, and laid up logs for his home. From other trees, he secured materials for much of his furniture, farm equipment, and fencing materials. The woods also furnished fuel for his hearthside, drugs for his medicine chest, dye for his clothing and coverlets, and a lot of food for his table. Beech, acorn, and hickory nut mast helped fatten his hogs and poultry. Chestnuts and red-berried holly, ginseng, pelts of possum, raccoon, and skunk—all gathered from the woods—were traded at the crossroads store for coffee, salt, soda, axes, nails, grubbing hoes, and other exotic things he could not make or grow. The young were often set to work splitting shingles, which could be sold for cash.

It was from the dynamic community of trees that the settler predicted the weather. By noting how high the bald-faced hornets built their nests from the ground, he more or less accurately predicted the depth of winter snows. By counting the gnats inside black oak galls in spring, he forecast rains or lack of rains in summer, and by observing the thickness of black walnut hulls and other natural signs found in the woods in autumn, he confidently predicted the length and severity of the coming winter weather.

Was the settler insensate to the virgin beauty of the surrounding land? To him, a woodland, like money in the bank, was simply a resource upon which he could draw as the occasion demanded. To him, a tree represented so many board feet of timber, a piece of wood for the beam of a bull-tongue plow, the runner for a sled, or a railroad tie that could be sold for fifty cents. The somber, melancholy beauty of a hemlock etched against a winter sky meant absolutely nothing to him. Its importance to him was sawtimber, tanbark, and medicine when his children came down with the croup. He never exulted in the flowering beauty of the dogwood or redbud or considered the graceful "instep of the beech" which so impressed Henry David Thoreau. To him, the myriad wildflowers of the woodland floor held little, if any, attraction. At the grim business of making a living in a harsh and often unproductive land, he was interested only in utility.

Perhaps the settler deserved more, deserved a better knowledge and a deeper understanding of the significance of his trees—how they lived, breathed, and responded to the eras, the epochs, and the seasons, how they put forth new leaves, why their tops were alive with warblers in spring, and why in autumn they changed from green to glorious hues of russet, scarlet, purple, and gold. He never learned to see trees as things of dignity and beauty or as things that helped purify the air that he breathed for the years that he lived among them. As before, he saw trees only as material objects that he could use for creature comforts. He lived a long life and in many respects, a full life, but in his patch of woods he missed many things that could have made his life much more meaningful and enjoyable.

The fruits of the Industrial Revolution allowed the settler's ancestors a more gracious life, with which came the chance to view trees as more than an economic resource. Perhaps school had a hand in the changing attitude toward the woods. The young people of settled areas could begin to see the woodlands as places of inspiration and repose, as a cool retreat in summer, and as shelter in winter. Now that starvation was no longer just outside the door, the settler's children had the luxury of sketching the trees and listening to their soft music in the wind.

The awed nature worship of Thoreau and others could only have come after the first wave of homesteaders had made the wilds habitable. Now, after many years of change to our landscape and ways of making a living, we seek in the woods just those things that made them a formidable scene for our ancestors. The settler had solitude in big doses, was all too familiar with the change of seasons, and spent most of his time outside at the mercy of the weather. These are things that lure us out of the warm living room for a moonlight tour on skis, that make us respond to the maple's first spring stirrings at sugaring-time, that cause us to hike the two-thousand-mile Appalachian Trail. The time and ability to enjoy the woods truly is a luxury.

WILD GREENS

There's a lot of good eating and drinking in the woods. Starting with wild greens—creasies, crow's foot, fiddlehead ferns, poke, speckled britches, morels, and sassafras tea in early spring—you wind up with wild grapes, pawpaws, persimmons, and nuts of various kinds in late autumn. In between times there are mulberries and sarvisberries for dessert.

Not everyone likes wild greens, of course, but there is a lot that can be said for them, especially if gathered and prepared in the old-fashioned way. They are high in vitamins A and C and will stick to the ribs as well as a kettle of soup beans seasoned with a chunk of what used to be known as sow bosom. For the best and tastiest results, wild greens should be gathered soon after they appear at the first touch of spring. Then they should be thoroughly cooked and washed to get rid of grit, sand, and any insects that may be hiding within. Hasten the greens and a little water to a bacon-greased covered skillet. Cook until tender, remove, salt to taste, add a dash of vinegar, and eat with green onions, cornbread, and a cup of steaming sassafras tea. With a noon meal such as this under the belt, you can clear off a half acre of new ground or chop up two cords of firewood without feeling the least bit tired.

PAWPAWS AND PERSIMMONS

Nearly every stand of timber in the eastern and central United States will have a few persimmon and pawpaw trees growing somewhere along its edges. These two fruits alone can make the ownership of a patch of woods worthwhile. North American Indians called the pawpaw Assimin, from which likely comes the botanical name, *Asimina tribola*. The tree was cultivated by some tribes of Indians who used its soft, pliable inner bark for weaving a coarse cloth. They also crushed the seed and used the powerful alkaloid derived from them for stupefying fish. It is recorded that, in 1541, explorer Hernando de Soto's Mississippi Valley expedition was saved from starvation by the pawpaw.

The pawpaw prefers to grow on fertile hillside benches and along alluvial bottomlands but does well enough along woodland edges. If it can get sufficient sunshine, the tree often reaches a height of from twenty to thirty feet and is characterized by a smooth grayish green bark and large dark green leaves which turn to a brilliant yellow in autumn. The pawpaw blooms in early spring with cup-shaped green flowers that turn to a deep velvety purple and assume an odor not unlike that of ripening grapes.

Although many forms of wildlife take an interest in the pawpaw when it starts ripening in late September, not all humans share the sentiment. Pawpaw connoisseurs say that the main trouble lies in the fact that few know how and when to eat the fruit. In the first place, they maintain, the pawpaw is a wild fruit and therefore is best when eaten in the wild. It should never be picked from the tree but be allowed to drop of its own accord and lie for at least a week among the autumn leaves; when its tough, green skin has taken on the color and texture of a piece of well-tanned horsehide, the fruit is ready to eat.

The best way to eat an odoriferous pawpaw is first to mash it gently between the fingers to soften up the yellow pulp. Then bite off the end and, when the wild and tangy odor assails the nostrils, suck the kneaded pulp from the skin as a gourmet might draw off the juice from a boiled lobster claw. You get the delightful bouquet and the taste at the same time.

Some romanticists call the pawpaw the fruit of reminiscence; indeed, if found rich ripe and eaten alone in the solitude of the woods, it is an experience to long remember. Thereafter the taste and smell of a pawpaw will bring back recollections, because no one who learns to relish a pawpaw can ever eat or smell one again without being just a little bit happy.

The pawpaw is distinctly plebian and was once known as the

poor man's banana. But even so, a lot of people in high places have a taste for it and never let an autumn go by without taking to the hills to search for it. No patch of woods should be without a tree or two. The tree is easily transplanted or seeded—the Indians did it all the time. Many tree nurseries sell the tree, too.

Like the pawpaw, the unripe persimmon has such a gosh-awful mouth-puckering taste and imparts the sensation of feathers sprouting on the tongue because of an excess of tannin. Some varieties never lose this astringency even when ripe, but fortunately these varieties are rare. Most ripe persimmons, as Indiana settler Elias Pym Fordham once wrote, taste as sweet as "raisins dipped in honey."

In the early years of North American exploration and settlement, Indians were found making good use of persimmons. After removing the seed, Indian women dried them for winter use. By mixing the dried pulp with a little water and meal pounded from parched corn, they baked a delicious cake.

According to the culinary history of the United States, the persimmon also contributed immensely to the diet of early settlers. They improved somewhat upon Indian cookery and used persimmons for other than bread. A delightful dish known as persimmon butter was made by mixing the dried pulp with honey and then cooking the mixture down for a little while over a slow fire.

PERSIMMON PUDDING

A special treat was persimmon pudding, which many people still enjoy. For the benefit of readers who might like to sample this dessert, here is a recipe that has been handed down from early Virginia settlers:

Take 3 eggs, ½ teaspoon of salt, 2 cups of sweet milk, 3 cups of flour, 1 quart of ripe persimmon pulp, 1 teaspoon of soda, 1 cup of sugar, and 1 pint of water. Mix well with a spoon, pour batter into a greased pan, and bake for 1 hour in a very hot oven or until the pudding turns a dark brown. Serve with whipped cream.

Another name for the persimmon is Indian raisin, perhaps because the fruit, if not shaken off by the wind or gathered by persimmon lovers of one kind or another, will often hang on the tree until late winter, turning sweeter and drier becoming like a raisin.

The persimmon was once widely employed in the treatment of certain ailments. Rich in tannin, pectin, malic acid, and sugar, the unripe fruit made a gruel which Kentucky pioneers took when suffering from diarrhea and dysentery. A tea from the bark was used as a gargle for sore throat. In case anyone is inclined to ridicule these old treatments, a pharmacopoeia of recent origin lists both the unripe fruit and the bark of the persimmon as valuable in the compounding of medicine.

WILD GRAPES

In your sorties into a woodlot, you will likely come upon what the Norse voyagers discovered when they first set foot on North American shores—the wild grape. The story is that the Norsemen found this fruit in such fantastic abundance that they named the new land Vinland.

Wild grapes are still abundant and constitute a valuable natural resource. More than seventy different species of song and game birds and thirteen species of wild animals feed with relish on the dark fruit of the untamed vine. To be fit for human consumption, wild grapes must first be subjected to the ripening influences of autumn and the alchemy of several hard frosts.

Farm wives once set great store by wild grapes. From them they made jellies and marmalades of incomparable tang and flavor, and a strong vinegar valuable for pickling—or for use as a liniment. A bandage of brown wrapping paper soaked in wild grape vinegar has eased the pain of many a farm workhand suffering from a sprain or broken bone.

According to the travel writings of William Bartram, American Indians also made good use of wild grapes. "They gather them in

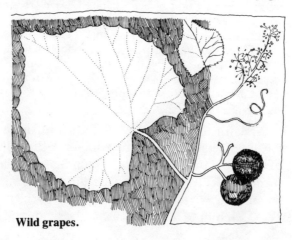

Wild grapes.

great quantities," he wrote in his journal, "and prepare for keeping by first sweating on hurdles over a gentle fire, and afterwards drying them on their bunches in the sun and air, and store them up for provision."

It must be admitted that most people find wild grapes are inferior to domestic varieties. Yet, horticulturists say, had it not been for the native plants, we would not today have the magnificent Concords, Niagaras, and Muscadines that grow in our vineyards. When the first English settlers along the Eastern seaboard tried to transplant and establish Old World varieties, they met with utter failure. Fungus diseases and insect pests of the New World were just too much for the transplants to withstand. It took a combination of the old and the new to produce the hardy new species now found in American vineyards.

Today, there are nearly eight hundred varieties of grapes in America developed either by selection and cultivation of native stocks or by grafting European varieties on the roots of wild American vines. Most varieties grown in the eastern United States are of the former kind.

Before the day of the ubiquitous hairdresser and tremendous arrays of shampoos, tonics, and other forms of scalp cosmetics, country maidens, especially of Appalachia, used the sap of wild grape vines to soften and beautify their tresses. In spring they went into the woods, cut through a finger-sized vine, caught the soapy sap in basins, and used it to wash their hair. The sap was also believed beneficial in stimulating hair growth. As a consequence, bald-headed rustics with a touch of vanity in their souls used gallons of it in attempts to restore foliage to their shining scalps. Unfortunately, research has revealed that the juice is about as effective in hair restoration as shaving the scalp in the light of the moon, another old remedy for restoring fallen locks.

Nevertheless, a wild grape vine or two is a good and interesting thing to have or establish in a patch of woods. Aside from the good jellies, marmalades, and vinegar they can provide, the vines attract wildlife and provide safe refuges for nesting birds.

THE NUT TREES

Although for all practical purposes the American chestnut has long since vanished from the woodlands, you may occasionally come upon a small tree springing from the hardy roots of an old dead tree. Such a tree may even grow a few nuts, but it probably will not live many more years because the blight that laid low its mighty ancestors is still as virulent as ever. The story of the American chestnut is a tragic one, but you can still grow a reasonable facsimile in the form of the Oriental variety or hybrids that are highly blight resistant. These varieties will grow and produce on various types of well-drained soil, but unlike the native species they will not do well at all in the woods, being intolerant of much competition and requiring almost full exposure to the sun.

In taste, nuts produced by the hybrids compare favorably with the native kind. They are generally larger and do not keep as well in dry storage, but the yield is as great and they too can be roasted, boiled, eaten raw, and made into stuffing.

CHESTNUT STUFFING

To make chestnut stuffing in the good old-fashioned way, husk a quart of boiled chestnuts, and thoroughly mash them in a mixing bowl with a potato maul or masher. To the mashed chestnuts, add a couple of tablespoons of butter, two tablespoons of chopped onions, two tablespoons of cream, and a big handful of corn bread crumbs. Salt and pepper to taste, thoroughly mix all the ingredients together, and then stuff inside a baking hen or turkey. This stuffing can also be squeezed out in the form of biscuits and baked in a shallow bread pan. Either way, it's delicious.

Though the American chestnut is gone, an abundance of other nut trees can be found in most woodlots, especially butternuts, black walnuts, hickories, and beeches. Nuts from these trees are delicious, nutritious, and can be used in pastries and candy making. Beechnuts, although a bit more tedious to prepare, can be made into a dressing every bit as tasty as that made from chestnuts.

The husks from black walnuts and butternuts, when boiled in water and strained, make a dye as enduring as anything purchased in packages at the store.

A venerable Kentuckian, known locally as Old Man Roberts, often appeared at the country church attired in an ancient linsey-woolsey suit dyed with black walnut hulls. He was very proud of this suit and claimed he had worn it for fifty years. His wonderful, industrious, and capable wife had made it from wool sheared and woven into cloth soon after their marriage. The suit was a little bit shiny, but the color was as steadfast as ever. He often boasted that it could be soaked in all the hot water between here and Hades without fading.

BLACK WALNUT DYE

Just for the sake of keeping the old art of black walnut hull dye alive, here is the recipe Mrs. Roberts used and passed along to younger housewives in her neighborhood. First she chopped up about a gallon of black walnut or butternut hulls, soaked them overnight in about two gallons of water, drained off the water, and simmered them outside over a slow fire in a cast-iron wash kettle for another two hours. Next she soaked whatever she wanted to color in clear water to which alum had been added (as a mordant) at the rate of one ounce of alum per gallon of water. Then the cloth or garment was taken out, rinsed, and soaked in the walnut water overnight. The result was a dark brown that never faded. As she explained it, the alum caused the dye to penetrate deeper into the wool fibers.

There are dozens of barks, berries, roots, and plants growing in any forest boundary that make dyes in nearly every color of the spectrum. To list them all and give directions for their preparation would take a book-length manuscript; see Chapter 11 to learn of the better-known tree dyes.

BEVERAGES FROM THE WOODS

A woodlot can provide some excellent brews to substitute for store-bought coffee, tea, beer, and soda. For instance, a delightful substitute for lemonade can be made from steeping the scarlet seed tapers of the staghorn sumac for several hours in water and then serving up the strained ade in tall glasses filled with ice cubes. The process can be stepped up by crushing tapers in water with a potato masher. The tapers ripen in midsummer and can be gathered, dried, and stored away for winter use.

In the early days of Kentucky, coffee was almost as precious as gunpowder—and much harder to come by. But settlers found a passable substitute in the large dark seed from the pealike pods of the locust, *Gymnocladus dioicus,* thereafter to be widely known as the Kentucky coffeetree. Although this tree grows all the way from central New York to Tennessee, it is not as common as most other trees. Its leaves and seedpod clusters resemble those of a locust, but the seed are much larger. The black brew is made by grinding the ripe dry seed and boiling them in water. Some who have imbibed it hot from the pot around a campfire say it is indeed innards warming, but others have described it as tasting like something drawn from a tanning vat.

Then there's the delightfully aromatic spicebush, long used as an infusion to break out the measles and as a pepper-upper for those coming in from a long day of cutting logs or grubbing out sprouts from a hillside pasture. Long used by country people to accentuate the taste of baked groundhog and parched possum, the spicebush prefers to grow in damp places in the woods and along woodland watercourses. It reaches a height of about fifteen feet, has dark green aromatic leaves, and in the fall, produces beautiful, bright red but inedible berries. A handful of bark scraped from spicebush twigs and boiled for a short time in a quart or so of sap drawn from a tapped maple tree makes a hot springtime tea fit to revive winter-wilted spirits and give the drinker a much brighter outlook on life.

Another old standby beverage from the woodlands is a pungent brew made by boiling the roots of the sassafras. Traditionally the tea has been imbibed by country people not so much because it is pleasant to drink, but as a springtime tonic. An old folk-belief holds that drinking sassafras tea tones up the system and thins down winter-thickened blood, thus making it easier for a person to withstand the heat of summer. Old Man Roberts was a firm adherent to this philosophy and claimed that it also helped his "rheumatiz." From January to June he kept a big pot of tea on the cookstove and three times a day would drink down a big mustache

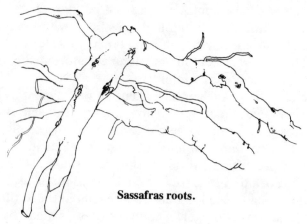

Sassafras roots.

cup of what he called hot toddy. This was a sort of highball composed half of hot tea and half of hot yellow-corn moonshine. His neighbors always claimed it was the ''corn likker'' in the tea that eased his pains and lubricated the stiffness in his joints; they urged him to drink plain willow bark tea instead, but he wouldn't. He knew what helped him and, although often told that his rheumatism medicine was endangering the future safety of his immortal soul, he stuck with it until he passed on.

Just about everybody knows about the sassafras tree and how to make the tea by boiling its roots in water. But what some may not know is that it was once considered very unlucky to use the tree for stovewood. In the arcane lore of some tribes of American Indians, the sassafras was as sacred to the Great Manitou as ambrosia was to the gods of Greek and Roman mythology. Manitou was jealous of this tree and to burn it was to risk his displeasure. Burning wood can be unlucky today, too, as it pops and cracks and cuts up like a package of Chinese firecrackers on the Fourth of July. The explosions shoot out sparks and red hot coals in all directions. Many times in backwoods history these sparks landed in strawtick beds, on rips in the wallpaper, or on some other combustible household material, setting the house on fire.

Another woodland tea-making ingredient is worthy of mention. Although not brewed nearly as often as sassafras, monkeying around with it entails no risk of stirring up the wrath of the gods. This is wintergreen or teaberry, or as many people in Appalachia call it, mountain tea, an evergreen plant that grows close to the ground in many dry woodland areas throughout the United States. In winter it bears an attractive red berry that, while edible, doesn't

Teaberry.

really have much taste. The shiny oval leaves, however, are very aromatic. The three- to five-inch plants can be easily identified by their distinctive smell. Plucked fresh from the woods and boiled for thirty minutes or so in water, these leaves turn out a flavorful, heart-warming winter beverage.

In times past, bashful rustic swains with romance on their minds often made good use of mountain tea plants. To get up enough nerve to approach and ask a young maiden's permission to walk her home from church or somewhere, they often took a swig or two of corn squeezings or pawpaw brandy purchased from a factory hidden deep in some rhododendron thicket where it was safe from revenuers. To mask the odor of this inhibition-banishing, but socially frowned-on elixir, they would chew a handful of mountain tea leaves, better whisky killers than cinnamon berries, cloves, or any of the high-priced lotions and breath sweeteners on sale at the drugstore, then or now.

If you own a patch of woods or have the privilege of wandering over woodlands belonging to somebody else, you will do well to watch for oak galls. There is much more to them than at first meets the eye. These somewhat unnatural spongy, puffy, or bladderlike egg-shaped critters are usually found on the twigs of white oaks or black oaks and in the main, according to entomologists, are caused by the larvae of certain flies, wasps, or other insects. These insects sting and lay their eggs in the tissues of the plant. When the eggs hatch and the larvae start eating into the tissues of the twig, they secrete an irritating substance that causes vegetable fibers to grow around the wound and the larvae. This continues until the larvae are completely enclosed and protected by a palace almost as magical as that of Aladdin of *Arabian Nights*. The larvae live within until they pupate and emerge as adult insects.

In pioneer times oak galls, or oak apples as they were generally known, were gathered and used in the manufacture of homemade ink. Some of the oldest American documents, it is said, were written with the bright and unfading ink from these growths. An old recipe for making oak gall ink calls for a pint of the spongy galls most often found on white oak twigs. Crush these galls and steep in just enough hot water to cover the pulp in the container. Squeeze the water from the pulp, mix with several teaspoonfuls of copperas and, if available, a half teaspoonful of gum arabic. If the gum arabic isn't available, an equal amount of castor oil will serve very well. The result will be a fine brownish black ink that, while rough on steel pens, is all but permanent. On the flyleaves of many a schoolbook of yesteryear, one can still see the name of the owner and bits of sentimental doggerel inscribed with gall ink.

Oak galls once figured prominently in backwoods medicine, being recommended for internal use in cases of diarrhea. For a sore throat, a gargle made from oak galls steeped in water might be suggested. A bath of the same concoction was recommended in cases of the seven-year-itch and other cutaneous diseases. "Oak galls," as an old country doctor's book described, "are slightly tonic, powerfully astringent, and antiseptic. They can be used whenever an astringent is called for but only when ordered by a physician."

Oak galls are products of spring but as folk weather lore has it, the state of the coming winter weather can be predicted with great accuracy by examining the insides of those found in black oaks. If, upon tearing open one of these leathery-skinned growths, a flock of gnats is found inside, then the coming winter will be mild and lacking in big snows. On the other hand, if a spider or spider-looking insect crawls forth, look out—the coming winter will be a stemwinder with blizzards galore, snows belly deep to work-oxen, and winds sharp enough to shave the teeth from an old-fashioned A-frame harrow.

There are many other galls to be found, of course. Some appear on roses, goldenrods, hoss weeds, willows, and witch hazel bushes. Each has its own particular form and history and each, as a poet once wrote, is "a little house of magic."

THE WOODS AREN'T QUITE TAMED YET

Except for poison ivy there are not many hazards to be encountered in the woodlots of today. One of the few left is the bald-faced hornet, a stinger that lives in colonies in great pumpkin-sized nests, often seen hanging from limbs of trees. Stirred to anger by a threat or presumed threat, this stinging insect will attack with a vengeance and fight to the bitter end. Its sting can be exceedingly painful, so should you spot its neat paper condominium, it would be wise to keep at a distance. But before leaving the scene, check the height of the nest in the trees. If it is high, you can safely prophesy that the snows of the coming winter will be deep. If low, vice versa. At least, so says another age-old weather sign.

If there are some nubile maidens of acquaintance or in the family, it will also be well to make note of the site of the nest. According to an old amorous superstition, a small piece of one of these nests pinned to the nether garments of a young girl of marriageable age will make her so attractive that young swains will flock around her like yellow jackets around a cider mill.

If the hornet and its nest have figured in romantic folklore, they have done the same thing in American history. In the words of one imaginative historian (whose name, unfortunately, has been forgotten), the hornet may have been an indirect cause of the British burning Washington, D.C. It was in August 1814 during the War of 1812 that a squadron of British warships dropped anchor near Lower Marlboro just off the coast of Maryland. A group of officers from the flagship of the fleet came ashore and, spotting a huge hornet's nest among the branches of a nearby tree, inquired of a small boy who had been observing the landing party what it was. Recognizing the officers as enemies of his country, the quick-witted lad told them it was the nest of a rare species of hummingbird. He told them that if they would come back at night when the birds were inside, plug up the entrance to the nest with a wad of leaves, and take it back to the ship with them and keep it for two days, the birds would stay with them as pets.

The officers did as instructed. Nobody ever knew for sure what happened, but two days later while watching the ships through a spyglass, an observer on shore saw a group of officers on the flagship suddenly go into a wild dance and then dive into the sea, dress uniforms, swords, and all. The historian in question surmised that, stung to the quick by the "hummingbirds" and in high dudgeon over this Yankee trick, the British retaliated by putting the capitol city to the torch.

Another potential hazard of the woodlot is the skunk, but if a pair takes up residence, don't panic and rush for the old shooting iron. Leave them alone and they'll return the favor. They prey on the moles and grubworms from the lawn and garden.

For those unacquainted with the skunk, it is a small black creature, often with a white stripe down its back, that comes with a squirt gun loaded with a chemical that has an odor like nothing else on earth. In its refined intensity, the aroma approaches the sublime, and once smelled, can never be forgotten. Once this attar is sprayed on a person or dog, the smell is exceedingly difficult to remove. A bath in tomato juice will help out a dog, but a person has two options: either bury or burn the foul clothes.

Some quaint humans claim skunk juice has rare medical virtues, producing a tonical and bracing effect and relieving rheumatism and failing eyesight. This may be true, but no physician from Hippocrates on down has ever recommended it. In this respect, though, it must be recounted how Old Man Roberts was inadvertently treated for eyesight failure with skunk lotion. Aroused one warm early springtime night by a terrible hullabaloo in his hen house, the old man sprang from bed, snatched up his shotgun, and scatted out barefoot to see what was causing such an unholy commotion among his poultry. In his furious rush to catch red-handed the hen roost sacker, he demonstrated an inexcusable lack of caution, stepped on the culprit which was a skunk, and for his pains, received smack in the face a full load from the varmint's vials of wrath. Totally blinded by the blast, the half-crazed man rolled on the grass in agony, during which time the animal scampered to safety in a nearby thicket with hen feathers clinging to its chin. The pain was awful, he later said, and for about the space of a half hour, he was blind as a bat. His eyeballs felt like they had been dipped in lye water, but after they quit hurting, he found to his great joy that his sight was much clearer.

WOODS WITCHERY

Most folks appreciate the magic of the change of seasons, but few these days know the magic of the witch hazel. This is a medium-sized shrub, common to cut-over woodlands. It grows from six to ten feet high, has leaves resembling those of a hazel, and blossoms in late October or November in curious, bright yellow starlike flowers. After the slender petals fall, the calyx forms a beautiful little urn which holds the developing fruit and which, according to folklore, wood elves use for drinking cups. For generations, witch hazel twigs have been used by dowsers to devine the location of underground streams of water and precious metals. But more importantly, perhaps, from its leaves and twigs is distilled a healing extract, an age-old remedy for cuts and bruises and for chapped or sunburned skin. It is said that the Oneida Indians passed the information along to early settlers.

The fruit of the witch hazel comes in the form of a nut that requires a year to reach maturity. The nut is about a half inch in

Witch hazel.

length; until the frosts of November turn it brown, the nut is covered with a velvety green husk. Cuddled deep in the close-fitting, bone-hard cells of the husk are two highly polished brown seeds decorated with a white dot. Frosty nights and sunny days of November cause the husks to break open with popping sounds like those made by a jaybird cracking beechnuts. The edges of the cells curl inward with such force that the seeds are sometimes ejected as far as twenty feet.

Contributing to the witchery of the woods is that peculiar member of the mushroom family, the wood witch. Some know it also as stinkhorn, and either name is appropriate. Possessing a fetid odor and thus repulsive to most hikers and wanderers of the woods, it is nevertheless a joy to blue-bottle flies, carrion beetles, botanists, and nature writers. To them it is an enchantress and therefore witch of the woods.

Despite its evil odor, the wood witch is curiously beautiful and a most interesting example of Old Mother Nature's glorious handiwork. Springing from an object which in color and shape first appears as a small hen egg buried in the earth is more ephemeral than the day-long life of the mayfly. After reaching maturity, the wood witch lives only a few hours and then falls apart into a jellylike glob. But these few hours are glorious. Wild and uninhibited carrion flies and beetles pay homage and assure propagation and perpetuation of the species. Below the truncated, evil-smelling cap of the wood witch there hangs a wide skirt resembling finest Mechlin lace, and in the hour or so before the cap turns a messy black, this curious fungus gives the earth a touch of beauty.

In its egg state, mushroom gourmets say, the wood witch is delicious as indeed many of its kin are excellent to eat. But here

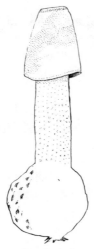

Wood witch.

would be a good time to make mention of the fact that while your woods may contain many edible mushrooms, never eat one without knowing exactly what you are doing. Mycologists say that while many of the hundreds of varieties are harmless and edible, many more are deadly. So if you don't know your mushrooms, then enjoy them by sight rather than by taste.

Not so common among the magical things of the forest is the witch's broom, a strange, dense growth of slender twigs that sometimes emerges from the limbs of trees. While not very threatening in summer, on a winter's day they take on a weird aspect when silhouetted against a pale moonlit sky, and resemble the business end of that legendary vehicle of superstition. There was a time when residents of the deep hinterlands believed any area in which a witch's broom grew was haunted. Less superstitious botanists and dendrologists say there's nothing particularly evil about the witch's broom beyond the fact that it is a product of unregulated bud development, presumably brought about by some injury, fungus, or parasite. Instead of a few buds developing while the rest are inhibited, as is customary in the normal processes of growth of a plant, many or all of the buds on a single branch develop independently and all at the same time. It is known that this condition is sometimes caused by a parasite that paralyzes the method of correlation by which adventitious buds on trees are controlled.

Not every patch of woods will have its witch's broom, but if you have black gum, elm, or black walnut trees, chances are good that there will be clumps of mistletoe sprouting from their limbs. If so, a sprig or two of this parasitical plant nailed to lintel pieces of doors at Christmas will facilitate amorous activities. But better still, perhaps, mistletoe can mean extra spending money. In most places gift shops, flower shops, and dealers in holiday greens will pay good prices for all the mistletoe they can get. Removing the mistletoe will harm neither the plant nor the tree. When cut from a limb, it will immediately grow back.

Witch hazel, wood witches, witch's brooms, and mistletoe—decades after the land has been groomed of any real threats to life, the woods continues to thrill the imagination.

Mistletoe.

CHAPTER 7 Harvesting
the Sugar
Orchard
by GUY THOMPSON

Long before the white man arrived on the shores of North
America, Indians were tapping maples for their sweet sap. It is
thought that they broke off branches or slashed trunks with axes to
cause the trees to flow and used birch bark troughs and containers
to direct and hold sap. The sap was poured into hollowed-out logs
and brought to a boil by dropping fire-heated rocks into the liquid.
Until recent times, the Iroquois celebrated a thanks-to-the-maple
festival in spring.

Today, the first warm, sunny days of spring still cause something to stir within the residents of sugaring country, just as the
warmth awakens the flow of sap in the maples. Perhaps it's the
urge to get outside after being cooped up all winter. But sugarers
get a bug that smites them each February, a spring fever that hits a
month or two early.

Although the tools of sugaring have progressed a good ways
since the red man ruled the sugarbush, collecting and boiling down

the sap is still hard work. Even a backyard operation involves most of the physical labor and time that commercial operations require. Still, sugarers would agree that the end sweet is well worth the sweat. Maple syrup and sugar have a distinctive flavor that precious few don't like, and maple products reflect this popularity in their price. Despite the valiant effort of chemists to duplicate its flavor, real maple syrup continues to be in demand. And it tastes even better if you make it yourself.

The maple flavor is subtle, and nobody is sure just how it comes about; strangely, the sap is faintly sweet but otherwise tasteless as it flows from the tree. No matter what the explanation, maple syrup can be substituted for cane sugar and honey in many everyday recipes. How much maple syrup should you use? The best proportions can only be worked out by trial and error, but $^3/_4$ cup of syrup is roughly equivalent to one cup of sugar. Also, the liquid in the recipe should be reduced by about three tablespoons for every cup of syrup used. Common uses include glazing ham and carrots, and flavoring baked butternut or acorn squash, baked beans, meatloaf, cookies, cakes, candy, and pies. The possibilities are endless; if something sounds like it would be good with maple syrup, give it a try. Tree sap has long been brewed into beers, especially in Scandinavia, and Vermont stores sell a maple syrup wine.

If you have a good number of sugar maples in your woodlot, you might consider making syrup commercially. A relatively small investment can yield a respectable profit. The operation looks more attractive when you consider that sugaring happens at a time of year when there aren't many other activities to compete for one's time. Aside from the profit motive, it's likely that most commercial sugarers are just plain more susceptible than most others to the romance of this ancient art. The special requirements of a big-time operation will be dealt with later in the chapter.

When maples go dormant in the fall, the sap leaves the branches and goes down into the roots for winter storage. Come spring, when the temperature rises above freezing and into the upper thirties and forties, the sap starts its flow back up the trunk. The sap may run occasionally in late fall and winter, but the modest flow isn't worth the effort of hanging out a bucket until the middle or end of February, depending on location. You should be tapping when 40°F. days are followed by cold nights—a time of season that has a special feel to many backyard and sugarbush operators.

GETTING PREPARED

Of the great many species of native and imported maples growing in the United States and Canada, only two species have enough sugar content in their sap to make them worthwhile to commercial and backyard sugarers. These two, the sugar maple and black sugar maple, are so much alike they may be considered the same species for the purposes of maple sugar production.

The sugar maples are native to the northeastern and north central states and adjacent parts of Canada. In addition, they are found and are tapped, south into the mountains of Kentucky and Tennessee. The trees can be most easily identified by their leaves. While other maples will work (as well as the sweet birch and several nut trees), they are usually passed by because of their low sugar content and because syrup made from the sap may have an off taste.

It is best to identify the sugar maples in summer and to mark them at that time with paint or tags of some sort (see the illustration of the leaf in Chapter 11). After the leaves fall off, maples look a lot like most other trees, and it's downright embarrassing to find that you've tapped a beech or a linden when the leaves come out the next spring.

Any sugar maple measuring more than 10 inches in diameter at chest height (four feet above the ground) can be tapped. A tree of 10 to 15 inches around should have only one taphole, a 15- to 20-inch tree may have two, a 20- to 25-incher may have three, and those over 25 inches may have four. Size the trees with a flexible tape measure. Another way to gauge the number of tapholes a tree should have is to simply divide the circumference by three. Record the suitable number of tapholes when you identify and mark the trees, either with coded paint marks or on tags. You might paint a spot on the tree for each taphole.

The sugar in maple sap is produced by photosynthesis in the leaves. The more leaves on a tree, the more sugar will be produced. Therefore, the best trees are those with wide, deep crowns. These trees not only yield more sap, but the sap is sweeter as well. Maples edging a road or in a fencerow have room to spread out and are usually better producers than those deep within a woodlot. How much syrup can you expect from your trees? For a rough estimate (and only a rough estimate is possible), figure that each taphole will yield from five to fifteen gallons of sap per season; when boiled down, the sap will end up as a quart or so of syrup. As you can see, there's a lot of work ahead of you.

In starting out, it's best not to be overly ambitious. Heavily running tapholes may yield up to two gallons a day, and five-gallon collection buckets get awfully heavy if you have to carry them very far, especially if the snow lies deep. Start off by tapping a few maples at a reasonably close distance.

If you must lug the sap a good distance, consider placing one or two twenty-gallon trashcans on a sled or toboggan. Tie the cans down well, and do not fill them more than half full to avoid spilling much precious sap. Of course, rough terrain will make such a labor-saving conveyance impracticable.

The sap begins to run at any time between the middle of February and early May; the season may end as early as March or as late as May. Note that a long season is not necessarily a highly productive one.

THE EQUIPMENT

Each taphole requires a spile (or spout) and a bucket to collect the sap. Spiles can be made by whittling and reaming sumac stems, which involves a modest amount of fireside labor (see illustration). If you can't locate a sumac or are knife shy, you can buy spiles from a maple equipment supplier or from some hardware stores. A number of different designs are on the market, fashioned from rolled sheet metal, cast iron, and various plastics, and all are efficient. Some have hooks from which to hang the bucket.

Practically any plastic or metal bucket will do for a collecting vessel, although steel buckets should be galvanized or tin-plated to avoid imparting a metallic taste to the sap. Do not under any cir-

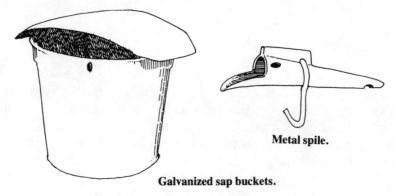

Metal spile.

Galvanized sap buckets.

cumstances use a bucket that may be coated with lead paint, as some of the lead will likely end up in the syrup. The buckets should have some sort of cover to keep rain, bark, twigs, and bugs from landing in the sap. Covers ought to fit closely while allowing enough space to permit some ventilation. Buckets with a two- to three-gallon capacity are best; smaller containers may not be able to hold a good day's run and should be emptied more often. In a pinch, even fruit jars and tin cans will do. Maple equipment suppliers sell special buckets. The plastic ones are lighter and easier to clean but blow around in the wind. So, if yours is a windy site, it's best to use metal buckets. Stainless steel buckets are easy to clean and impervious to the elements, but most backyard producers find them prohibitively expensive.

Large commercial operations now usually use plastic capillaries to transport sap from the taphole to the central collection tank. Tubing eliminates the tedious and time-consuming task of emptying buckets.

You should provide for some way to hold sap until it can be boiled. Since each taphole may yield up to two gallons of sap a day during a good run, plan on a storage capacity of at least two and preferably three or four gallons for every hole you drill. Small operations can get by with twenty- to thirty-gallon trash cans. If the cans have to be carried very far when full, it is best to use heavy galvanized ones, as plastic cans may not hold up under the weight. For larger capacity, consider the oval watering tanks sold by farm supply centers; they are sturdy and relatively inexpensive and the one-hundred-gallon size is practical for storing up to eighty gallons.

THE FIRST STEPS

Drill the holes with a $7/16$-inch wood bit. A hand brace will work, but a heavy-duty breast drill is easier to use. Sink a three-inch hole at a slight upward angle so that the sap will drain and at a height that makes emptying buckets as easy as possible. Knock in the spile snugly, but not so hard that it will split the surrounding wood; the feel of driving spiles in just right comes with practice.

Collect the sap at least once a day, preferably carrying two buckets at a time for balance. If any ice has formed in a bucket, throw it out, as the sugar doesn't freeze and will be left behind in the liquid at the bottom. Rain water that collects in buckets must be dumped, as you will have enough water to boil off without it.

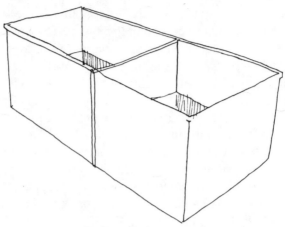

Rectangular storage tank.

Bacteria and yeast are present in the sap even as it comes out of the tree. The more these organisms work on the sap before it is boiled, the lower the quality of the finished syrup. Keep bacterial and yeast action to a minimum by making sure the equipment is as clean as possible. Scrub out storage tanks and collection buckets between sap runs, and clean out the tree buckets at least twice during the season. Bacterial growth is discouraged by low temperatures, so keep sap that is stored for boiling as cool as possible. It is also important to boil the sap soon after collection.

BOILING DOWN THE SAP

For the sake of everything and everyone in the kitchen, plan to do most of the boiling outdoors. Some sugar is carried off with the steam, and a sticky deposit is left wherever the steam condenses.

In a small operation, a deep, large pan such as an old wash boiler will serve as an evaporator. Maple suppliers offer a 2-by-4 foot pan, one foot deep, and made of tinplate. To make efficient use of the fire's heat, this boiler comes with a special arch and grates. However, you should have a fair number of tapholes to justify the considerable expense of such a custom-made boiler. A still more expensive model has a corrugated bottom for added heating surface and operates with a continuous feed of sap, which flows from an elevated storage tank through a series of five partitioned sections in the evaporator. A 2-by-4 foot model now brings about six hundred dollars, and you should have at least fifty tapholes to benefit from this investment. Large syrup producers use evapora-

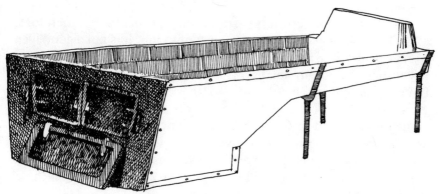

Evaporator for wood or coal.

tors of this type that measure up to six feet wide and twenty-five feet long and are capable of boiling off five to six hundred gallons per hour.

As was said earlier, it takes time to boil down sap. If you are using a wash boiler or washtub, you can figure that it will take you all day to reduce twenty to thirty gallons of sap to syrup. Generally, the sap should be boiled as soon as possible after collecting, as bacteria will turn it sour if given time and the right conditions. Sap can be stored a week or more if ultraviolet lamps are beamed at it; the USDA has information on this technique. The real advantage of using these germicidal lights is that the bailing time (the period in which buckets are emptied) can be extended over several days before boiling is necessary.

Making syrup is like any other agricultural operation in that it is dependent on weather conditions. There are good years and there are bad years, and the profitability of an operation for any given year is an uncertainty. In recent years, another variable factor has been the cost of fuel. Propane and fuel oil have risen sharply in price, and even the cost of the traditional fuel, cordwood, has been high—so high, in fact, that a sugarman would likely save money by selling his wood for firewood and then using the money to buy fuel oil or propane. This is assuming you can market the firewood; if you can't, burn it in the evaporator.

The best way to determine when the sap has boiled down into the desirable density of syrup is to check the temperature with a thermometer. The thermometer should read up to at least 250°F. and should have a scale open enough that the temperature can be determined within one degree.

The sap-to-syrup ratio starts out at 40 to 1; therefore, 10 gallons of sap will end as one quart of syrup. It is not a good idea to mix nearly finished syrup and fresh sap (row sap) when boiling; if you have to do any mixing, it is best to mix batches of partially boiled sap having nearly the same density. So, if you have 15 gallons to boil off and the pan will only hold 10, start with 10 gallons and add the other 5 in small batches of about a gallon as soon as there is room. If you have 20 gallons, boil down 10 as far as possible, store it, and boil down the second 10 gallons. Then mix the two to complete the boiling. If you have 30 gallons, run three batches and then mix.

You should keep some butter or cooking oil on hand to prevent boiling sap from foaming up. A little butter held on a stick in the boiling sap or a few drops of vegetable oil will do the trick. Never leave a boiling pan unattended; as many veteran sugarmen can attest, it is heartbreaking to return to the scene to find that the sap has boiled over and caught fire, giving a scorched taste to the batch. Another danger is that the sugar sand which forms at the bottom of the tank may burn and ruin a batch. Baked-on sugar sand can be removed by boiling *soft* water in the pan and scrubbing with a stiff brush.

In a small operation, it is best to finish off the syrup in a small pot on the kitchen stove. When the syrup has reached the proper density, it will boil at 7.5°F. above the boiling point of water. The boiling point of water changes from day to day with atmospheric pressure, and you should therefore boil a pan and check its temperature at the time you will be finishing off a batch of syrup. As an example, if the water boils at 210°F., then the syrup will be finished when its boiling temperature reaches 217.5°F.

To produce a clear, clean syrup, pour it through $1/4$-inch felt filter material, available from maple equipment suppliers in 36-inch-square sheets. Although expensive, the felt can be cleaned and reused many times. To support the felt, use a large strainer or a deep-fat fryer basket. The syrup will run through the filter much faster if poured when boiling hot. The hot syrup should be put into jars or bottles while it is still at least 180° to 200°F., and the containers must be sealed immediately and turned upside down to sterilize the entire inside. Put up in this way, syrup should last in a sealed container indefinitely at room temperature.

When felt filters get plugged up, hang them over the outdoor

boiling pan and pour boiling sap through them to reclaim the sugar. Then run clean, hot water through them backwards.

A number of different plastic and metal jugs are available for marketing maple syrup. For your own use, the best and cheapest containers are soda or beer bottles with reclosable tops. Regular screw-top canning jars work well, too. Just be sure you have enough containers before the season starts so that you don't get caught short at the last minute, and see to it that they are clean and dried before use.

At the end of the season, all the equipment should be thoroughly cleaned before it is put away. Dirty equipment may breed bacteria, making a mess for the next season.

MAPLE SUGAR

Maple sugar is a delicious confection sold in the form of bars or molded shapes. If less water is evaporated, a product known as maple cream or maple butter is produced. There is a good demand for these products, and they bring a good price, but their manufacture requires special equipment. If you are interested, first visit the candy kitchens of several maple producers for a look at what is involved. Much of the equipment can be homemade (such as beating and whipping equipment), and many producers have been quite resourceful in designing machines using materials they have on hand. You'll find what you need to know in the USDA's *Maple Syrup Producers' Manual*, Handbook No. 134. Order it from the Superintendent of Documents, U.S. Government Printing Office, Washington, DC 20402.

COMMERCIAL PRODUCTION

The USDA's manual is also an excellent introduction to producing syrup on a commercial scale. It is well organized, easy to read, and inexpensive.

You should visit producers in the area before investing much money or time. Examine the equipment and talk to them about the maple business. Everyone in the business has his own methods that he feels work best.

It is difficult to say just how much work or investment is involved in a small commercial setup, but you should probably aim at a thousand tapholes for a start. With this size, you should be able to cover the depreciation of new equipment and still make a respectable profit. An operation with only one hundred or two hundred tapholes will make enough syrup for home use with enough left over to help defray expenses but will not generate any appreciable income.

Most syrup producers have other jobs to tend to, and because time is a precious commodity they have to find ways to make the operation as efficient as possible. The first important consideration is boiling capacity: the larger the evaporator, the shorter the time required to boil down a given amount of syrup. For example, a 4-by-8 foot evaporator will boil down seven hundred gallons of sap in about nine hours, while an evaporator measuring 5-by-14 feet would only require three hours. So, don't skimp on an evaporator if you have the few extra dollars to invest. Secondly, a great deal of time and effort can be saved by using plastic tubing to carry sap from the tapholes to collecting tanks. Although it takes time before and after the season to install and take down the system, tubing saves time when time is at a premium, doing all of the work that would otherwise be done by men lugging buckets through the snowy woods. Techniques for the use of plastic tubing have evolved considerably in the past few years, and printed instruction tends to go quickly out of date; it would therefore be wise to check out the systems of nearby producers.

MARKETING

Most sugarers with modest-sized operations sell their syrup either from the house or by mail. As the demand for syrup has far exceeded the supply in recent years, you shouldn't have much trouble selling all you can make. Producers who lose money on their operations either use wasteful and out-of-date methods or aren't charging enough—and often one mistake is coupled with the other. If you're in doubt about how much to charge, check on the pricing of those producers in the area who are making a substantial profit.

If you find it more profitable to sell syrup in bulk, pour it off into drums instead of tins and jugs meant for retail trade; if the bulk deal doesn't work out, you can always package it for retail instead.

Should you find yourself with questions that the local operators can't answer, turn to the USDA's publications or to the local county agent.

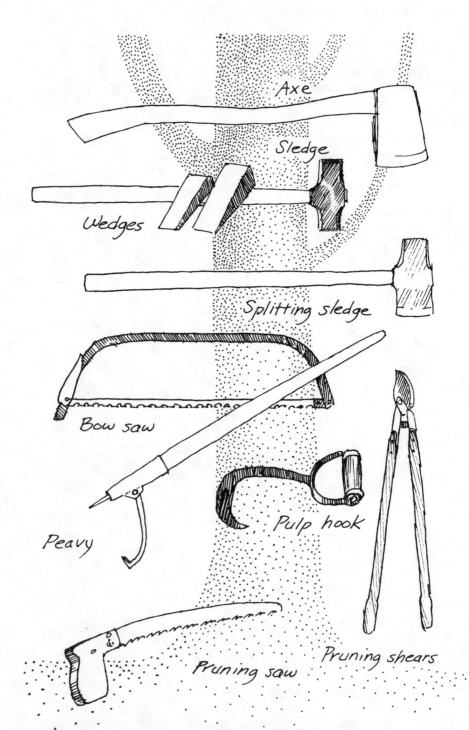

Axe

Sledge

Wedges

Splitting sledge

Bow saw

Peavy

Pulp hook

Pruning shears

Pruning saw

The tools.

CHAPTER **8** Trees and Homestead Economics: Trees Once Made Self-sufficiency Possible, and Can Again

by JIM RITCHIE

What is a woodlot worth on a modern-day homestead?

In the next chapter we discuss how to manage a home woodlot as a source of income. But these pages are aimed at those tree owners who want to produce a little or a good share of their livelihood directly from their acres; it speaks to those who would rather put timber directly to work then sell timber products and buy those wooden items ready-made.

This flies in the face of the bigger-is-better schools of eco-

nomics which preach ever-faster cash flows and ever-larger invest-
ments in capital equipment. Most homesteaders are mavericks who
rebel at the spend-yourself-rich philosophy, as a basic principle of
homesteading is to trade labor for capital expenditures. Expressed
in another way, homesteading is largely an exercise in not buying
what you can produce.

A tree takes on a different appearance in this light of true economic reality. You cut a tree only after you're convinced that you
will replace it with something of even more real worth, and you do
not waste the wood the tree contains.

So, your trees will not die in vain. Not with fences to build,
compost heaps and outbuildings to construct, and cordwood in
high demand in today's fuel-short homes. Each tree that must give
way is a potential fence rail or clothesline pole. Nothing need be
wasted, not even the smaller limbs and brush, which can be piled in
hollows and gullies to thwart erosion and provide cover for rabbits
and quail.

The raw material most in evidence on the typical homestead is
timber. Let's survey an imaginary—but typical—plot of land. The
trees are mostly second-growth oak and hickory, with a sprinkling
of ash and black walnut. Here and there along the hillside, an
absolutely uncuttable dogwood or a sarvisberry pins a welcome
bouquet to the early spring woods. In the hollows, maple, sycamore, and mulberry trees play along a gravelly branch. Rounding
out the woodlot are a few sassafras and persimmon trees, and an
occasional cedar whose seed had been air-freighted in by the birds.
It's not particularly valuable, as timbered tracts are evaluated.
Neither Weyerhauser nor Georgia-Pacific would get excited over
such a mix of trees. But on these acres grow fence rails, gates, hay
racks, tool handles, outbuildings, cordwood, and furniture.

Since it is often necessary to clear trees and sprouts to make
room for gardening, animal husbandry, and recreation, why not invest a little more time and labor to turn this timber into fixtures
needed around the place?

A funny thing happens to a person who brushes shoulders with
a woods. After a while, he starts to gather new meaning from the
old phrase, "You can't see the forest for the trees." It's no longer a
woods. Each tree is an individual, a well-known acquaintance: the
big hollow white oak that serves as home for a family of flying
squirrels; the red oak with the dead snag where woodpeckers hold

drilling maneuvers. You get to know them all, to know their moods and seasons, and it adds peculiar pleasure to the joys of living close to the land.

You acquire a kinship with the trees that share your land. You develop racial prejudices, becoming partial to some species rather than others. Blackjack and postoak are beneath respect, while black walnut and mulberry find obvious favor. This kinship doesn't mean that you mourn those trees you cut for firewood or those you use to build a fence, a barn, or a hay rack—no more than you grieve for baby chicks that have grown into fryers that must be butchered for the family table.

But you learn to care for your trees (and for the birds and animals that live in, around, and under them) with more of a feeling of family than of property. It's a closeness that makes you feel a personal kind of rage when a careless hunter's or hiker's match threatens your woods. It's an appreciation for the time and patience and care nature uses in making a tree—or a man. It's a conviction that to waste even one tree is the basest sin.

Converting standing timber into useful, needed homestead fixtures involves no great skill, but it does call on imagination and hard work. A tall, straight, limb-free red oak is potential framing material for a hen house or calf shed. Mulberry, black locust, pine, and fir make long-lived fence posts. Scrubbier trees can become bean poles, tomato stakes, or hen roosts. Any kind of wood will make a warming fire, although oak, fruitwoods, and hickory are best. But how best to put the wood to work? To come up with the most practical answer, it is necessary to apply a rudimentary "homestead economics" to the situation at hand. Suppose you must clear timber for pasture and fields, and at the same time need to build fences to enclose livestock on those areas. Should you cut the timber into firewood lengths, sell the wood, and then buy fencing materials? Or, should you use the wood to build the fence?

Granted that firewood is a more marketable commodity in some areas than others, let's say you could sell fireplace wood for $15 per cord (4-by-4-by-8 feet of wood) f.o.b. your homestead. In wood-scarce regions the price may be higher; in other areas it may be lower. The timber in a cord of wood will provide enough rails to construct about seventy feet of durable fence. However, it takes less time, labor, and other resources to turn small, pole-sized timber into fence rails than into firewood.

With hog wire costing $40 or more per 330-foot spool, barbed wire at $25 per quarter-mile roll, and steel fence posts at $1.50 each, seventy feet of fence built with purchased materials will cost about $18. On the other hand, after deducting the extra out-of-pocket costs of sawing timber into firewood lengths (rather than ten-foot fence rails), the timber in one cord of wood is worth $4 to $4.50 more as fencing materials than as firewood sold to pay for commercial fencing materials.

Also, by building the fence of native materials, you have created something that fits and complements the setting. A metal-post-and-wire fence would look pretty much like fences everywhere—businesslike but not very attractive. And most people who enjoy their land would agree that their acres should not only produce food and shelter, but beauty and joy as well.

Perhaps most important of all, by building your fences from materials produced on your homestead you have weaned yourself from dependence on wire manufacturers and merchandisers. You are not at the mercy of tight-supply situations that seem to generate shortages—real or invented—of a great many products nowadays. In short, you have achieved a measure of self-reliance.

As you cut and split rails and weave them into a fence, still another value is harvested from the woodlot: you gain a personal satisfaction in building something useful with your own two hands. This is an intangible but very important benefit; an economist would have a tough time putting a dollar value on satisfaction of that sort, but it adds up to real worth.

TOOLS YOU'LL NEED

For most homestead timbering purposes, you will need a small investment in tools: a lightweight chainsaw or bow saw, an axe, at least two steel wedges for splitting logs and rails, and a sledge to drive the wedges. You may prefer a splitting hammer, a sledge with a hammer face on one side and a wedge-shaped splitting blade on the other; once you get the hang of using it, this tool can speed up timber chores.

You may also find a use for a machete, brush hook, grub hoe, mattock, power circular saw, and bucksaw. Other, more specialized tools and equipment are occasionally called in for particular jobs around the homestead, but unless you'll use a specialized piece of equipment enough to justify the investment, you may want to borrow or rent, rather than buy.

All woodcutting tools should be kept sharp and out of the rain. Well-maintained equipment is not only easier to work with, but safer as well. A sledge or axe that is loose on the handle is a hazard both to the operator and to fellow workers or bystanders. A dull axe blade may bounce or glance off the log and into a human limb.

Saws. For most homestead work a lightweight chainsaw with a fourteen- or sixteen-inch cutter bar is sufficient. You can buy heavier, more powerful models if you need to do a lot of heavy work. But by notching and undercutting with smaller saws, you can fell trees up to three feet in diameter. If you've never operated a chainsaw, try out two or three different models and sizes. Also, consider the availability of parts and service before you buy.

Chainsaws aren't for everybody. Many people object to the cash investment, the stink or the noise, or the gas and oil consumed. You may prefer to work with a crosscut saw—either the two-man variety (if you have a steady helper) or a one-man saw. The rhythmic sound of a crosscut has a soothing quality, something that certainly cannot be said of a chainsaw.

Two-man saws are typically six to seven feet long and have cutting teeth alternated with drag teeth to remove sawdust from the saw kerf (or slot). These saws are made of high-quality steel and are too limber and springy for handy operation by one man. However, it is possible to use a two-man saw by yourself if you remove the handle from one end and support that end of the saw with a slender, limber stick cut to just the right length. Poke the

**Two-man saw on branch
for operation by a single person.**

stick into the ground at the midpoint of the saw's travel, on the opposite side of the log (or tree) from the sawyer and tie the upper end of the stick to the saw where the handle was removed. The stick then supports the saw so that the blade doesn't flop and wobble. It's not as handy as a sawing partner, but it works.

One-man crosscut saws are shorter, about five feet in length, and are made of heavier metal than two-man crosscuts. They are not as likely to buckle when pushed and pulled from one end.

Because of the chainsaw's great popularity, manual crosscut saws have all but disappeared from some areas—even in regions of heavy timbering. And, as with most steel products, prices have climbed rapidly the past few years. To find a used saw, check classified ads in local newspapers and visit a few farm sales. (You often can also find reasonably priced axes, sledges, wedges, files, and other timber equipment at these sales.)

For lighter work, a bow saw or bucksaw is more convenient than a crosscut. These have two or three-foot sawblades stretched in a metal or wooden frame, hacksaw fashion. They're ideal for bucking off cordwood cuts, limbing, and other light timber work and can be used to fell smaller trees. They also come in handy for pruning fruit and ornamentals.

With all saws—power or manual—the condition of the cutting teeth has a big influence on the condition of the sawyer at the end of a day's work. There's an art to filing and setting saw teeth, and no two timbermen file a saw the same way. You'll need a good, clean file—about a number 10 bastard flat file for crosscut saws. Chainsaw chains have teeth of various sizes, so you'll need to buy a file to fit your particular saw. Bow saw blades can be easily replaced.

You'll also need gauges to show the length and set of the saw teeth. (Turn the saw teeth up and sight lengthwise along the blade or chain; the angle of the cutting teeth from the plane of the saw blade is called the set.) For cutting fibrous wood, such as green oak or hickory, you'll need to set a greater angle than normal into the saw's teeth.

For clearing brush and small trees from land to be cultivated, a wheel-mounted circular power saw can come in handy, particularly if you're clearing large areas. These saws are fast and effective in cutting top growth. Some models are self-propelled but shouldn't be used on steep slopes.

Axes. A good single- or double-bitted axe is a necessary homestead tool. Keep the blade sharp on the job with a small pocket whetstone.

Some woodsmen prefer to use a double-bitted axe, with one blade honed sharp and the other allowed to dull slightly; the dull blade serves well for grubbing out roots and cutting off sprouts below ground level, while the sharp blade is never used for such rough work.

Leaving one blade slightly dulled gives a measure of protection when chopping among limbs that might catch the axe and divert your swing. If the axe glances into your leg or foot (an occurrence to be avoided at all costs) at least you have a fifty-fifty chance that the dull blade will make contact.

HOMESTEAD USES OF TIMBER

A homestead woodlot can provide shelter, fuel, tools, equipment, and outbuildings—depending on the size of the woods, the kind of trees grown, and the imagination and skill of the landowner.

Firewood. Trees are most often cut for burning. Even if you cut timber for other purposes, you'll find that much of your firewood supply—perhaps all of it—can come from the leftover portions of the harvested trees.

Wood varies in heating value with the species used and the degree of seasoning. Wood that has been allowed to air-dry for a year or more after cutting has a moisture content of twenty to twenty-five percent and will burn better and produce more heat per unit of wood than freshly cut, green wood. Also, dried wood does not deposit as much creosote on flue walls, lessening the chance of a chimney fire.

The best firewood burns steadily but not too quickly, produces a lot of heat for the amount of wood used, and burns cleanly with

To fell a tree properly, cut wedges as shown.

little creosote deposit and little ash. The table below gives the heat equivalents of the most common firewood species (based on air-dried wood) as compared with fuel oil. The heat values are given in millions of Btu's (British thermal unit—the amount of heat required to raise the temperature of one pound of water by one degree per cord of wood).

Softwoods generally make poor firewood. They burn too quickly, produce relatively little heat, and often give off unpleasant odors. For example, air-dried red pine has but 12.8 million Btu's per cord as compared with 24 million Btu's per cord of white oak.

HEAT EQUIVALENTS OF WOOD, BY SPECIES

Wood (1 standard cord)	Available heat of 1 cord of wood (Btu's)	No. 2 fuel oil (gallons)
Hickory, shagbark	24,600,000	251
Locust, black	24,600,000	251
Ironwood (hardhack)	24,100,000	246
Apple	23,877,000	244
Elm, rock	23,488,000	240
Hickory or butternut	23,477,000	240
Oak, white	22,700,000	232
Beech, American	21,800,000	222
Oak, red	21,300,000	217
Maple, sugar	21,300,000	217
Birch, yellow	21,300,000	217
Ash, white	20,000,000	204
Walnut, black	19,500,000	198
Birch, white	18,900,000	193
Cherry, black	18,770,000	191
Tamarack (eastern larch)	18,650,000	190
Maple, red	18,600,000	190
Ash, green	18,360,000	187
Pine, pitch	17,970,000	183
Sycamore, American	17,950,000	183
Ash, black	17,300,000	177
Elm, American	17,200,000	176
Maple, silver	17,000,000	173
Spruce, red	13,632,000	139
Hemlock	13,500,000	138
Willow, black	13,206,000	135
Pine, red	12,765,000	130
Aspen (poplar)	12,500,000	128
Pine, white	12,022,000	123
Basswood	11,700,000	119
Fir, balsam	11,282,000	115

You can compare the heating value—and the relative costs—of wood with other fuels by computing the price for each Btu of available heat. For example, a gallon of home heating oil produces about 140,000 Btu's. Which would be the better buy—oil at 30 cents per gallon or white oak wood at $30 per cord?

The wood, with 24 million Btu's per cord, costs $1.25 per million Btu's (24 million Btu's divided into $30), whereas the heating oil (at 30 cents per gallon) costs about $2.70 per million Btu's. Or, a cord of air-dried white oak wood has a heating value of about 168 gallons of fuel oil. At 30 cents per gallon, 168 gallons of fuel oil cost more than $50. Even if you charge yourself wages for the extra work of carrying out ashes, wood is a better fuel buy. You'll need to check on the relative prices of firewood and other heating fuels in the area before figuring your own price comparisons.

To dry wood, stack it log-cabin style in as dry a place as possible. If that place is outside, the wood pile can be shielded from the elements by placing a tarp, plastic sheet, or odd piece of metal over it. How long should wood be aged? A year, if possible. Green wood will burn but uses up much of its energy in turning moisture to steam. If you must use green wood, allow the leaves and branches to remain on a felled tree for at least two weeks before sawing it up; this draws off much moisture from the log. Ideally, you should be diligent enough to have at least a year's worth of wood salted away so that you are never forced to burn unseasoned wood.

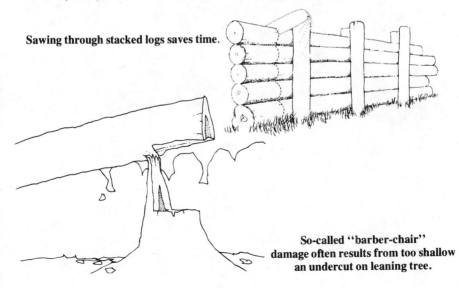

Sawing through stacked logs saves time.

So-called "barber-chair" damage often results from too shallow an undercut on leaning tree.

In addition to its greater efficiency, dry wood is not as apt to line a chimney with creosote. Creosote is the highly fragrant, tarry stuff that causes chimney fires. (It can serve, however, in the garden: string soaked in soupy creosote will keep away rabbits when strung up like small-scale wire fence.) Creosote may blacken ceilings and walls if it leaks out of stovepipes or chimneys which are in disrepair.

IN CASE OF A CHIMNEY FIRE . . .

Although every source agrees that chimney fires are a terrible thing, few offer a hint of what to do when one strikes. Our one experience suggested what seems to be a good answer for exposed portions of stovepipe.

I knew we had trouble when the stove suddenly started crackling excitedly and I could hear the air being sucked in around the doors and mica windows. Then, as I watched, the silvery pipe turned a matte gray. I yelled to my wife to get old sheets and soak them. I half-filled a bucket and doused the fire, and the wet sheets were wrapped around the pipe. Since that time, we've taken care to disassemble the pipe every month or so through the winter, and soak and scrape out the accreted creosote and soot. A long-handled wire brush works well. While a messy job, it allows us to sleep better at night.

We've heard that creosote deposits are discouraged by occasionally throwing a handful of salt on a hot fire. Another tip: if you must burn wet or green or rain-soaked wood, use it on a hot fire so that the creosote has less of a chance of condensing on the pipe.

R.B.Y.

Fencing. For a good rail fence, you'll need to split rails from relatively straight-grained timber. The rails may be eight, ten, or twelve feet long—or whatever length best suits your purpose. Split rails thick enough so that they will not settle and warp after you've laid them up into a fence—at least four or five inches wide at the smaller end.

When you're splitting rails, start a wedge into the smaller end of the log, perpendicular to the growth rings of the tree and aligned directly with the heart of the log. Drive this wedge almost home, within a half inch or so, and then start the second wedge down the log where the crack is about ¼ inch wide. By the time you've struck this wedge two or three blows with the sledge, the first wedge should drop out of the widened crack. Use the wedges al-

Zig-zag fence, with view from above.

ternately to split the log from end to end, cutting hanging splinters with an axe.

How should a rail fence be laid up? Old-timers built fences with a ninety-degree worm or zig-zag. However, you can use a shallower angle by cheating a bit, nailing together the top two or three courses of rails. This takes fewer rails, fencing goes faster, and the fence will be sturdy enough for most purposes. Bottom rails will last longer if they don't come in contact with the ground, so set them on flat stones. Make your fence only as high as it needs to be; seven or eight rails high will turn cattle.

Post-and-pole fencing can take any form or shape you wish. You can use split rails nailed to posts, round rails mortised into posts—or whatever best suits your sense of design. Peeled poles may make a more attractive fence than poles with the bark left on, but the peeling involves extra work.

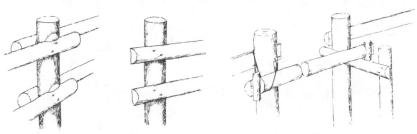

Post-and-pole fence.   **Gate.**

Some timber species have better resistance to decay than others and have a longer life as fence posts. The best species for untreated posts are black locust, Osage orange, white cedar, red cedar, southern cypress, catalpa, sassafras, redwood, and mulberry. The life of wood placed in contact with the soil can be extended by treating the posts with chemicals such as creosote, penta, or zinc chloride. These products often are expensive, make the wood messy to handle and, by their nature, are more or less toxic to humans. Some can cause skin irritation by just brief contact with the treated wood. A cheaper but less effective method of preserving wood is to soak the ends of fence posts in used engine oil. Into an open-ended barrel, pour enough used oil to cover that part of the post that will be in the ground. Stand the posts in the oil for forty-eight hours or more, and then lift them out and let them drip dry over the container for a day or so. This messy procedure is more effective with seasoned posts than with green wood.

Livestock Equipment and Other Projects. Simple but effective structures can be built from posts and poles with a small out-of-pocket cost. While a pole barn, calf shed, or hay rack represents a goodly investment in labor, aching joints and blisters yield to time, and there's real satisfaction in looking about the homestead and knowing that most of the man-made structures in sight were built by you, from timber that grew on your land.

Need a livestock shelter? Cut four posts with forks on the top end, place them in the ground with the forks up, and then place

Livestock shelter. Roof with a thatch of long grass hay or straw.

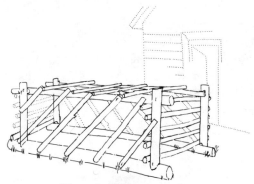

**Hayrack. Slant manger bars
for strength and to save hay.**

frame members across the forks, as illustrated. Use more poles for rafters, thatch the top with straw or hay, and you have a cheap calf shed. You can use this same idea to provide a shade arbor for livestock where there are no trees. Instead of straw, cover the rafter poles with leafy boughs.

Have you priced custom-made wooden or metal hayfeeding racks lately? You can make your own from poles, as large or small as the purpose demands. The rack can be designed for feeding either bales or loose hay, can be made portable or fixed, roofed or open topped—and the savings will buy much of the first winter's hay supply.

Bridges can take any size and dimension, from a single tree felled to make a foot bridge to a kingpost truss that would support a freight train. You can also construct cattle guards of logs and poles,

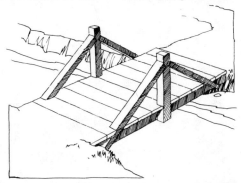

Kingpost truss bridge utilizes angled notches to hold pieces in place and to distribute weight evenly. The truss is designed so that each timber both pushes down and pulls up, transferring weight from the center to the ends of the bridge.

saving a lot of gate opening and closing. (Cattle guards should not be installed where property fences are adjacent to busy public roads. Now and then, a cow will learn to cross a cattle guard as nimbly as a mountain goat.) Even the saplings and small limbs that are not suitable for fencing, building, or burning find uses as bean poles, hen roosts, tomato stakes, and so on.

Grape arbors, hay barns, rose trellises, lawn swings, log cabins, furniture—hundreds of homestead fixtures are growing out there in the woods. Need a harrow to smooth a field or cover a seedling of winter wheat? Cut a couple of bristly trees and leave the limbs six inches or so long all along the trunks. Pulled behind a tractor or pickup truck, those trees make a passable homemade tillage implement.

Trees, a few tools, and imagination—basic resources for the do-it-myself homesteader.

Simple post-and-crosstree clothesline poles.

Feeding Livestock with Tree Crops. The recent interest in foraging for wild foods ensures that some free and very good delicacies will no longer go unnoticed. But what of the long-forgotten practice of grazing livestock under a grove of nut, locust, or mulberry trees? In Europe of the Middle Ages, farmers let their animals feed beneath the trees while the animals in turn left their manure to nourish the trees. What the animals couldn't eat was gathered up and stored for winter feeding.

Tree farming became a thing of the past as farmers gave up the nomadic life of herdsmen and turned their attention to grains. But it's worth a few paragraphs to examine several tree crops and see just how they stack up against more conventional feeds. Credit for gathering much of the information that follows goes to the late J. Russell Smith, author of *Tree Crops* (Devin-Adair, 1953). Unfortunately, his hope that trees could someday provide an important source of animal food has yet to come to be. That's not to say, however, that you can't start to put trees to work feeding livestock.

• *Honey locust.* Edible for humans, the pods of this legumous tree appeal to a variety of animals as well. Dairy cattle will pick those they can reach and forage from the ground. Some farmers gather the pods for winter feeding, and one dairyman made a feed made of equal parts honey locust, bran, and shorts (a by-product of wheat milling), all run through a hammermill. The locust is also valuable in that its nitrogen-producing nodules improve the soil. The tree is attractive, as well. Some trees bear better than others, and good qualities can be passed on to trees propagated either by grafting or from root suckers.

• *Mulberry.* The mulberry is a tree fruit that appears in profusion each year, only to fall and stain the surrounding earth. The fruit intrude into the consciousness when berry-eating birds color cars with their purple droppings; otherwise, little notice is given to the berries. But the mulberry can be an important food for both swine and poultry. Although the fruit cannot be stored, it takes little to establish trees over the pigs' yard or the chickens' run. Earlier in this century, farmers in the Carolinas and the Cotton Belt made good use of mulberry trees as hog feed, planting orchards for hogs to run in. Mulberries are easily transplanted.

• *Persimmon.* Like the mulberry, the persimmon tree is a proven hog fattener. But while the berries fall early in summer, persimmons are ready to be eaten from September through as late as

November. Cows and horses enjoy the fruit, too. Once hogs acquire an ear for the sound of the dropping fruit, they will trot away
from their feed to pick them up.

• *Carob*. Carob is popularly known as a substitute for chocolate,
and this attractive tree has long been used to feed sheep and cattle
in Europe, especially on farms of the Mediterranean.

• *Mesquite*. In areas of the Southwest prone to drought, the mesquite has shown its value as a feed for cattle, horses, goats, and
hogs. It is able to survive where other trees cannot because of a
very deep root system and modest need for moisture.

• *Chestnut*. Smith suggests that Japanese and Chinese varieties
could be bred as a food source for hogs; even turkeys could
benefit, by picking up escaping worms and beetles and any crumbs
the pigs may have missed.

• *Oak*. Smith refers to the oak as the corn tree. It's a productive
tree, with acorns rich in food value. "As the pioneer farmers of
Pennsylvania pushed aside the flowing stream of oil from their
springs so that animals might drink water," says Smith, "so the
modern world has pushed aside this good food plant, the oak tree."
Along the moving frontier of this country, acorns were known as a
valuable feed for fattening up hogs. In 1916, it was reported by the
Kentucky Agricultural Experiment Station that hogs in that state
were fattened on acorns, and then finished on corn to harden the
fat—"Lard of the acorn-fed hog will not, of course, congeal."
Hogs let out to forage on their own in the woods can be trained to
report back at the barnyard once or twice a week to pick up corn as
a supplement and to keep them tame.

Is the meat of an acorn-fed hog different than that of animals
raised on corn? Smith says that the former is softer in consistency
and brings lower prices. But if properly prepared and regarded with
an open mind, he suggests, the acorn pork should be just as good in
every way. A closed mind is apt to consider acorn pork an ersatz
meat, or a novelty at best; the same was true of reindeer meat when
offered instead of beef during the meat shortage of World War I.

As hog feed, a gallon of acorns may be equal to eight or ten
ears of yellow corn—at least in calories of energy. Acorns are low
in protein, however—typically from two to three percent protein
by weight. For a balanced livestock ration, some protein supplement such as soybean oil meal would need to be fed (to about a
fourteen-percent level for hogs, for example). But, consider this:

suppose a pork producer grew soybeans around the edges or in the spaces between his oak trees. Might not the combination produce a "self-feeding" balanced ration for producing pork? This is the kind of possibility—perhaps far-out sounding at first—that needs poking into by minds unfettered by conventional ways of thinking.

Other lifestock relish acorns, too. But under some conditions, acorns are toxic to ruminant animals. This hazard appears to be greatest during warm, damp autumns when the fallen nuts begin to sprout. Cattle, sheep, and goats readily eat them, however—even when the acorns do not agree with their several stomachs.

Dried acorns apparently hold no hazard to ruminants. Perhaps the acorns could be gathered, dried, and ground into a coarse meal to be used as a carbohydrate base for ruminant rations. Poultry also thrive on cracked or ground acorns. In fact, acorns are the basic natural food of wild turkeys.

• *Black walnut.* Although the walnut is high in protein, its use as cattle feed is discouraged by the difficulty in extracting the kernels.

• *Beech. Nut Trees* records the practice in Kentucky of fencing in woodlots with woven wire and then turning the hogs loose when the ripe beechnuts start to drop.

CHAPTER **9** The New Trend
in Woodlot
Management

by JIM RITCHIE
and ROGER B. YEPSEN, JR.

Like a garden, a woodlot can be cultivated to produce a crop. The trees are thinned, the undesirable or "weed trees" are removed, and the valuable species are harvested. But while gardening is enjoying great popularity, woodland owners have come to place less and less importance on making use of the wood. In an economy that places such a premium on wood, this declining role played by small landowners is unfortunate, especially when you consider that close to three-fourths of forests in the East occur in privately owned pieces of from three to five hundred acres.

Why are landowners passing up the chance to market a valuable commodity? For one thing, they just don't stand to make that much profit. Owners of modest wooded acreage have found that the value of their timber doesn't make up for the high price of woodland and the steep taxes that go along with it. A second reason is that the public is more than ever aware of the noncommercial worth of woodlands. Browsers, bird watchers, hunters, hikers, and ecologists all find values in the forest that cannot be measured in terms of lucre.

What appears to be a standoff between lumberman and nature lover is quickly dispelled by talking to the new breed of forester who hastens to explain the concept of multiple use of family forests. With his guidance, you should be able to enjoy a modest income while improving the wildlife habitat, harvesting firewood, protecting a watershed, and making the forest more pleasing to the eye. In addition to selling timber, monetary reward is realized from rising land values and from government subsidies. In most counties, the U.S. Forest Service's Agricultural Conservation Program shares with owners the cost of improving existing stands of trees and the cost of planting trees and shrubs on farmlands for forests, windbreaks, shelterbelts, wildlife food and shelter, and erosion control. Cost shares are paid upon completion of the approved project, and payments typically cover from fifty to eighty percent of the cost.

But financial gain shouldn't be your only motive. It's likely that the harvested timber won't pay off the interest on the loan taken out to buy the land. A couple of decades ago the value of timber growth per ten-year period was generally twice the cost of well-managed woodland. Today, the timber growth value per ten years is usually less than half the cost of the land. And of course, all of the fixed costs, including interest, taxes, and insurance, have gone steadily up.

DESIGNING AN INTEGRATED PROGRAM

The first step in a woodlot management program is deciding just what you want from your acres of trees. Fortunately, wildlife, recreation, aesthetics, and watershed protection all tend to be compatible in a hardwood forest. And with a bit of intelligent compromise, valuable timber trees can be cultivated at the same time. It may seem contradictory, but there are several ways in which selective logging can keep the woods a happy place for man and animal. For one, cutting timber and cull trees (those that are misshapen or in poor health) leaves holes in the woods that support small trees and small bushes, which in turn support wildlife. The new growth that comes up provides excellent browse for deer. Ruffed grouse benefit when the density of the forest is reduced,

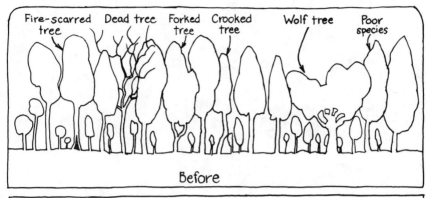

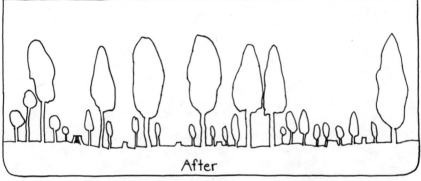

Timber stand improvement involves removing some trees.

and nesting areas can be created by piling up slash (logging or trimming debris) in bramble thickets that run along the forest's edge. Such openings also encourage tree reproduction, as most species need a good deal of light to get started in life. Cull trees should be removed to encourage the growth of nearby timber trees, but as culls often serve as den or feed trees for wildlife, care should be taken to leave those that figure importantly to animals and birds.

Species diversity favors a variety of wildlife and is aesthetically pleasing, especially when trees flower in spring and turn their colors. While it would seem that lumbering mixed stands would be difficult or impractical, this is not so. And, differing species provide an interesting variety of woodlot chores. Pines require pruning, hardwoods do not. Pines yield earlier cuttings, while hardwoods take their time in growing to marketable size (but furnish firewood as they mature).

Clear-cutting is somewhat of a dirty word to many, and it can't be denied that deforested areas are ugly to the eye and inhospitable

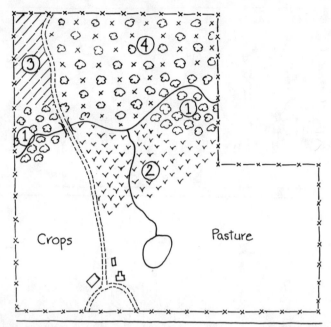

Crops

Pasture

Sample planning map for a homestead forest. 1) is a stand of bottomland hardwood, uneven-aged; 2) is a new planting of pines that will need improvement work; 3) is a newly cut area that need reforestation; and 4) is a mixed pine hardwood stand that needs release cutting.

to a variety of wildlife. So, while clear-cutting may yield an immediate and considerable profit, it is inimical to integrated use of the woodlot.

TAKING A LOOK AT WHAT YOUR WOODLOT CAN PROVIDE

Make an appointment with your county forester, and together take a walk through the woodlot to inventory what you have. Although he is likely most concerned with getting timber on the market, the forester should be able to help you plan a variety of uses. So, before he arrives, it would be good to decide just what uses you're interested in.

Income. The county forester can help you find mills that will come in and take the trees he has marked. Or, a private consulting forester can be hired to handle the sale and collect the bill. Either way, you save yourself a lot of effort.

But some people enjoy the effort. They take much personal satisfaction in being part-time foresters. What does it take to ready trees for market? You should be fairly certain that you really enjoy being in the woods, that your vision of vernal employment is more than a pipe dream. And, you should be in fairly good physical shape, although age hasn't much hampered sexigenarian Rockwell Stephens, author of *One Man's Forest* (Stephen Greene Press, 1974), who with his wife takes on ten-acre plots of Vermont woodland. Sales of hemlock and poplar have proven that their project is more than just fun and games in the woods.

How much can you expect to make? Count satisfaction as part of your wage, and you'll be doing all right. Stephens' first logging experience netted him an amount "far from subsistence income," but "an occasional sale of quality logs plus the smaller but more frequent payments for poplar and the small annual amounts from the Agricultural Conservation Program definitely covered out-of-pocket expenses for all our work."

The value of the trees on your woodlot is influenced by the local market for wood. Ask area industries, sawmills, and pulp mills about species purchases, prices, and means of transporting the wood. Logs bought for sawtimber and veneer bring more than those bought for pulp. And of course the species has a lot to do with price. For example, the Michigan State University Cooperative Extension Service gives the current prices for quality veneer

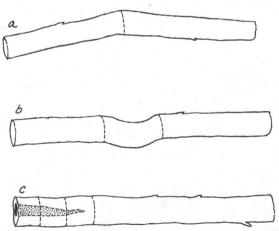

How a tree is cut into logs has a big influence on its value as veneer or saw timber. Trunks with bends (a) or crooks (b) should be cut so as to give the greatest length of straight log. Rotten butts (c) and serious defects should be bucked off.

logs as ranging from $100 per thousand board feet for red oak to over $500 per thousand board feet for black walnut. At the other end of the scale, an excelsior mill mentioned in *One Man's Forest* offered $20 a cord for poplar, plus a transportation allowance of a dollar or two.

Choice species bring good prices as sawtimber and as veneer (which is shaved from the revolving log). One such species is sugar maple, usually occurring in mixed stands. It is a heavy, hard, close-grained wood that is highly valued by the lumber industry, being used for furniture, veneer, flooring, and woodenware. Certain trees produce wood with a highly decorative figuring known as bird's-eye, which is prized for cabinetmaking. Sugar maple is the source of another potential source of income, maple syrup. Yellow birch ranks as the most important North American member of the birch family, its heavy, hard wood being used for furniture, veneer, interior trim, woodenware, and handles. The tops of the species have been distilled to produce the traditional essence of birch and root beers. The reddish brown heartwood of black cherry is used for fine furniture and veneer. This tree is typically found in mixed forest stands, where close neighbors cause it to grow straight and tall. Northern red oak and white oak are used for construction, flooring, furniture veneer, and railroad ties. Red and white pine are good choices for plantings on open land. Unlike most of the hardwoods, pine is of no use as firewood but grows quickly and can

Highly valuable figured wood is obtained from crotches and burls. For greatest return, such trees should be harvested by digging out the entire lower log with stump attached.

be cut early for posts or pulpwood (providing you have enough trees to bother with). The first choice of cabinet and furniture makers is black walnut. It grows best on deep, rich, moist, river-deposited soils. Other choice species that command high prices include loblolly, longleaf, shortleaf, and slash pines in the South, the southern cypresses, sweet gum, cucumber tree, basswood, white ash, and the cedars and catalpas.

Recreation and Aesthetics. You can make your woodland a place of enjoyment and beauty with minimum impact upon the environment. Ponds, roads, structures, and even new plantings should be planned with a thought to harmonizing with the surroundings. Ideally, the woodland environment should exemplify the harmony that is possible between man and nature. While it seems man has accepted it as his manifest destiny to manipulate his habitat, this manipulation needn't spawn ecological blunders if we can understand and sense our role in the natural scheme of things.

HOW PUBLIC AND PRIVATE FORESTERS CAN HELP

The hour I spent with the service forester for Berks and Lancaster Counties (Pennsylvania), Robert Schweitzer, was of great help in understanding the workings of the dense woodlot that surrounds my house. I had a lot of questions for him when he arrived for our appointment. What could I do about the thicket of spicebush that makes the woods nearly impenetrable? Which trees should be felled to admit more light to the house and cut down on the humidity indoors? Where were the nearest sawmills, and would they bother ripping up a few logs for me? How long ago was fieldstone gathered to make the low walls that now bordered woods from woods? Where could I find black spruce for brewing spruce beer?

I got my answers, and the offer of more help should I decide to make a clearing around the house or market some of the trees. There is no charge for a service forester's time. He will mark trees, take inventory of the woodlot, make a rough estimate of the worth of a cutting, and give you a list of sawmills in your area. To find the local public forester, check with the state department of forestry, conservation or environmental resources.

If you are interested in harvesting a sizeable acreage, or desire help in making financial arrangements with a sawmill or pulp mill, consider hiring a private consultant forester. They can transact a sale, while a public forester cannot, and receive a commission on the sale. A list of consultant foresters is available from the state office

R. B. Y.

SIZING UP THE WOODLOT

Woodlands tend to be one of three types: those with few commercially valuable trees, with cordwood trees only, and with sawtimber trees only. Of course, these are very general categories, and most lots likely have all three characteristics to some degree. But, a knowledge of what sort of trees you have can help in planning what to do with the woodlot.

Few Commercially Valuable Trees. That a woods has few valuable trees doesn't hamper recreation—hiking, hunting, foraging, fishing, birdwatching, and so on. But you might make the woods more easily enjoyed by clearing away underbrush or blazing trails for hiking or cross-country skiing.

The woodlot can be made valuable in the future by artificial forestation. Christmas tree plantings offer an income that is realized in only a few years; see Chapter 10. You might also plant for pulp mills, if any are in the area. In New York and New England, the best species for pulp are the spruces and northern pines. In the Middle Atlantic states, the usual choices are Virginia and loblolly pines. Southern pines predominate in the Coastal Plain and Piedmont regions.

Certain species are highly valued for fence posts, including black locust and eastern red cedar. If erosion is a problem on your land, consider black locust, hybrid poplars, sycamore, and jack, shortleaf, and Virginia pines. For sawtimber and veneer, the recommended species are white and red pine in the North, and loblolly and slash pines in the South. As for the hardwoods, red oak, tulip poplar, and ash are sometimes chosen, and black walnut is valuable as a veneer tree.

A planting of mixed species has its advantages, aesthetic, economic, and ecological. One plan might include Christmas trees, which are ready for the market in ten years, pulpwood, which could be taken out in twenty-five years, and sawlogs, large enough for the saw after three decades or more. Such mixed plantings favor wildlife, as they provide a variety of foods and habitats. Finally, most people would agree that a variety of trees is more appealing than neat rows of like-sized pines or hardwoods.

Undesirable tree species often compete with marketable trees for space, light, and nutrients, and can be weeded out from time to time. Also, large but undesirable species can be removed in what are known as liberation cuttings. Either fell the unwanted trees or girdle them all around the trunk.

Cordwood Trees Only. As defined by Reginald D. Forbes in *Woodlands for Profit and Pleasure* (American Forestry Association, 1971), cordwood trees range in diameter from four-inch saplings to young trees of up to eight or ten inches. They may either be cut to realize an immediate profit or be allowed to grow. Some species should be cut now, as they will not increase in value with time; these include aspens, jack pine, Virginia pine, and sand and timber pines. These species rarely reach sawtimber size, points out Forbes, and usually are finished growing by thirty-five years. So, they should be clear-cut for fuel or pulpwood. The value of cordwood stands can be improved by weeding, improvement cuttings, and pruning valuable species.

Sawtimber Trees Only. If many trees in the woodlot are more than ten inches in diameter, the time may be right for a harvest cutting—especially if you find coniferous trees with a diameter of eighteen or so inches and valued hardwoods measuring at least twenty inches. Many woodlot owners would rather just sit back and enjoy such fine trees, and this is all right so long as it is realized that such a stand will deteriorate in value if left alone. Big trees will begin to break up, and rot will enter injured trees. Forbes suggests cutting overmature trees of all species, all marketable trees of poor species and seed-bearing size, and marketable trees of valued species that are crowding out other trees in better shape. Trees above a certain diameter can be saved—say, broad-leafed trees of more than sixteen inches in diameter.

TENDING YOUR TREES

Trees, like a garden, will grow by themselves after they have been planted. But an unmanaged garden will not produce nearly as well as one that is carefully tended, and the same is true of a woodlot. The big difference is that with a garden you can enjoy the fruits of your labor in one season, whereas a forest takes years to start producing marketable results.

Generally, the goal of woodlot management is to keep the timberland producing the maximum quantity of highest quality products. Of course, you may want to modify your management to accommodate other uses you will make of your woodlot—wildlife, recreation, or whatever other purpose you wish.

To keep your woodlot growing according to your plan, you will need to make some maintenance cuttings and prunings from time to time. Professional foresters call this nonharvest saw work "timber-stand improvement" (TSI). TSI means weeding or cleaning out undesirable species of trees so that they do not compete with more useful trees. It involves thinning crowded trees so that those left have more space, light, and moisture to grow more vigorously; it involves making release cuttings—that is, removing larger trees that overtop seedlings or saplings; and it involves pruning those trees which are potential sawlogs, veneer, or other wood products that require big logs of high quality.

Most young, second-growth stands suffer from crowding, which slows down growth. You can roughly gauge a tree's rate of growth by the ratio of the length of its live crown and its overall height; if branches on more than half the length of the tree are dead, chances are crowding is having an ill effect. Trees grown at a uniform rate typically produce the best wood, although notable exceptions to this are oaks, hickory, and ash, which yield a superior wood if grown quickly.

Forests in Japan and Europe are kept properly thinned, partly because the trimmings are marketable as fuel. In this country, however, the cost of labor and low fuel wood consumption mean that thinning has long-term benefits only. There are exceptions to this. For example, in southern New Jersey, white cedar trimmings are extensively used as bean poles, tomato stakes, and various other products.

How much TSI should you undertake? Again, it depends. How much time and labor do you have available to work your trees? What species do you grow, and for what ultimate market? What other, nontimber uses will you make of your woodlot? Here's where planning can be a big help, as can that fellow we introduced earlier—the extension forester.

If you own a large forested acreage but have limited time to tend it, you may want to concentrate only on the most productive areas. It's more profitable to have a few fast-growing, valuable trees than to have hundreds of acres of stunted, gnarled, worthless shrubs. Perhaps you'll want to leave some areas in brushy undergrowth anyway, if part of your goal is to provide wildlife cover. The open floor of a mature forest offers little shelter to rabbits, quail, and other small game.

For a smaller woodlot—say up to thirty acres—and for woodlands with only young timber (no trees that will need to be harvested for several years), your plan can be fairly simple. Draw a rough map of the property, showing any areas that need replanting, thinning, weeding, or release cutting. For areas needing reforestation, the map should indicate the number and species to be planted and when they will be planted.

For larger forests, particularly where some timber is approaching maturity, the plan should include a harvesting schedule, based on your inventory of the timber and local markets. Again, a map is a useful tool. Plot in the location of any haul roads, fire breaks, or other features.

Whatever size and stage of maturity, whatever species and market your trees have, *permanence* is a major consideration in woodlot management. That is, the forest must be kept fully stocked to be constantly reproducing. Even if you start with a woods of mature trees of little commercial value, with time you can convert your acreage to species that will return bigger profits to your time, labor, and investment.

PREPARING FOR PAYDAY

You've worked hard and long, and now you have trees approaching marketable size. Payday is in sight. The first buyer cruises your woods and offers you a lump sum for your trees as they stand on the stump. Should you take his offer?

No! Selling timber without measuring the products it contains is like selling livestock without weighing the animals. Timber sales made without an idea as to the volume, quality, and value of the wood are unwise—and usually unprofitable to the seller. Know how much timber you have to sell and what it's worth on the local market. Consider the care and management you provided the trees, interest and taxes on the land where they grew, and the risk of fire or other damage. Don't be in too big a hurry to sell. Unlike a bushel of tomatoes, those trees will keep until you've done your merchandising homework.

Let's say you planted that acre of seedlings twenty-five years ago. Today, you have the equivalent of thirty cords of wood on that acre. As firewood, you might gross anywhere from $15 to $70 per cord, depending on how much of the cutting and hauling you did yourself, and on what kind of market prevails in your locality. To get toward the upper end of that price range, you'll need to be in a wood-deficit area, fairly close to big-city fireplaces.

The price a pulpwood operator would pay to come in and harvest your trees depends on your proximity to a papermill, competition for wood in your area, and several other factors. In many sections of the country, you might receive only $4 per cord. The thirty cords, then, could return you an income of $120 per acre in twenty-five years, if purchased and harvested by a pulpwood cutter. This is virtually clear income, as you will be out little if any harvesting costs.

Or, you might realize as much as $2,100 gross income if you cut, haul, and sell the thirty cords as firewood. That sounds like much the best profit, but you will be out the time, labor, and expense of harvesting and delivering the wood. That cost can amount to half or more of the gross income, which would leave you about $1,050 clear. Sounds a lot better than selling your trees as pulpwood, doesn't it?

But don't stop figuring yet. The value of a tree changes abruptly as it moves from pulpwood size (five inches or more in diameter measured at 4½ feet above the ground—called diameter at breast height or DBH) to sawtimber sizes (ten inches or greater DBH for softwoods, twelve inches or greater DBH for hardwoods). For example, a pine tree nine inches in diameter might increase in value from fifty cents for pulpwood to two dollars for sawtimber in the two or three years it takes to gain another inch or more in diameter. That's a four-fold increase in value, just for waiting another couple of years or so.

How To Measure Trees. Knowing what you have to sell and securing bids before you sell can mean additional dollars from your timber. Decide which trees are ready for market, measure them, and mark them with paint spots at breast height and below stump height. Or, if trees are already cut, scale the logs before you send them to the mill.

To compute the volume of standing trees you need to know two dimensions: the diameter at breast height and the usable length of the tree. To make a close estimate, you'll need a cruising stick and the volume table shown later in this section.

However, you can make rough estimates of timber volume quickly and with no equipment other than your thumb and a straight stick. By using formulas you can estimate sawtimber and cordwood per acre accurately enough to get a good idea of what you have to sell.

First, you'll need to calibrate your thumb. Place a one-foot-wide target 4½ feet above the ground on a tree or wall. Extend your arm at full length, hold up your thumb, and back away from the target until your thumb appears to just cover the target. Measure the horizontal distance from your eye to the target. Use this distance to find the basal area factor (BAF) for your thumb, from the following table:

Distance (ft.)	BAF	Distance (ft.)	BAF
20	27	31	11
21	25	32	11
22	22	33	10
23	21	34	9
24	19	35	9
25	17	36	8
26	16	37	8
27	15	38	8
28	14	39	7
29	13	40	7
30	12		

Remember you thumb's BAF. To estimate the basal area of a stand, pick out a number of representative points in the woods—preferably widely separated locations on fairly level ground. At each point, count the number of trees which appear larger at DBH than your thumb. Each time you stop to take a measurement, turn a complete circle, using your eye as the pivot point. Count every tree that appears to be just equal to your thumb's width. Then, estimate the square feet of basal area per acre as:

$$\frac{\text{Number of trees counted} \times \text{BAF}}{\text{Number of points measured}}$$

For example, suppose you count 150 "in" trees at 30 different points and your thumb's BAF is 11. Then,

$$\frac{150 \times 11}{30} = 55 \text{ square feet of basal area per acre.}$$

This figure, basal area per acre, does not mean much in itself, but you'll need to use it to compute sawtimber or cordwood volume per acre, after you've estimated tree height.

To do that, you'll need a straight stick about four feet long. Measure the distance from your sighting eye to your fist when your hand is extended horizontally. Mark on the stick a length equal to that distance. To use this homemade gauge, hold the stick straight up with the mark just even with the top of your hand. Back away from the tree, on relatively level ground, until the lines of sight over your fist and the top of the stick intersect the tree's base and the top end of the usable trunk, respectively. The distance between you and the base of the tree should be the same as the tree's height. Remember, you want to measure the *usable* height of the tree rather than the topmost branches.

Sawtimber volume usually is measured in board feet (a board foot is equal to the volume of a board 12 inches square and one inch thick, or 144 cubic inches of wood). To estimate board feet in a tree, choose a number of representative points on relatively level ground in the tree stand. At each point, use the stick method to determine the number of usable 16-foot-long logs larger than 10 inches in diameter. You can determine this after you've found

the usable height of the tree by pacing 16 feet of the distance between you and the base of the tree. Measure the distance to the nearest half-log, or 8 feet.

For hardwoods, you can estimate board foot volumes by:

$$\frac{\text{Number of logs} \times \text{BAF} \times 67}{\text{Number of points measured}}$$

For example, say you count 130.5 logs, each 16 feet long, at 30 different points in a hardwood stand.

$$\frac{130.5 \times 11 \times 67}{30} = 3{,}206 \text{ board feet per acre}$$

For softwoods, the formula is:

$$\frac{\text{Number of logs} \times \text{BAF} \times 60}{\text{Number of points measured}}$$

You can estimate cordwood volume per acre in much the same way. Determine the average basal area per acre, with your calibrated thumb and the formula above; then determine the average usable height of trees, using the stick. Rough cords per acre can be estimated as:

$$\frac{\text{Basal area per acre}}{100} \times \frac{\text{Average height}}{2}$$

For example, if the average basal area per acre is 55 square feet and the average usable height of trees is 60 feet, then:

$$\frac{55}{100} \times \frac{60}{2} = 16.5 \text{ cords per acre.}$$

Once you commit these formulas to memory, this technique will be a fast way to roughly estimate the volume of sawtimber or cordwood in your woodlots.

The Cruising Stick—A Forester's Slide Rule. For more accurate measurements, you should use a cruising stick and a volume table, such as the International Rule printed below. Cruising sticks can be purchased from most timber equipment supply firms, and extension foresters in many states will provide one free of charge to landowners.

To use the stick to measure tree diameter at breast height, use the scale marked "Diameter—Inches." Face the tree and hold the stick at arm's length (about twenty-five inches from your eye) with the edge of the stick against the tree. Close one eye and move the stick sidewise until the left end is even with your line of sight to the left edge of the tree. Read outside the bark, since volume tables allow for a normal sawmill slab.

Without moving your head, and still using the same eye, shift your vision to the right edge of the tree. The point where your line of sight crosses the stick is the diameter in inches. It's important to move your eye, rather than your head; otherwise the reading will not be accurate. Read the diameter to the nearest even inch.

To measure the usable height of a tree, use the scale on the stick marked "Number 16 foot logs." With your heel against the base of the tree, pace off a distance of fifty feet—about twenty thirty-inch steps. Pace toward an opening which will let you see the tree you are measuring and, as nearly as possible, stay on the same level as the base of the tree.

Decide where the last cut will be made when the tree is sawed into logs—at a fork or where the diameter of the tree is reduced to about ten inches. Again hold the stick twenty-five inches from your eye, but this time in a vertical position. Measure with that part of the stick marked off in sixteen-foot logs. Move the stick up or down until the lower end is even with your line of sight to the stump height of the tree. Then, without moving your head or the stick, shift your vision upward to the point you decided was the usable height of the tree. The point where your line of sight passes the stick amounts to a reading in terms of sixteen-foot logs. Read to the nearest log or half-log.

With practice, you'll find that you need not measure the usable height of every tree. You'll want to measure a tree now and then to check your eye, of course.

To convert the diameter and number of logs to the volume of sawtimber in standing trees using the International Rule table, below, read down the left-hand column, headed DBH, and find the diameter of the tree. Then, read across the table to the column for the number of sixteen-foot logs in the tree. The result is the volume in board feet. The International Rule is very accurate, and sound trees will saw out close to the number of board feet indicated. Crooked or defective trees or logs will reduce the volume accordingly, however.

BOARD FOOT VOLUME OF TREES* BY DIAMETER AND HEIGHT CLASSES
International Rule

DBH in inches	Number of 16-foot logs in trees						
	½	1	1½	2	2½	3	3½
10	21	34	44	55			
12	30	52	68	85	98		
14	42	74	99	124	143	162	
16	59	100	134	169	198	226	246
18	74	129	175	221	259	297	325
20	92	162	220	279	328	377	413
22	112	198	271	344	406	467	514
24	133	237	326	415	491	567	622
26	158	284	392	500	592	684	755
28	187	331	458	585	696	806	888
30	220	381	529	677	805	933	1029
32	254	435	606	776	926	1077	1192
34	291	493	687	881	1054	1227	1359
36	333	559	782	1006	1205	1404	1557
38	374	624	874	1125	1354	1582	1754
40	415	693	974	1256	1510	1764	1962

*For estimating board feet in standing trees.

HARVESTING THE CROP

You can either sell your timber as standing trees (called stumpage) or harvest them yourself and sell the logs and by-products. If you do your own harvesting or contract to have it done, you have an opportunity to increase your profits by converting timber to products that will return the most income. For example, you can separate veneer grade logs from saw logs, or cut pulpwood from those trees not quite of sawtimber caliber. But you'll need to own or hire heavy timbering equipment to get even a few logs out of the woods, so the best bet may be to sell stumpage.

Always locate a market first, though, and have a complete written sales agreement signed before any trees are cut. Check out all likely markets before closing a deal. Your local forester will know markets and prices. Ask around to learn the going prices for the kind of timber or products you have to sell.

If you decide to sell stumpage, you can sell for a lump sum or for a price per unit of measurement—so much per thousand board feet or cord. If you sell for a lump sum, you'll still want to determine the price on the basis of your measurements, however. Don't be afraid to haggle with buyers when you're sure of what you've got growing out there in the woods. After all, you don't *have* to sell the trees today.

If you have the time—and the necessary skills—to produce

your own timber products for sale, you may want to go that route. This doesn't mean you'll need to get into the sawmill business, but you should know how to harvest trees to get the most value from each individual tree.

At the top of the price list for timber products is veneer logs, those high-quality hardwoods that are sliced into veneer for panel-ing, furniture, and other uses. A top-quality black walnut tree that is cut and handled right may bring several thousand dollars. The same tree, hacked into odd-length logs by an inexperienced tim-berman, may be worth only the going rate for sawtimber.

In most areas, sawlogs are the second most valuable timber commodity. However, tall straight pines, firs, and even oaks may net more as poles or pilings than as sawtimber in some locales. White oak and burr oak also are in great demand for staves for bourbon-aging barrels.

Several markets may exist for wood products of less-than-sawtimber quality. In mining regions, for example, smaller trees can be converted to pin ties, props, lagging, caps, and sills. Or, you may be in the proximity of an excelsior mill, pallet mill, or charcoal kilns. Fence posts and rails find a ready market in most regions. Or, you may have a market for naval stores (turpentines and resins), chemical extract wood, or tanning bark.

The Fine Print. Always get a written sales agreement that covers all items agreed upon between you and the buyer. A reliable buyer and a reliable seller should not have great difficulty finding a happy meeting ground of agreement. It's wise to check on the past perfor-mance of the buyer to make sure he has a reputation for good busi-ness dealings.

Verbal agreements, even between honorable men, hold the risk of misunderstandings. The contract should include:
- a legal description and location of the timber.
- the price and manner of payment.
- the method of determining quantities to be sold.
- conditions for cutting and removal.
- the duration of cutting rights, and responsibility for taxes on timber before cutting.
- how the slash will be disposed of.
- a means of settling disputes.

A written sales contract alone does not automatically guarantee a good sales agreement, however. A contract is not worth the paper it's written on if one or both parties fail to live up to the agreement; if you have a large volume of timber to sell, you may want to require the buyer to post a performance bond or place partial payment in escrow before cutting begins.

Of Taxes and Such Things. Before you sell your timber—or before you agree on the manner of payment—you should give some thought as to how the income will affect your income tax situation. Normally, sales of forest products qualify for taxation as capital gains, rather than as ordinary income. If you've worked and waited years to grow timber to marketable size, it's hardly fair to have Uncle Sam dip his hand into your profits as if all the income were produced in one taxable year.

On the subject of taxes, many states have special property tax provisions for land put to improved forestry uses. This relief usually is in the form of a reduced real estate tax on land devoted to timber. Check to see if your state has such a tax policy to make sure you're not paying more taxes than you need to. Also, if you own or rent equipment for woods work, learn if the state tax on fuel you use qualifies for a nonroad exemption.

Much of the work you'll do in the woodlot—reforestation, timber stand improvement, etc.—will qualify for cost-sharing financial assistance under the federal Rural Environmental and Conservation Program. For some forestry practices, the federal government will stand up to eighty percent of the out-of-pocket costs you incur. Check with your county Agricultural Stabilization and Conservation Service to see which of your timber practices might rate cost-sharing.

HOW TO RESTOCK YOUR FOREST

Whether you begin your forest management program with a stand of mature trees or with bare land that needs to be planted, restocking will be a constant chore for as long as you manage the woodland.

The cheapest way to reproduce a stand is through natural reseeding. However, this is not always possible. Natural forest reproduction depends upon the species grown, availability of seed, soil moisture, summer temperature, rodents, insects, and diseases. Also, you may want to restock your woodlot with species other than those presently growing there.

Most uneven-aged forests will reseed themselves, unless new seedlings are killed by fire or grazing. The kind of trees to be reproduced following a harvest can often be influenced by timing the cut to coincide with a good seed crop of a desirable species and by cutting less desirable species more heavily. Or, you can leave seed trees standing after harvest.

In fully stocked stands of even-aged trees, the dense overstory prevents seedlings from developing because of lack of sunlight. But in most cases of this kind, you will not worry about reproduction—at least until after trees have been thinned by cutting.

If natural seeding will not do the job, artificial seeding can be done a number of ways. Seed can be broadcast from the ground by hand or with a hand-operated seeder. For larger areas, you may want to use a tractor-drawn row seeder or have the seed broadcast by hired aircraft.

Perhaps the most successful way to restock your woodland is by planting seedling trees. Seedlings, in a variety of sizes and species, are grown by the millions in private and public nurseries. Seedlings are the surest way to convert a forest acreage to a different, more profitable species of tree.

State or federal nurseries will provide seedlings of many adapted species free, or at cost of production—depending on the use you plan to make of these trees. These are usually 1-0 seedlings, wrapped in bundles of one thousand trees. The 1-0 refers to a seedling tree that was grown one year in a seedbed, with no time as a transplant. A 2-1 tree, for example, was grown two years in a seedbed, then transplanted and grown with more space the third year. Older seedlings and those that have been transplanted once are more costly than 1-0 trees.

The best time to plant trees varies with the character of the soil and the local climate. In the South, trees can be planted throughout the winter as long as the ground is not frozen. In more northerly areas, planting usually is done in spring, before new growth starts.

Ordinarily, you will be planting trees for timber production on land that is better suited for trees than for other crops. But you may want to change the use of land, from cultivation or open pasture to timber production. Planting either in established forests or in open areas is much easier than planting tree seedlings in areas overgrown with brush or worthless trees. See Chapter 4 for methods of planting trees.

CHAPTER 10 Growing Christmas Trees for Market

by LESTER A. BELL

Christmas trees have been used, loved, and admired by Western peoples for centuries. In fact, the exact beginnings of the custom are lost to antiquity; but many historians credit Martin Luther with developing the tradition of celebrating yuletide with a freshly cut, decorated evergreen, back in the early sixteenth century. Whatever the origin of the Christmas tree, it is now a deep tradition in many countries of the world. Something like thirty-seven million trees are used in the United States alone each Christmas.

Virtually all of those trees grow on Christmas tree planta-tions. Could you successfully grow evergreens to help supply the demand? It's a specialized kind of business and requires a commit-ment of management, land, and trees. But the market is there, and you can scale tree plantations to fit about any size tract of land. Various species of evergreens are adapted to nearly all sections of the country.

Scotch pine, the most popular plantation-grown Christmas

tree, is adapted to a wide range of climates and soil types. Douglas fir, balsam fir, and the spruces (black, white, red, and blue) follow in order of popularity. In the Pacific Northwest, many true firs are grown, while eastern red cedar and Fraser fir are front-runners in the southeastern states.

Remember that it takes from eight years (for Scotch pine) to twelve years (for the firs) to produce a six-foot Christmas tree. And trees don't stop growing at six feet. So, to insure having a tree crop each year, you'll need to plant an annual crop of new seedlings.

MAKING PLANS

Rotational Planting. Say you'll plant a species that takes ten years to grow from seedling to six-foot tree. To have a marketable crop every year, you'll need to divide your area into ten equal blocks. (Actually, you'll need more than ten. We'll get into just why later.) If two-year-old seedlings are planted, a new block of trees must be planted each year. After ten years, you can harvest the first group of trees, with the younger trees coming on for harvest in succeeding years. Of course, you replant new seedlings after each harvest. This kind of rotation works with either a few trees or many—depending both on your land area and the scale of your Christmas tree business.

In selecting a place to plant your trees, you'll want to choose land that will not be needed for other uses for the length of the rotation. In the backyard or garden, trees might be planted along the back fence. On wild land or abandoned farm acreage, be sure the land use will not change in the near future.

In any case, plant trees in the open where they will get full sunlight. Christmas trees will not grow well in the shade or in competition with other trees.

Where to Plant. The location of your Christmas tree planting should be well planned, as once trees are planted it's difficult and costly to move them or shift to another area. During the development of the plantation, you'll need access to plant, cultivate, shape, and ultimately harvest the trees, and a good road to the property is therefore essential. Often the late-fall and early-winter harvest season for Christmas trees unfortunately coincides with poor road conditions.

If the trees are planted near your home, you will get more enjoyment from them—and probably do a better job of growing them. You'll be close enough to watch for trespassers, fire, animal damage, and insect and disease outbreaks. A plantation of evergreens, whether large or small, adds greatly to the aesthetic beauty of property, improves the habitat for birds and small animals, benefits the environment, and even helps hold down landscaping costs.

Most species of evergreens will grow on a variety of soils. They all grow best on well-drained but moist sandy loams, while few do well on fine-textured, heavy clay soils. You should choose a species well adapted to your soil type, rather than try to change or add amendments to the soil to suit the requirements of the tree.

Most evergreens prefer a slightly acid soil, with a pH range of 5.6 to 6.0, and some will do well at higher levels of acidity. One notable exception is eastern red cedar, which prefers an alkaline soil and grows best on limestone soils throughout its natural range.

Christmas trees do not require highly fertile soil and will grow well on soils of relatively poor fertility. In fact, overly fertile soils will produce heavy weed and grass growth which then competes with the trees for soil moisture and plant nutrients. Grass and weeds also harbor damaging insects and rodents.

Very rocky soils or thin soils over bedrock are difficult to plant and till. Avoid flood plains along streams, where trees may be flooded for part of the year. Poorly drained soils are also a bad choice, as are tight, shallow clay pans and coarse droughty sand.

Topography is a minor consideration; you'll have to plant your land as she lies. Nearly level terrain or rolling plains are ideal, of course, but trees will grow on steep mountain slopes where there is little soil and the rocks are nearly perpendicular. This is not to recommend such sites for a Christmas tree plantation; steep, rough land limits access and the use of implements.

Good air drainage is important. Avoid low, frosty areas, as stagnant chilly air can damage new growth in the spring. Very droughty areas are not recommended unless irrigation will be practiced. In the arid Plains and southwestern states, some growers use irrigation to produce Christmas trees.

So, if you avoid extremes and select a deep, well-drained soil that is easy to work, you should be successful in growing good Christmas trees. The area needed for the planting is entirely dependent on the scale of your plans and the amount of land you can devote to trees. The range of involvement runs from one specimen tree in the dooryard (to serve as a living Christmas tree year after year) to many thousands of trees on hundreds of acres. Choose the area on the basis of your expected size of enterprise. You can grow about one thousand trees per acre, with seventy-five to ninety percent of them marketable. This assumes a 6-by-6 foot spacing, with access lanes about every twelfth row of trees.

SELECTING THE SPECIES

If you are looking for the perfect Christmas tree, forget it—there's no such thing. However, one or more of the many species being planted should grow well in your locality and develop into satisfactory, marketable trees. Visit other growers in your region to find out what species they prefer and which they have best success with. You might also check with your local extension forester and take a look at trees used for ornamental plantings in yards and parks in the neighborhood.

CHRISTMAS TREE SPECIES RECOMMENDED BY REGION

Species	Normal Rotation (years)	Geographic Regions Where Recommended
Scotch pine (*Pinus sylvestris*)	6–8	Central, Great Lakes, New England, Northeast, Plains, Southwest.
White pine (*Pinus strobus*)	6–8	Central, Great Lakes, New England, Northeast, Southeast.
Red pine (*Pinus resinosa*)	6–8	Same as white pine.
Austrian pine (*Pinus nigra*)	6–8	Same as white pine.
Lodgepole pine (*Pinus contorta*)	6–8	Same as Scotch pine.
Blue spruce (*Picea pungens*)	9–11	Central, Northeast. Great Lakes, Rocky Mountain, Southeast, Southwest.
Black spruce (*Picea mariana*)	9–11	Great Lakes, Northeast.
Norway spruce (*Picea abies*)	9–11	Central, Great Lakes, Northeast, New England, Southeast.

White spruce (*Picea glauca*)	9–11	Same as white pine.
Engelmann spruce (*Picea engelmannii*)	9–11	Rocky Mountain, Pacific Northwest, Southwest.
Balsam fir (*Abies balsamea*)	11–14	Great Lakes, New England, Northeast.
Douglas fir (*Pseudotsuga menziesii*)	11–14	Central, Great Lakes, New England, Pacific Northwest, Rocky Mountain, Southwest.
Fraser fir (*Abies fraseri*)	11–14	Central, Southeast, Northeast.
Red fir (*Abies magnifica*)	11–14	Pacific Northwest, Southwest.
White fir (*Abies concolor*)	11–14	Pacific Northwest, Southwest, Great Lakes.
Eastern red cedar (*Juniperus virginiana*)	9–11	South Central, Southeast.
Arizona cypress (*Cupressus arizonica*)	6–8	South Central, Southwest.

Remember that the one most important point is to select a species that is adapted to your climatic conditions. Here are some other factors that should influence your choice of what to plant:

• Adaptability of the species to your soil conditions.
• Natural resistance to insects and disease.
• Growth rate or length of rotation.
• Availability of nursery stock of proven genetic excellence.
• Transplantability.
• Good growth habits, straight stem, compact crown, pleasing green color.
• Needle-holding ability, when the tree is cut and placed in a heated room.

Studies conducted in different localities around the United States point up some consumer preferences in Christmas trees. Generally, the species or type preferred depends on the tree customarily used in that locality in the past—tradition plays a big part. If a long-needled tree was used in the home during one's childhood, the adult probably will prefer a long-needled tree today. Likewise, the short-needled spruces and firs have their champions.

Local preferences aside, there are certain characteristics of a good Christmas tree that prevail everywhere. They are:

• Height. Most people prefer a tree of between 5½ and 7 feet.

There is also a market for smaller quantities of apartment-sized trees of 3 to 4 feet in height and of 7- to 9-foot trees for use in large houses, churches, schools, and commercial buildings.

• Shape. A tree with 66⅔-percent taper is ideal (⅔ as wide at the base as it is high).

• Stem. Straight stem with a well-developed handle at the base that should be one inch in length for each foot in height.

• Branches. Whorls of branches uniformly distributed on stem, strong enough to support ornaments, limber enough to pack well for shipping or transport without breaking.

• Density. A compact crown with four good faces is preferred. No large openings or flat faces.

• Needles. Good, healthy, vigorous, fresh-looking growth is more important than length or size of the needles. The tree must possess the ability to hold its needles when displayed in hot, dry living rooms.

• Color. Dark green, slate green, and blue green are preferred over light green or yellow green foliage.

• Aroma. Species that impart a very desirable fragrance when brought into a heated home are favored ones with no fragrance or undesirable fragrances.

PLANTING

The Shape of Things to Come. Good growth habits, straightness of stems, compact crowns, and green color all tie back to genetic excellence of the species. But there are other things to consider, too.

When you buy seedlings or transplants from the nursery, sort them for uniformity of growth. Planting trees of the same size helps maintain uniform growth throughout the life of the planting. Dwarfs or runts at the seedling stage may be inherent slow growers, so cull them out. Crooked-stemmed or multiple-stemmed seedlings also should be sorted out. Crooks in the lower stem may be caused by improper planting, too. Plant all trees straight up. If they are tilted or planted crooked, they will grow toward the sun and create a bend in the lower stem. The number of buds on a seedling, especially on terminal whorls, indicates how compact the crown will be. If you find a spindly seedling with few buds, cast it out, as it likely will not grow into a good tree. You can influence tree color at the seedling stage, too. Many nurserymen rogue out off-color seedlings, but if this hasn't been done you should do so before planting. Some growers select only the better-colored seed-lings (called shiners) from a nursery bed and plant them in selected plantations for fine specimens.

Some species have superior needle-holding ability, and a valuable trait it is; most trees are cut several weeks before Christmas, shipped, held a few days (or weeks) on a retail lot, and are then placed in heated homes. Certain species shed needles within a few days if exposed to temperatures of above 70°F. and humidity below thirty percent.

Pines are the best needle holders. Next in order are the firs. Poorest are the spruces, cedars, and cypress, none of which hold their needles well when exposed to high temperature and low hu-midity. A tree will hold its needles better if the butt is placed in a container of water as soon as the tree is brought inside. This also helps reduce fire hazards.

The Planting Plan. In nearly every chapter of this book we've em-phasized planting trees according to a plan. Planning is doubly im-portant with Christmas tree growing, whether you plant a few trees on a one-time basis or plant many trees on a rotational basis.

If you will be growing one to ten trees in a garden location, first determine the species, rotation age, and spacing between trees; then divide the area available into equal-sized plots, one for each year of the rotation plus an extra plot, the purpose of which is explained below. Make each plot large enough to plant the number of trees desired.

For larger-scale planting, the plan will need to be more so-phisticated but will cover the same basics. It should include all ap-proaches, plus access lanes for cultural work, management, pro-tection, and eventual harvest. Make a base map of the area to be planted, with access roads, fire lanes, planting divisions, and se-quence of plantings drawn in. It's easier to make changes on the map than in the field when the trees are already in the ground.

The number of trees planted in any one block depends on the species selected, the land area available, the growth rate or number of years in a rotation, and the amount of time you can afford to devote to shearing and shaping, cultivation, insect control, harvesting, and marketing.

The extra plot in addition to the rotation plots, mentioned earlier, allows for one year of fallow to remove brush and weeds and clean up the land before a new crop is planted there. Another planning consideration is that some species tend to reach the six-foot height with irregularity and require two or three years to harvest. In this case, additional years (and blocks) should be added to the plan.

Here, then, is a formula for figuring the size of each planting block (with area in acres, time in years):

$$\frac{\text{Total land area} - \text{wasteland} - \begin{array}{l}\text{roads, lanes,}\\\text{building sites}\end{array}}{\text{Average rotation} + \text{harvest period} + \begin{array}{l}\text{fallow or}\\\text{cleanup time}\end{array}} = \begin{array}{l}\text{Area to be}\\\text{planted annually}\end{array}$$

For example, assume you have 40 acres, less 3 acres for a building site and garden, 4 acres of access roads and lanes, and 3 acres for a pond—for a total of 30 acres of plantable area. If you choose Scotch pine, you can figure an average rotation of 7 years, plus 2 years to harvest, and 1 year of fallow before replanting. Your formula would look like this:

$$\frac{40 - 3 - 4 - 3}{7 + 2 + 1} = \frac{30}{10} = \begin{array}{l}\text{3 acres per block}\\\text{planted each year}\end{array}$$

Following this plan, you would plant 3 acres of trees the first year, 3 acres the second year, and so on. At the end of 10 years, all blocks will have been planted.

Harvesting should begin on the first block in December of the seventh year, when the larger trees are cut. Harvest in that first block will continue for two more seasons, when the last of the trees are cut and the block is lain fallow to be cleared of brush, grass, and weeds and is prepared for replanting in the eleventh year to start a new cycle. In the eighth year from planting, some trees from the second block will be ready to harvest, as well as those trees from the first block. Thereafter, trees will be harvested from each of two blocks annually.

If you plant spruce or fir, species that take longer to develop, you will need more blocks; given the same land area, each block would be smaller than for Scotch pine. Remember that regardless of the size of the planting blocks, every twelfth row should be left open for access.

The Best Tree for Your Site. In addition to the limitations of climate and soil mentioned earlier, you'll want to evaluate Christmas tree species on the basis of the ecosystem into which the trees will be introduced. For instance, you would not want to plant frost-tender species such as balsam fir, Douglas fir, or Norway spruce in a frost pocket or in low, cold spots. These species do better on higher areas having good air drainage. Nor would you plant a limestone-loving species like eastern red cedar in highly acid soil. If your soil is alkaline, however, eastern red cedar may be the very species that will do best.

Don't plant Scotch pine or balsam fir in areas of high deer population. Deer find these trees delicious and often eat the tops to cause deformed trees. Neither will you want to plant dry-land species such as Scotch pine in low-lying, poorly drained soils. Winter hardiness (how well the tree can withstand the rigors of winter climate) is another consideration, particularly in northern states and areas of high elevation.

No species of tree is completely free of insect attack or of disease, but some are less susceptible than others. Resistance to insect and disease problems is more important to Christmas tree growers than to forest owners. So, if you have a choice between two or more species for your site, choose the one less susceptible to trouble. (This doesn't mean you can relax your vigilance in preventing insect and disease invasions; nor does it substitute for good housekeeping practices, such as elminating infested or infected trees, cleaning up dead or damaged trees, and removing areas where insects can hibernate or multiply.)

Length of Rotation. Some Christmas tree species grow rapidly, and others rather slowly. The growth rate makes a big difference in the number of years it takes for trees to develop into marketable products. Most species grow slower the first couple of years after transplanting and then speed up as they develop better root systems and become established on the site. Weed control helps speed up the growth rate; cultivation, mulching, or other methods of weed and grass control mean more moisture and nutrients for the trees.

The faster-growing trees such as Scotch pine will reach a height of six feet in seven to eight years on good sites. Trees of a medium growth rate, such as Norway spruce and white spruce, will produce six-foot trees in eight to eleven years. The firs take twelve to fifteen years to grow into six- or seven-foot trees.

Note that faster growers are often chosen because they produce a quicker return on the investment in land, trees, and labor. Longer-rotation species may appeal to some growers if the market value is enough higher to compensate for the longer production period.

Nursery Stock. Within most tree species, there are wide variations in inherent genetic traits. For instance, Douglas fir seedlings grown from seed collected in the southern Rockies of New Mexico are usually winter hardy and not likely to freeze back in the spring, even when planted in New England, the Lake states, or other areas having severe weather. On the other hand, Douglas firs grown from seed collected along the coastal areas of Oregon and Washington are not so winter hardy.

Frost resistance, winter hardiness, drought resistance, disease and insect tolerance, rate of growth, color of foliage, needle size and length, size and number of buds, size of twigs, straightness of stem—all are traits that may vary by seed source within the same species. This makes it vital that you check with experts before ordering trees to plant. Find out what seed source is recommended for your locality, and then check with local nurserymen to see if they grow seedlings from that source.

Beware of bargain-basement nursery stock—it's rarely a bargain. Buy stock with a pedigree from a nurseryman who stands behind it. Also, check the stock for vigor, uniformity of size, and freedom from insects and disease. It's possible to buy an insect or disease epidemic along with nursery plants.

How well a species transplants may be more a factor of quality and size of the root system than of genetics. But it is usually easier to transplant the pines than the spruces, and the spruces more easily than the firs, all other conditions being equal. And ease of transplanting is something to consider when you're ready to select a species.

Spacing and Number of Trees. The distance between trees in a plantation should be the minimum that will let them grow properly while enabling you to move among them. And this spacing determines the number of trees per acre.

Most growers plant as many trees as possible per acre, and some overdo it. At seedling size, trees with six-foot spacing look far apart, but they'll close the gap each year to eventually cover the site. Spacing depends on the species grown, the size of Christmas tree to be harvested, the amount of land available, the value of the land, and the suitability of the soil. Trees must have ample room to develop good, healthy branches and needles. If they crowd too tightly, the lower needles will be shaded, causing them to shed and reducing the quality of trees.

Pines normally have a wider taper to the crown and usually need wider spacing than the straighter-tapered spruces and firs. And with pines, air drainage is important to lessening the chance of spring frost damage and to reduce conditions favorable to the spread of fungus diseases. The wider the spacing, the better the drainage.

You may want to plant trees rather closely and then thin alternate trees for table-top or apartment-sized Christmas trees, if you have a market. Then let the remainder of the trees grow into six- to seven-foot sizes. Generally, a 5-by-5 spacing is the minimum for firs and spruces, and a 6-by-6 interval is best for pines. However, such plantings should be done only in coarse, sandy soils, on sites protected from drying winter winds. Unless the trees will have a blanket of snow during colder months, they can suffer severe drying by winter winds. Fall-planted trees in clay soils are subject to damage from frost heaving during late-winter freezes and thaws, and at times this heaving action can lift newly planted trees completely out of the ground. The one big advantage to fall planting is that the roots will continue to grow; the tree becomes well imbedded in the soil during winter and will start growth two to three weeks earlier the following spring and be better able to withstand summer dry spells.

Whether you plant trees in spring or fall, you'll have best results if planting is done on cool, moist days during the rainy season. At such times, the soil is moist and roots will not be as likely to dry out during the transplanting process.

Site Preparation. You don't have to work up a finely pulverized seedbed to plant Christmas trees. But the planting site should be cleared of all competitive trees, brush, and weeds. On larger acreages, this is best done by plowing and tilling the soil for as long as a year before the trees are planted.

You will be growing those new trees for seven to fifteen years, with the goal of producing specimen trees—each one a symmetrical jewel. They'll need full sunlight to produce thick foliage and vigorous growth, so trees or brush that shade the new seedlings and rob them of soil moisture and nutrients must go. If these weed trees are allowed to live, they too will grow during the seven to fifteen years, creating more and more competition for your Christmas trees.

Plowing the area deeply and tilling it for a year will get rid of heavy weed growth and also allow time for the sod to decompose and settle. This makes a better medium in which to plant new trees, one that holds moisture and is easy to cultivate after your trees are planted.

Quality Stock and Where To Get It. The Christmas trees you sell years from now will depend in large part on the quality of nursery stock you plant. Choose healthy, well-grown trees with large stem diameter, a short fibrous root system, and good bud formation, rather than spindly seedlings with small stems, long roots, and poorly developed buds.

Stock is listed in nursery catalogs as either seedlings or transplants, with the code designation explained earlier (1-0 means trees grown one year as seedlings with no time as transplants). Because of extra care and age, transplants are more expensive than seedlings and will be larger with more compact, fibrous roots. Because

SIZES, TYPES, AND AGES OF NURSERY STOCK

Species	Height in Inches	Types and Years
Balsam fir	6 to 14	2–2
Douglas fir	6 to 14	2–2
Fraser fir	6 to 12	2–2
Red fir	6 to 12	2–2
Concolor fir	6 to 12	2–2
Eastern red cedar	8 to 12	2–1 or 2–2
Blue spruce	6 to 12	2–1 or 2–2
Black spruce	6 to 12	2–1 or 2–2
Norway spruce	6 to 12	2–1 or 2–2
White spruce	6 to 12	2–1 or 2–2
Lodgepole pine	6 to 14	2–0
Red pine	6 to 14	2–0 or 2–1
Scotch pine	6 to 16	2–0
White pine	6 to 12	2–0 or 2–1

some species (pines, for instance) grow rapidly, transplants soon become too large for easy field planting. You'll be money ahead to use seedlings rather than transplants for these species. It's not necessarily true that the larger the tree the better, as far as planting stock is concerned. The following table shows recommended sizes, types, and ages of nursery stock for the more common Christmas tree species.

Many commercial nurseries in the United States and Canada specialize in producing seedling and transplant trees for Christmas tree growers, and most produce species adapted to their area or region. They usually will have several species to select from and often will have two or three seed selections of each species.

Because of high shipping costs and the danger of seedlings drying out in transit (as well as differences in climatic conditions at time of shipment), you should buy trees from a nursery relatively near your planting site. However, you may want to go farther to find good stock if there are significant differences in quality. Visit a few nurseries before placing your order to examine the color, vigor, size, and general quality of each offering.

In any event, estimate your needs and place your order early to be sure you'll get the species, seed source, and size you wish. If you don't know of nurserymen in your area, contact your local extension forester or state department of agriculture.

Planting Pointers. When your planting stock arrives, care for it as outlined for bare-root stock in Chapter 2. The sooner trees are planted after being removed from nursery beds, the better they'll do. To boost your chances for success, heed the following:

• Take good care of planting stock.
• Remove competition so trees can grow.
• Make the planting hole large enough and deep enough to fully accommodate the tree's root system.
• Pack soil firmly around roots.
• See that the tree has its roots in direct contact with moist soil; in order to survive, newly planted trees need all the soil moisture they can get.

In small plantings, trees can be hand-planted with a shovel, spade, planting bar, or mattock. Hand-planting is necessary on very steep sites, rocky soils, and when interplanting among growing trees or in small spaces. Each planter has his own favorite planting tool. Select whichever implement serves you best.

For larger plantations, you may want to use machine planting. The various machines on the market are all designed to perform the same basic functions: open a hole, place the tree into the hole, and tamp the soil around the tree. Some machines are tractor mounted; others are pulled behind a vehicle. Most machines work fairly well on coarse, sandy soils with few rocks, where the topography is level to slightly hilly. None are designed to plant very steep sites. In some communities, custom operators plant trees for hire. Your extension forester can give you specific information on this service in your area.

Several weeks after the initial planting, and prior to the next regular planting season, you should check the plantation for survival of the seedlings. Replant failures as soon as you can.

TENDING THE TREES

Policing the Plantation. As a long-term crop, Christmas trees are subject to damage from many sources, especially fire, trespassers, livestock, rodents, vegetative competition, insects, and diseases.

The best fire protection is prevention. Avoid locating your trees in areas prone to high fire hazard, such as along railroads and highways or near areas frequented by large numbers of people. The second line of defense is fire lanes—areas of raw soil both around the edges and within the plantation. You should also have a fire-fighting plan, just in case fire does strike.

An increasingly serious threat to Christmas tree plantations—and a sad comment on human nature—is thieves and vandals. Some tree rustlers swipe but a small tree or two, perhaps to take home as ornaments. Others wait until trees are ready for harvest and then steal a truckload at a time for sale. If your trees are planted some distance from your home so that you cannot keep a watchful eye on them, perhaps a neighbor could help stand guard.

Livestock can cause heavy damage to trees. They trample young trees, lie on them, and even eat them. Livestock also trample the ground and compact it, causing excessive rainfall runoff and depriving the roots of oxygen. By and large, Christmas trees and livestock are not compatible on the same acres.

Rodents (meaning rabbits, mice, and squirrels) can damage Christmas trees, too. But trees on a weed-free site that is kept cultivated or mulched are not as likely to be damaged. Most rodent injury occurs in winter months, when snow covers the ground. You can help prevent high rodent populations by encouraging those elements of the ecosystem that serve to control their numbers—coyotes, foxes, owls, and hawks.

Other forms of wildlife damage are minor, except for that done by deer and grosbeaks. Deer can ruin an entire plantation of young trees, especially Douglas fir, Fraser fir, balsam fir, and Scotch pine. The evening grosbeak, a lovely bird about the size of a robin, normally feeds on weed and tree seed. It has a heavy, strong beak designed for cracking seed. A northern bird, it may invade Christmas tree plantations in Canada, New England, and the northern Lake states when other foods are scarce. It also eats the buds of trees, causing serious deformities.

Insects can wreak havoc with Christmas trees by chewing roots, needles, twigs, and stems; by girdling the stem or boring holes inside it; and by sucking the sap from needles and twigs. Insects apt to do economic damage vary from one part of the country to another. A number of controls are discussed in Chapter 5. In each state, land-grant universities publish bulletins and descriptive materials on forest insects. You should get copies of these publications from your local extension agent or forester.

Disease usually is no serious threat to Christmas trees because of the short rotation period and the vigor of young trees. Trees are most susceptible when their vigor is reduced by drought, overcrowding, low soil fertility, injury, or insect attack.

Shaping Christmas Trees. After your trees have grown for a couple of seasons, you can safely assume they are established. Now comes the fun—and the work—of developing them into true specimen trees.

Walk each row of two-year-old trees and look for multiple stems and multiple leaders. With pruning shears, reduce each tree to a single stem and a single leader.

While trees are still small, perhaps during the third growing season, prune the lower branches of each tree to form a clear "handle" of six to ten inches at the base of the tree. Prune from the ground up to the first complete whorl of basal branches. This makes cultivation easier and reduces the change of rodent damage. It also will make harvesting easier.

Shearing trees improves their quality by making them more

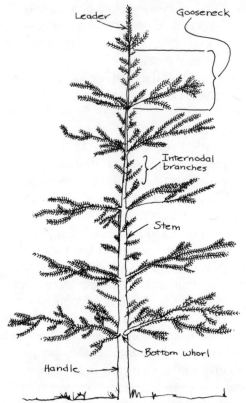

Parts of a Christmas tree. A whorl is a point at which several branches radiate from the same level. The distance between whorls is one year's growth.

compact, uniformly tapered, and well balanced. (It can also turn what otherwise would be culls into marketable trees.) The familiar conelike Christmas tree shape does not necessarily come naturally. An ideal tree is about two-thirds as wide at the base as it is high, and tapers uniformly to the tip. This is a 66⅔-percent taper. A 40- to 70-percent taper is acceptable on spruces and firs, while pines usually have greater width at the base and look better with a wider taper—up to a maximum of 90 percent.

Your shearing should be designed to control height and width growth; stimulate bud formation and increase the branches and density of foliage; and remove multiple leaders and branch deformities. Start shearing when the average tree in the block is

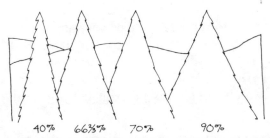

Acceptable tapers for Christmas trees: 40 percent minimum; 66²/₃ percent ideal for all species; 70 percent maximum for spruce and fir; 90 percent maximum for pines.

twenty-four to thirty inches tall, and continue each year until trees are ready to harvest.

Pines should be sheared in early summer, when the new growth has elongated but is still soft and succulent; this will be mid-May in the South, and as late as mid-July in northern states. Spruces and firs may be sheared any time, but it is best done between October 1 and March 1, while the tree is dormant.

Most growers prefer to shear with either a lightweight knife having a thin blade about fourteen to twenty inches long, or two-handled hedge shears with blades a foot or so long. Both work well, provided the blades are kept sharp and free of pitch. Kerosene, fuel oil, or mineral spirits will remove the pitch.

To shape pines, start by cutting back the terminal leader to the desired length—about twelve to fourteen inches. Next, cut the laterals of the terminal whorl so that they are three to five inches shorter than the terminal (see illustration). Then proceed around the tree, cutting tips of lateral branches to conform to a cone. Any branches that are too long or too irregular can be cut back to a line extending from base to tip.

When shearing lateral branches, cut them at an angle that lines up with the contour of the cone. Second, third, and fourth shearings are done the same way, but care should be taken to maintain a single terminal leader. Red, white, and Austrian pines normally do not produce as long a leader as does Scotch pine and need not be sheared as heavily.

With spruce and fir, start by cutting back the terminal leader to about eight to twelve inches. Make this cut at an angle, ¼ to ⅜ inch above the single lateral bud. This bud then will grow into next year's terminal. Next, shear and shape the lateral branches into a cone shape, without regard to individual branches. Dormant buds will grow branchlets that cover up the shearing points. The second, third, and succeeding shearings will be similar to the first.

Shearing is hard work but one of the most satisfying chores a tree grower performs. With every slash of the knife or snip of the shears, you watch your trees take on that distinctive Christmas tree shape.

HARVESTING THE CROP

When trees are six- to seven-foot specimens, they are ready to harvest. You can best measure, grade, and inventory them while they stand on the stump. If you have but a few trees, this is a simple task. If you have several hundred, typing colored tags or plastic tape leaders will speed up the process of grading, handling, and pricing the trees.

For fresh trees of the best quality, you should cut them as late as possible and still get them sold or delivered. If only a few trees are to be cut, a small bow saw is adequate to the chore. If many trees need harvesting, you might be better off with a lightweight chain saw.

After the trees are cut, drag them to the edge of the plantation. There they can be bundled or wrapped with twine, or pulled through a large funnel into a sleeve of plastic netting made especially for bundling Christmas trees. If you need to store the trees before delivering them, pile or deck them with the tops in and the butts out, one on top of the other. Piles should not be more than about five feet high, as the weight of the top trees might otherwise break branches and compress foliage on trees underneath. These storage piles should be in the shade to prevent drying of the needles. Covers of black plastic or tarpaulins help prevent drying and also protect the trees from snow and freezing rain.

The USDA publishes grade standards for Christmas trees: U.S. Premium, U.S. No. 1 (or U.S. Choice), U.S. No. 2 (or U.S. Standard), and culls. These grades designate size limits, freshness, cleanliness, health, density, shape, taper, color, handle length, and freedom from defects. If you grow only a few trees primarily for family and friends, you probably will not be greatly concerned with grading standards. But if you plan to become a large grower, you should be acquainted with tree grades. A copy of *United States Standards for Grades of Christmas Trees* is available from the Agricultural Marketing Service of the USDA, Washington, DC.

MARKETING

You have many marketing options with Christmas trees. You can retail them on the stump, on a choose-and-cut basis. Or you can wholesale trees on the stump to another retailer or to a Christmas tree broker.

You can retail the cut trees yourself, at your dooryard or on a rented lot. Still another method is to sell to a retailer or broker for whom you agree to cut, bale, and deliver the trees or make them available at roadside.

Regardless of the sale method, unless you retail the trees yourself, be sure you have an agreement that covers terms of sale, date of delivery, species and quality of trees, grades, price per tree, delivery point, and when and how payment is to be made. You are dealing with a perishable commodity for a short market season. Returned merchandise after December 25 is less than worthless—it costs you money to dispose of it.

If you like dealing with people and live close to a population center, you may want to consider a cut-your-own marketing plan. Grower Bill Blackwell, who lives near the sixty thousand people of Columbia, Missouri, sells four thousand to five thousand trees this way every year. He runs ads in local newspapers, showing directions to his farm. Trees are priced at a flat rate, whether large or small, to save time measuring and arguing over what to do with fractions of a foot. Blackwell points out that people who come to cut their own tree will carry off more poorly shaped specimens than he could ever sell at a lot in town.

As a goodwill gesture, Blackwell cuts several misformed and oversized trees from which he invites customers to snip fronds and boughs for decoration. He admits that he could retail his trees for more gross income by other methods, but figures the savings in labor and transportation costs make his cut-your-own system break even.

Keeping Track of the Business. If you grow Christmas trees for market, you'll need to keep some records to find out how successful the operation is in terms of dollars spent and dollars earned. In time, good records can show you how to increase the profitability of your enterprise.

But when you're starting out, what can you expect? How large an investment will you need? How long before you can earn a return on that investment? Will Christmas tree growing be profitable for you?

A table from a 1972 Michigan State University research report helps answer some of those questions. Actual costs change from year to year, but by plugging in your own costs for each item you can figure pretty accurately what it will cost to produce trees on your own land. Since Christmas trees are a long-term crop, income from their sale is normally treated as capital gains. Some of the annual costs may be written off in the year they are incurred, while others should be capitalized and shown as a cost only after the crop is marketed.

COSTS AND RETURNS FOR SCOTCH PINE CHRISTMAS TREES FOR A 7-YEAR PRODUCTION PERIOD ON A PER ACRE BASIS AT 6% COMPOUND INTEREST

Item	Basis	Years	6% Interest Factor	Capitalized to the end of 7 years Costs	Returns
Management costs	$30 each year				
& taxes	$30 each year	7	8.3938	$251.81	
Land value or cost	$100	7	1.5036	150.36	
Planting stock &					
shipping cost	$33 per M × 1,090 = $35.97	7	1.5036	54.08	
Planting cost	$15 per M × 1,090 = $16.35	7	1.5036	24.58	
Weed control at planting	$10	7	1.5036	15.04	
2nd year	$10	5	1.3382	13.38	
Mowing between rows,					
1st year	$6	6	1.4185	8.51	
Insect control spraying	$10 each year	6	6.9753	69.75	
Shearing, incl. basal					
pruning	3rd yr. 4¢/tree × 981 = $39.24	4	1.2625	49.54	
Shearing	4th yr. 2¢/tree × 981 = $19.62	3	1.1910	23.37	
	5th yr. 2¢/tree × 981 = $19.62	2	1.1236	22.04	
	6th yr. 3¢/tree × 981 = $29.43	1	1.0600	31.20	
Trees sold, 6th year	½ = 490 × $2.75 = $1,347.50	1	1.0600		$1,428.35
Shearing	7th year 4¢/tree × 393 = $15.72	—	—	15.72	
Trees sold, 7th year	393 × $2.75 = $1,080.75	—	—		1,080.75
Cleanup costs—					
98 cull trees	$8	—	—	8.00	
Residual land value	$100	—	—		100.00
Total accumulated					
returns					2,609.10
Total accumulated costs				737.38	
Net income for 1 crop	In 7 years				1,871.72
Average per tree:					
returns					2.95
costs				.84	
net income					2.11

Production cost per tree sold in: 6 years = $.72
7 years = $.98

SUGGESTED FOR FURTHER READING

The American Christmas Tree Journal. 225 East Michigan Street, Milwaukee, WI 53202.

Bell, Lester A. *Shearing and Shaping Christmas Trees.* Extension Bulletin E-719, Natural Resources Series. East Lansing: Michigan State University, 1971.

Hasner, John and Harvey S. Woods. *Christmas Trees as a Farm Crop.* Carbondale: Southern Illinois University, 1958.

Rudolph, V. J. *Costs and Returns in Christmas Tree Management.* Michigan State University Research Report No. 155, Natural Resources Series. East Lansing: Michigan State University, 1972.

Sowder, Arthur M. *Christmas Trees—The Tradition and the Trade.* USDA Extension Service, Agricultural Information Bulletin No. 94. Washington, DC, 1966.

United States Standards for Grades of Christmas Trees. USDA Agricultural Marketing Service. Washington, DC, 1973.

Wallner, William E. and James W. Butcher. *Christmas Tree Insect Management.* Extension Bulletin E-353. East Lansing: Cooperative Extension Service, Michigan State University, 1973.

CHAPTER **11** Forgotten Uses
for 120 Trees: Food,
Furniture, Dyes,
Drink, Medication,
and More

by ROGER B. YEPSEN, JR.

Man spent tens of thousands of years learning to put trees to work
and has forgotten most of it all over the past several decades. The
American of one, two, or three hundred years ago—and the Indian
before him—was a good deal more familiar with the growing landscape than the American of today. Each tree had its own special
uses, even the less conspicuous species: the young pods of the
eastern redbud were once fried into fritters in the South; the hard
wood of the crab apple often served as mallet heads; and the flexible wood of the downy serviceberry made limber flyrods.

But as the manufacture of housing and furniture, teas, and
medicines have become the concerns of big business, such multi-
fold uses ceased to be common knowledge. Once possessed of

unique personalities, the trees around us have become strangers.

When business took over from the homesteader, it found ways to put cheaper, more easily worked materials to work. Take a look, for example, at the manufacture of furniture. The popular wood for early manufactured furniture was oak—not spectacularly figured, but solid and pleasing to the eye. But wood did not lend itself to the streamlined thirties, and oak lost its prominence to plastics, glass, and metals.

Trees have been supplanted in countless other applications. The tops of sweet birch once were used to flavor birch beer, but that wintergreenlike flavor now comes from the laboratory. Beer barrels, once fashioned from oak and other sturdy woods, are now stamped from stainless steel. Shipbuilding used to require the special talents of a great number of species, some well known and others quite obscure. Before barbed wire came to be, farmers grew living hedges of Osage orange; a few specimens are still to be seen on old farms, no more than useless curiosities, bearing their odd brainlike fruit into fall. The pages that follow abound with such quaint applications.

But "quaint" doesn't quite do these old friends justice. Today we are witnessing an awakened interest in the old ways of using the tall crops around us. The prodigious number of hand and power tools now being sold testify to the fact that wood is a more satisfying workshop material than metal or plastic. Layers of paint accreted in the thirties, forties, and fifties are being scraped down to bare wood, to receive a finish that makes the most of the natural grain and color; what was only a surface to cover up is now something to rejoice in. And through the writings of naturalists Euell Gibbons, Nelson Coon, and others, many have come to learn that trees are more than just the pawns of landscapers—they can be nibbled at, as well as looked at.

This chapter is written in hopes that you will take enjoyment and benefit in rediscovering what it has taken man so long to learn. Some of the bits of knowledge that follow are curiosities and little more: it's fun to brew a cup of spicebush tea and reflect that colonists experienced the same flavor in lieu of the imported stuff. But you may be able to pick up something of more value. Food and fuel are the applications that first come to mind. Many of the unusual fruit and nut trees that follow either grow in the wild or can be introduced to the orchard or yard. These include the beech, butternut, chestnut, chinquapin, hackberry, hickory, juniper, honey locust, honey mesquite, mulberry, pawpaw, persimmon, service-berry, and sugarberry. In the fireplace, apple, hickory, oak, and ash rate high. While it's true that a half-acre lot isn't likely to generate enough wood for more than an occasional winter evening fire, unwanted trees can often be found at construction sites.

If you aren't quite up to sawing up lumber from your own trees, you might throw the logs into a pickup and take them to an obliging local sawmill operator. For example, several hemlock can be ripped into enough siding to board-and-batten a modest-sized house or outbuilding.

Many of the trees in this chapter yield dyes, including the alders, sweet birch, cascara buckthorn, butternut, red cedar, dog-wood, eastern hemlock, black locust, red maple, the oaks, Osage orange, pear, poplar, sassafras, smoketree, and walnut.

Of the trees discussed here, a surprising number have medi-cinal talents, having been used to sooth sore throats, relieve canker sores, settle stomachs, prepare one's constitution for long hikes, stave off scurvy, induce sweats, and more. Much of this wealth of pharmacology was discovered by the American Indians. Among the medicinal trees are the hazel alder, red alder, white ash, quak-ing aspen, cascara buckthorn, butternut, southern catalpa, eastern red cedar, black cherry, cucumber tree, dogwood, elm, balsam fir, Douglas fir, hemlock, holly, California laurel, the oaks, persim-mon, the pines, poplar, sassafras, sourwood, spicebush, black spruce, sweet gum, walnut, and black willow. As some tree-based medicines are apt to be very powerful and even dangerous, it's best to try them out cautiously and with the guidance of an herbal you can trust.

So, here they are—120 trees, each with its own foliage, habits, and special applications. Maps show where the more common species are to be found, courtesy of the USDA. Alternate common names are listed in parenthesis, as are occasional alternate or disused Latin names.

ALDERS *Alnus*
The alder family has not found favor in this country. Its members lack somewhat as ornamentals, being without interesting fruit and producing no pyrotechnics in fall. The trees are suited to wet and moist soils and might be planted where other ornamentals wouldn't thrive.

ALDER, EUROPEAN (black alder) *A. glutinosa*
This alder was introduced to the United States in Colonial times but has little to recommend it as an ornamental. It will do well where the ground is too wet for other trees. The light, soft, pale brown wood has been used to make shoe soles and finds application in inexpensive cabinetry. The bark and fruit will tan leather, and the bark and leaves yield a yellow dye.

ALDER, HAZEL (common alder) *A. serrulata*
This is no more than a shrub or, at best, small tree—too small to be used much for its wood. However, it was used to make small barrels and charcoal for gunpowder and is a good fuel. In Scotland, the leaves were used to tan leather and to feed sheep. The French fed their cattle on the foliage. Tea made from the leaves was said to heal ulcers and relieve sore throats. Fishermen used the bark, added to ferrous sulfate, to stain their nets dark.

ALDER, RED (alder, Oregon alder, western alder) *A. rubra*
The red alder is a medium-sized to large tree found along the Pacific coast north to Canada and Alaska. Pyramidal in shape, the tree bears dense, dark green foliage that tent caterpillars find particularly appetizing. Like the other alders, this species grows well in moist soils. Although it has little value as an ornamental, it has been rated the leading hardwood for commercial purposes in

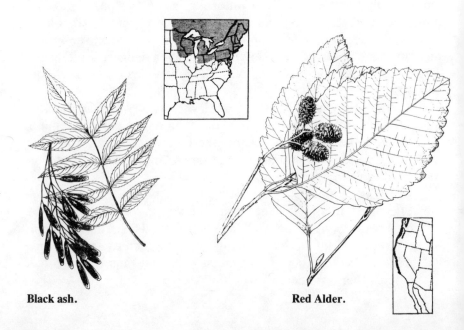

Black ash.   Red Alder.

the Pacific Northwest, the wood being used for furniture. This species has some talent as a dye plant; the roots produce brown, the leaves a yellow green, and the bark a yellow brown. The dyes are suitable for both wool and leather. The long birchlike fruit was once used by the Cree Indians to cure dropsy.

ASH *Fraxinus*
A good many species of ash grow in the United States and Canada. Some have a limited value as ornamentals. Others are important for their strong, elastic wood. Ash is a fine firewood, and if necessary can be burned green.

ASH, BLACK (basket ash, brown ash, hoop ash, swamp ash, water ash) *F. nigra*
Wet soils in the northeastern United States and adjacent Canada are the home of this species. As suggested by a couple of its common names, the wood was once used to weave baskets. It varies from grayish brown to light brown and often occurs in valuable burls. The wood finds use as veneer (marketed as northern brown ash), chair bottoms, and barrel hoops.

ASH, EUROPEAN (Italian olive ash) *F. excelsior*
The wood of this import is not used as packing material, as the Latin name might suggest, but is cut into a wavy, distinctly streaked veneer that brings a good price. While planted in this country as an ornamental, the European ash's foliage does not turn in the fall.

ASH, GREEN (blue ash, water ash) *F. pennsylvanica (F. lanceolata)*
Occurring in most of the United States east of the Rockies and in much of eastern Canada, the hardy, rapidly growing green ash often serves as an ornamental. It has an attractive rounded shape and turns yellow in the fall. This species is the most widely distributed of the ashes. In addition to its ornamental value, the tree's lumber is valuable and is often sold as white ash.

ASH, OREGON *F. velutina*
This species is notable in that it is the only ash that grows on the Pacific coast. It is happiest in rich lowland soils. A valuable hardwood in its area, Oregon ash wood is somewhat lighter than that of the eastern species but has most of the same uses. It often serves as a shade tree.

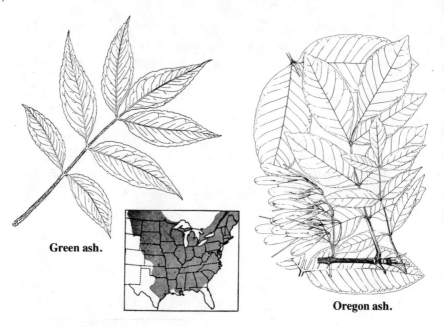

Green ash.

Oregon ash.

ASH, PUMPKIN *F. tomentosa*

This is a southern species, growing in the wet soils of the Mississippi Valley and along the coastal plain north into Virginia. The tree gets its peculiar name from the swollen base of the trunk. The wood is used in cooperage, furniture, boxes and other containers, railroad ties, and for veneer and fuel.

ASH, WHITE (American ash, biltmore ash, cane ash) *F. americana*

Much white ash lumber ends up as baseball bats, as the wood is strong and holds up well under shock. It's also the most popular choice for long tool and implement handles and for oars. Because it is an excellent wood for bending, white ash is often picked for the curved parts of chairs. The tree produces a yellow dye, and the inner bark was once collected for its medicinal value. This is likely the most popular of the ashes for landscaping. The seeds grow readily, and a tree often gives life to a great number of offspring in the immediate area—so many that the volunteer ashes may be looked upon as weeds. The compound leaves turn deep purple or yellow in the fall, and the tree grows to a height of 120 feet.

ASPEN, BIGTOOTH (aspen poplar, large poplar, largetooth aspen, popple, white poplar) *Populus grandidentata*

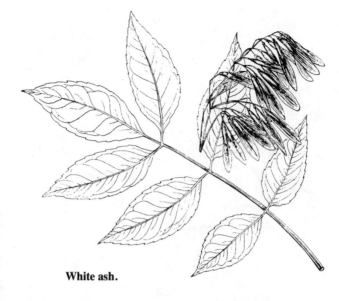

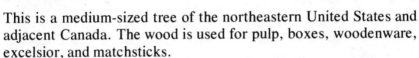

White ash.

This is a medium-sized tree of the northeastern United States and adjacent Canada. The wood is used for pulp, boxes, woodenware, excelsior, and matchsticks.

ASPEN, QUAKING (American aspen, aspen, golden aspen, mountain aspen, poplar, quaking asp, quiver leaf, trembling poplar, white poplar) *Populus tremuloides (P. tremuliformis)*

The most remarkable feature of this tree in the field is the way in which even a slight breeze will make the leaves flap back and forth with a restful hiss. A close look at the petiole, or leaf stem, shows why—it is flat in cross section, not rounded as on most trees, and therefore flaps in the wind. An extract of the bark contains a substance related to aspirin and was once used as we use synthetic aspirin today. (The active ingredient, salicin, can also be obtained from willow bark.)

The quaking aspen is distributed widely through the Northeastern, Rocky Mountain, and Pacific Coast regions, and across Canada to Alaska—in fact, it has been mentioned as the most widely distributed tree in nature across this continent. The foliage turns yellow with autumn, and the tree has value as an ornamental. However, it is short-lived and becomes increasingly susceptible to disease as it grows larger. One of the lighter hardwoods, the wood is often used for cheese containers because of its pale

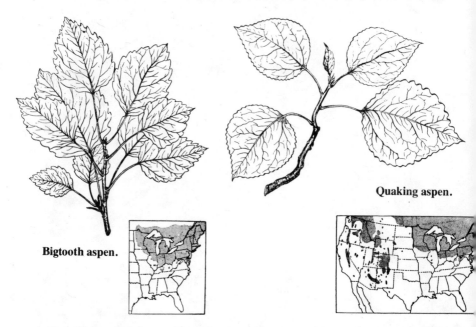

Quaking aspen.

Bigtooth aspen.

color, light weight, and lack of any perceptible smell or taste. The wood is also used as excelsior, pulp, and matches. Forked trunks and branches yield an especially valuable veneer. As for woodworking, the wood bends well and finishes to a smooth surface with either hand or power tools; however, nails and screws tend to split it, and the wood is better painted than stained.

BALDCYPRESS (black cypress, buck cypress, cow cypress, gulf cypress, red cypress, southern cypress, tidewater cypress, white cypress, yellow cypress) *Taxodium distichum*

If you find it puzzling that this one species could be labelled four different colors, the answer is that the tint of the wood varies with the locale from which it comes. Trees from southern swamps produce a darker wood than those grown on drier land in the northern part of the range. The wood has a reputation for durability, is strong and hard, and has a greasy feeling when rubbed, according to Albert Constantine, Jr. in *Know Your Woods* (Scribner's, 1975). He notes that attractive baldcypress crotches are sometimes offered on the market as faux satine. Because baldcypress is so durable, it finds application in coffins, greenhouses, and building and ship construction.

BASSWOOD, AMERICAN (American linden, basswood beetree,

black limetree, lime tree, linden, linn, whitewood, wickup, and yellow basswood) *Tilia americana*

The American Indians made twine by pulling apart the basswood's inner bark into strands and then twisting three together at a time. These strings could be twisted together to make cords, which were woven into mats. The wood is made into boxes (especially food containers), millwork, furniture (sides and backs of drawers), apiary supplies, and excelsior. Ship's figureheads were carved from basswood, and model makers still favor this lightweight, rather weak wood for carving. Strips of basswood are used as acoustically dead structural material in guitars. This species is a popular shade tree, and its fragrant yellow white flowers make it an important honey plant.

BEECH (American beech) *Fagus grandifolia*

This is a large, beautiful tree, with an attractive shape and foliage in summer. Its smooth gray bark suggests the skin of a large, sinuous sea creature and invites jackknife graffiti. The leaves turn a golden bronze in fall. All in all, this native beech is a fine ornamental. One word of caution is in order, however—the tree feeds close to the surface, making it difficult to grow other vegetation beneath the dripline. Also, it does not do well along city streets. You shouldn't

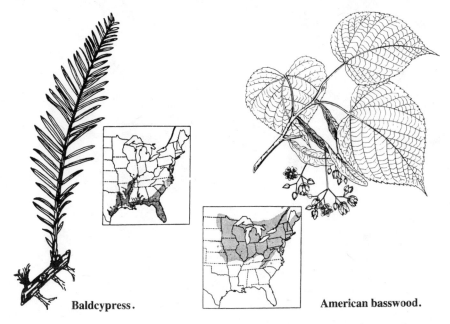

Baldcypress.   American basswood.

have much trouble in moving young beeches, as their roots are strong and fibrous.

The wood is heavy, strong, and bends well when steamed. As it dries, beech tends to shrink a good deal and may check, warp, or discolor. Its positive qualities make it good choice for furniture (particularly chair posts), food containers, handles, veneer, and firewood. The wood has tiny pores and rays that are easily seen.

The beechnut, known also as beech mast, was once marketed, but now you'll have to gather your own. At one time the nuts were dried and roasted to make a coffee substitute, and the young leaves once found favor in the South as a potherb. The trade name Beechnut harks back to the time when beech oil was used commercially as a butter substitute; the French used it for lamp oil. Should you find the times really hard, you might resort to boiling and roasting beech sawdust to add to bread recipes; the ground inner bark has also been used as a flour substitute. Hogs were once let loose beneath beechnut trees to fatten up on the nuts, records J. Russell Smith in *Tree Crops*. The beechnut might well be bred into something as fine as the Persian walnut, suggests Smith, but "thus far, scientific agriculture seems to have utterly neglected the beechnut."

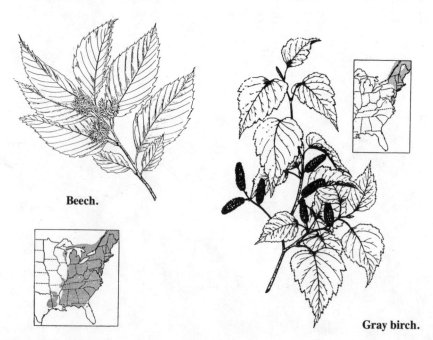

Beech.

Gray birch.

BEECH, EUROPEAN *Fagus sylvatica*

Several varieties of this imported species are used as ornamentals: the fernleaf beech, having feather foliage; the purple beech, so named for the purple leaves; weeping European beech, a wide-spreading tree with branches hanging to the ground; and a number of others. In all, sixty-seven clones of European beech have been named, such is their beauty and variety. As late as a hundred years or so ago, beech leaves were used in Europe to stuff mattresses, as they stayed fresher than straw.

BIRCH *Betula*

This family of trees is popularly grown as an ornamental for its graceful manner, gold autumn color, and the white bark on some species. On the debit side, birches are typically short-lived. They should be transplanted with roots balled and wrapped in burlap. They prefer a moist, slightly acid, sandy, light soil, and flourish best in those regions having plentiful rainfall.

BIRCH, GRAY *B. populifolia*

This species has an unspectacular dull white or grayish bark that does not peel. It is chosen for its habit of sending up several trunks with no large branches, thereby casting a light shade. The wood is used for spools and other turned articles, and for fuel. Gray birch is particularly susceptible to the birch leaf miner, which somewhat reduces its desirability as a shade tree.

BIRCH, PAPER (canoe birch, mother tree, silver birch, white birch) *B. papyrifera*

This attractive white-trunked birch is often chosen as an ornamental. Interestingly, great numbers of this beauty spring up where they're needed most—on the bare, steep-sided mountains of waste left standing in Pennsylvania coal country. When planted alongside other trees, the paper birch typically has one trunk, but it may send up several if grown along the banks of a stream or pond.

The bark was used by Indians as a covering for huts and for canoes. The largest and smoothest trunks were selected in spring, and cut sections were pried off with a wooden wedge; they measured from ten to twelve feet long and two feet nine inches broad. The sheets were stuck together with the fibrous roots of the white spruce, rendered supple by soaking in water. The seams were waterproofed by coating them with the resin of the balsam fir. The canoes weighed little—a four-passenger model ranged from forty to fifty pounds. At Hudson Bay posts, tents were sewn of birch bark. Canadians and backwoods Yankees would place large sheets under the shingles of their roofs to ensure a dry house. The bark was also placed between the soles of shoes and in hat crowns "as a defense against humidity," says an old source. Commercially, the wood has been used to fashion spools and toothpicks. One old book says that wood taken from the trunk where a branch issues is beautifully feathered and variegated, ideal for the front of a bureau or table top. Scandinavians at one time boiled and baked birch sawdust to a flourlike consistency, and used it as a supplement to real flour.

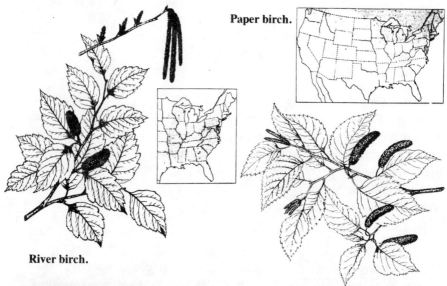

Paper birch.

River birch.

BIRCH, RIVER (black birch, red birch, water birch) *B. nigra*
This species is found in swamps and along streams through much of the eastern half of the United States. It bears decorative catkins in early spring. Logs of this wood have the curious property of storing well under water. Constantine says in *Know Your Woods* that "one large veneer firm recently learned of a large number of logs that had been buried in Lake Superior for sixty-three years on the site of an old sawmill. They had their men inspect the logs beneath water and then purchased the entire lot. They were fine, large logs of birch timber, and when they were taken into the mill

produced some very fine veneer.'' River birch can serve duty for erosion control.

BIRCH, SWEET (black birch, cherry birch) *B. lenta*
To find why the name sweet birch, just scrape a bit of the thin bark from a twig and sniff. The bark and other plant parts contain methyl salicylate, or oil of wintergreen. The oil is still distilled in some places to make medicines and good quality birch beer, although the natural oil has largely been supplanted by a synthetic preparation. (It is interesting that another forest plant also contains this aromatic oil. The little checkerberry, or teaberry, sends its shiny green elliptical leaves up but three or four inches. The leaves and berries have an unmistakably wintergreen taste.) An old Norwegian wine recipe calls for two pounds of sugar to be added to each gallon of sap. The liquid is boiled and skimmed as impurities rise to the top. After an unspecified period, the liquid is allowed to cool and then activated with yeast. A superior wine involved lemons and raisins, as well. The Norwegians have also made wine of sap from the poplar, willow, sycamore, and walnut.

The wood has a strong, close, hard grain, and is used in cabinetry; the heartwood is brownish red, and the sapwood varies from light brown to yellow. The wood sometimes shows a landscape effect and was once specified for the foot and headboards of

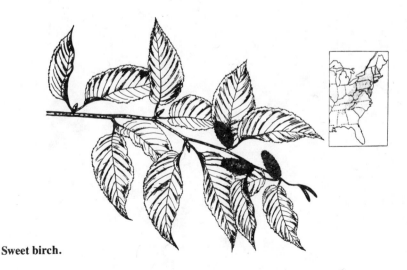

Sweet birch.

beds and in other furniture, including chairs, although it doesn't bend quite as well as yellow birch. The bark, decocted and combined with ferrous sulfate, was used to color woolens a beautiful wine drab.

BIRCH, YELLOW (gray birch, silver birch, swamp birch) *B. lutea*
This species derives its name from the color of the papery curls of bark that readily peel from young trees. Like the sweet birch, its young twigs are aromatic. The lumber is valuable, serving as flooring, woodenware, furniture, and veneers. It's easy to work, finishes nicely, and is light brown with white sapwood. Veneers often show off the wood's handsome wavy figuring.

BOXELDER (ash-leaf maple, black ash, cut-leafed maple, Manitoba maple, Red River maple, stinking ash, sugar ash, three-leaf maple, water ash) *Acer negundo*
This rapid-growing tree is best suited for areas where other ornamentals won't make it. Boxelder has been used in windbreaks in the Midwest and can act as a nurse tree for slower growing, more desirable species. When the boxelder is no longer needed, it can be cut for firewood. Good lumber is sometimes made into woodenware or interior finish. While it is hardy and long-lived, it is not as attractive as the other members of the maple family.

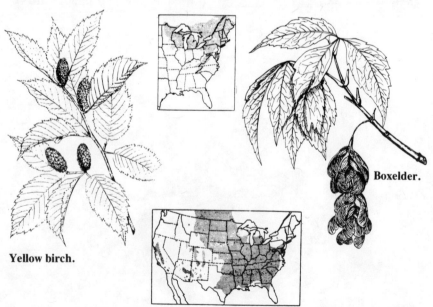

Boxelder.

Yellow birch.

Boxelders can be tapped for sap, although far less productive than the sugar maple. Still, this tree in its several varieties finds favor in areas with cold winters and hot dry summers.

BUCKEYE, OHIO (American horsechestnut, fetid buckeye, stinking buckeye) *Aesculus glabra*
This is a small tree, but it may grow to a height of fifty or sixty feet in areas favorable to it. Although the official tree of Ohio, this buckeye was brought to North America from Germany. As a couple of its common names suggest, the twigs and flowers put off a bad smell when crushed. To settlers, the seeds looked something like the eyes of buck deer and were carried around in the pockets to ward off rheumatism. These seeds are poisonous—in fact, the seeds of the California buckeye *(Aesculus californica)* were used by the Indians of the West as a fish-stupifying poison. The wood is lightweight, soft, and a pale off-white; it has been used for artificial limbs and woodenware. Lumber shows a characteristic ripple pattern, and veneers are sometimes available. The leaves turn bright orange in fall, recommending this tree as an ornamental.

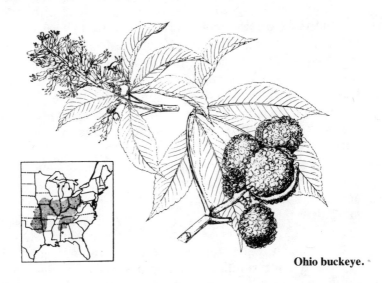

Ohio buckeye.

BUCKTHORN, CASCARA (cascara, cascara sagrada) *Rhamnus purshiana*
The bark of this small tree or shrub is the source of the drug cascara sagrada, a laxative (the bark can also be taken from the

California buckeye, *Aesculus californica*). To prepare the drug, the bark is dried over a long period and then soaked in water. You can still buy cascara in some drugstores, marketed under any of several names. Locally, the wood is used for fence posts and fuel. The bark can also be used to impart a variety of gray, brown, and yellow shades to wool; when used for this purpose, the bark sometimes goes by the name of chittam wood.

BUTTERNUT (filnut, lemon nut, oilnut, white mahogany, white walnut) *Juglans cinerea*

Although its wood is not as heavy and tough as walnut, butternut deserves the name white walnut, making fine-looking paneling and furniture, and working well with tools. The Shakers at Lebanon, New York, used butternut for the fronts of drawers, and it has also served in coffins, bowls, gun stocks, small house timbers, and posts and rails. It is a medium to large tree, with a lofty spreading form that looks good on a lawn. The tree is a good deal hardier than the black walnut. Its nut is easier to extricate, and the butternut taste is preferred to walnut by some people. The sap can be boiled down to a sweet syrup and is sometimes mixed with maple sap. A tea brewed from the inner bark is supposed to settle the stomach and act as a delicate laxative, but it has disappeared from the *Pharmacopoeia of the United States*. In the Revolution, physicians employed the bark as a mild cathartic. The leaves, bark, and unripe fruit were once used to dye woolens a dark brown, while the roots imparted a fawn color. Rebel soldiers were known as Butternuts in the War Between the States, as their clothes were often colored with this free dyestuff.

Unfortunately, the nuts are becoming somewhat scarce, disease and lumbering claiming a good number of the trees. There's no need to hull them; just spread them out to dry in the shade, no more than three deep. Soaking them overnight should make cracking easier. The nuts can be preserved by pickling. They should be young enough that you can lance them with a needle. First, soak them in a brine solution, keeping them covered and changing the solution every other day. Then wipe them off, pierce each several times with a needle, and put them in glass jars, sprinkling ginger, mace, nutmeg, and cloves between each layer. Finally, pour boiling cider vinegar to the top of each jar and seal. The pickles will be ready to eat in two weeks. An alternate common name for butternut is oilnut, and the once-valued oil can be released from the nuts by boiling them. The Indians did this to produce a hardened substance that was used much like butter. The dried and powdered leaves served as a domestic substitute for Spanish flies, a drug.

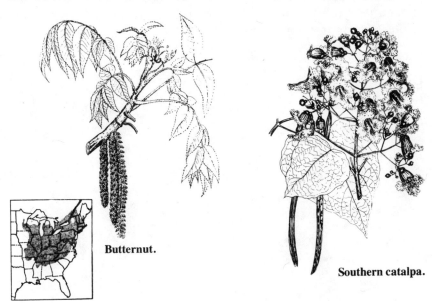

Butternut.

Southern catalpa.

CATALPA, NORTHERN (cigartree, hardy catalpa, Indian bean, smoking bean, western catalpa) *Catalpa speciosa*
This catalpa's showy white flowers and odd beanlike pods are responsible for it being planted far outside its native region, a small area in the Mississippi Valley. The tree is now to be found throughout the East. The wood is soft, brown, and durable, and is often used for posts. Children sometimes smoke the pods as cigars.

CATALPA, SOUTHERN (bean tree, candle tree, cigartree) *Catalpa bignonioides*
This is a smaller tree than the northern species, and it is less cold-hardy. The pods, reaching a length of twelve inches or more, were at one time smoked to relieve the symptoms of asthma. The wood is soft, mildly aromatic, and durable, and finds use as picture frames and tool handles.

CEDAR, ATLANTIC WHITE (false cypress, juniper, post cedar, southern white cedar, swamp cedar) *Chamaecyparis thyoides*
You'll find this medium-sized cedar in swamps and bogs on the Atlantic and Gulf Coastal Plains. When young, the tree is graceful and

can serve as an ornamental, but it loses its lower branches in time and the foliage becomes thin and ragged. As such, it is best suited for planting only in low wet places where other trees do poorly. Although it hasn't much of a reputation as a lawn tree, the Atlantic white cedar's fragrant, durable wood serves well for fence posts, rails, shingles, and small boat construction.

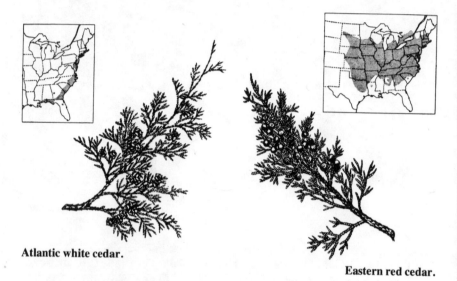

Atlantic white cedar.

Eastern red cedar.

CEDAR, EASTERN RED (pencil cedar, red cedar, red juniper, savin, Virginia cedar) *Juniperus virginiana*
This is a medium-sized tree of the eastern half of the United States and adjacent Canada. The wood is pale to bright red, sometimes streaked attractively with white. Aromatic and easily worked, it is used to make chests, cigar boxes, and pencils (the good-smelling ones). The wood is often picked for trim on boats and at one time was popular for both boat and ship construction. Although people find the cedar aroma enjoyable, insects are repelled by it, explaining why the wood is often used to make chests and line clothes closets. To make a repellent soil drench or spray for garden or house plants, brew a tea of cedar chips in water.

The bark, berries, and twigs of this species and several relatives can be used to dye woolens a khaki color. In Appalachian folk medicine, the various plant parts are boiled and the steam inhaled to relieve bronchitis. American Indians made a tea of the fruit and leaves that was drunk to relieve colds and coughs, and they inhaled small amounts of cedar smoke to help clear up stuffy sinuses. An oil from the berries was used by southwestern tribes as a cure for dysentery. Canker sores was relieved by washing out the mouth with berry juice. The oil from the wood, known as cedar oil or cedrol, is used to repel moths and is an ingredient of some insecticide preparations. This aromatic oil is also used to scent soap.

You have a choice of several horticultural forms to choose from. To transplant this attractive and useful species, leave a ball of earth around the roots. The horticultural forms are usually grown from cuttings or by grafting. If you're interested in harvesting the wood, be patient—the red cedar grows slowly and may live to be three hundred years old.

CEDAR, PORT ORFORD (ginger pine, Lawson's cypress, Oregon cedar, Port Orford white cedar) *Chamaecyparis lawsoniana*
Native to a small coastal area shared by Oregon and California, the tall Port Orford cedar is now grown in mild, moist climates as an ornamental. Several interesting varieties are available. The pale yellow to yellow brown wood has the smell of ginger and is a prime wood for arrows, boatbuilding, and furniture. A somewhat dated source gives this as the principal wood for battery separators. The resin has been used as an insecticide.

Western red cedar.

CEDAR, WESTERN RED (canoe cedar, giant arborvitae, Idaho cedar, Pacific red cedar, shinglewood, stinking cedar) *Thuja plicata*

This large tree is lumbered for shingles (of which it is the primary source), siding, millwork, and boatbuilding. It works well and looks good when finished. While the wood is aromatic, it isn't as pleasant to the nose as the eastern red cedar. Left on its own, the tree may grow to 180 feet high, but it can be kept trimmed to any desired height if you so wish.

CHERRY, BLACK (chokecherry, New England mahogany, rum cherry, whisky cherry, wild cherry) *Prunus serotina*

Originally more common in the East, the numbers of this valuable tree have been reduced by the demand for the wood in cabinetry. Cherry wood is heavy, strong, and light reddish brown, and responds well to working with tools. It has long been selected for tables and chests of drawers, window sashes, stair-rail posts, doors, and gun stocks. The most beautiful portion of the trunk wood is at the juncture of the branches. The pea-sized fruit is bitter to the tongue but can be made into jelly or added to rum or brandy to make cherry bounce. The cherries will add to the flavor of cider.

A scraped young twig gives off the almondy smell of hydrocyanic acid, a somewhat toxic substance that acts as a sedative and

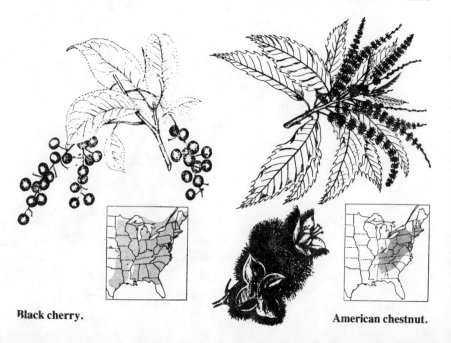

Black cherry.

American chestnut.

cough suppressant when taken in very modest amounts. The bark is listed in the *Pharmacopoeia of the United States;* the 1890 issue specifies that the bark be collected in autumn, and that bark of the very large and very small branches shouldn't be used. In any case, stripping the bark is very tedious work. A syrup of wild cherry may be prepared by this recipe from the book: mix 150 cc. of glycerin with 300 cc. of water; moisten 150 grams of powdered bark with a sufficient quantity of the liquid, and macerate it for twenty-four hours in a closed vessel; pack it firmly into a cylindrical percolator (or large funnel), and pour on the remainder of the water and glycerin. When the liquid has disappeared from the surface, follow it up with water until the percolate that drips from the bottom measures 450 cc. Dissolve the percolate in 750 grams of sugar by agitation, strain, add enough water to make the product measure 1000 cc., and mix thoroughly. At no time should a wild cherry preparation be heated, as this will dispel its medicinal properties.

CHESTNUT, AMERICAN *Castanea dentata*

This large, stately tree of the Appalachian Mountain and Ohio Valley regions has nearly been eliminated by chestnut blight. Worm-riddled logs are made into furniture and picture frames. On old furniture, you can expect to find chestnut in the frames of bureaus and sofas, and the bottom and sides of drawers were often made of it. Inexpensive chestnut items still abound at antique shops and flea markets. The bark is an important source of tannin and with iron makes a black ink. The Mohegans collected the leaves when still green in September or October for use as an astringent extract, a practice supported by the *Pharmacopoeia of the United States* until early in the century. The Iriquois liberated the oil from chestnuts by crushing them and boiling till the oil rose to the surface. This oil was served with bread or as a topping for pudding, and the nutmeat that was left over went into puddings or breads. Where do street vendors of chestnuts find their produce today? The nuts are imported from Europe, where the trees are resistant to blight.

CHINQUAPIN, GOLDEN (chinquapin, giant evergreen chinquapin, golden-leaf chestnut) *Castanopsis chrysophylla*

This Pacific Coast tree bears a very spiny burr containing one or two edible nuts that mature the second year. It does well on poor soils and bears its dark green foliage the year-round. The wood has been used to make furniture and is similar to that of the chinquapin *Castanea pumila,* found in the South and East.

COFFEETREE, KENTUCKY (American coffeebean, chicot, coffee nut, Kentucky mahogany, mahogany bean, stumptree) *Gymnocladus dioicus*
The podded beans of this tree were indeed once ground, roasted, and used as a coffee substitute. The beverage never caught on, perhaps because the beans are without caffeine. The Indians ate the roasted seeds. This tree is often grown outside its natural range as an ornamental, although it is not noted for its beauty. The brown wood is durable and strong, polishes well, and is marked with annual rings that give it interest as a cabinet wood.

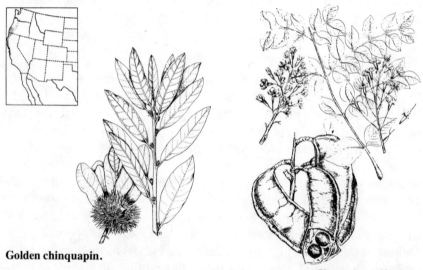

Golden chinquapin.

Kentucky coffeetree.

COTTONWOOD, EASTERN (aspen cottonwood, Carolina poplar, cottonwood, eastern poplar, necklace poplar, river poplar, water poplar, yellow cottonwood) *Populus deltoides*
A stately tree with foliage that trembles in the slightest winds, the cottonwood grows in almost any soil. It can be propagated by setting a section of branch in the moist ground. The heartwood is off-white to pale brown, the sapwood a creamy white. While not of much value for cabinetry, cottonwood is often selected for packing crates, as the smooth surface stencils well. It sometimes ends up as an indifferent veneer and makes a fair firewood.

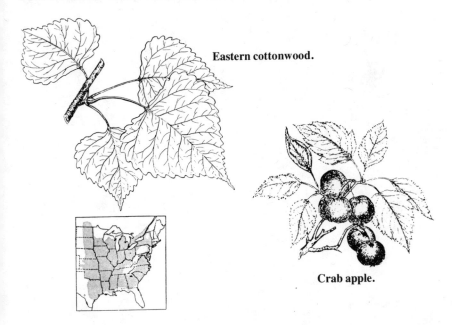

Eastern cottonwood.

Crab apple.

CRAB APPLE (crab, crab tree, garland, wild apple) *Malus pumila*
Unfortunately for Johnny Appleseed's beneficiaries, apple trees
grown from seed don't produce very good apples, and wild trees
have to be grafted in order to get a sizeable, sweet fruit. Crab twigs
and buds are typically hairy, and the twigs taste sweet when
chewed. Crab apples may not be much right off the tree, but they
make fine applebutter, cider, and jelly. The wood is difficult to
work with, although it turns well and is suited for carving because
of the very uniform texture. Crab wood is heavier and harder and
shows more variation in color than pear wood, ranging from
pinkish to gray brown. It is used for saw handles and mallet heads.

CUCUMBER TREE (cucumber tree magnolia, mountain magnolia)
Magnolia acuminata
A large to medium-sized tree, this species is so named because the
immature fruit looks somewhat like a cucumber. Settlers of the
Alleghenies picked the fruit in midsummer and soaked them in
whisky, believing that the bitter liquid that resulted would guard
them from "autumnal fever." The attractive shape of the tree and
its large elliptical foliage recommend its use as an ornamental. The
more exotic magnolias can be grafted on to this sturdy species. The
wood is much the same as that of the yellow poplar.

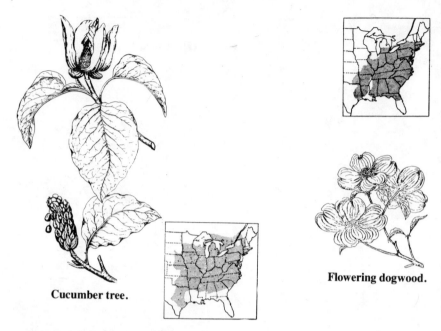

Cucumber tree.

Flowering dogwood.

DOGWOOD, FLOWERING (arrow wood, bitter redberry, cornel, cornelian, false boxwood) *Cornus florida*

One of the finest ornamentals, the dogwood is claimed by two states as their state tree—Missouri and Virginia. The yellow brown wood is the prime source of textile shuttles. It is much like maple and is the only wood of the dogwood family of any commercial importance. The wood also has found its way into golf club heads, wood engraving blocks, tool handles, and the cogs of wheels. The bark has some medicinal value. The Indians made a tea of it to reduce fevers, as did Southerners during the Civil War, when the then-current remedy, quinine, was unavailable. The bark was also supposed to ward off malaria. Although the dogwood is no longer mentioned in the *Pharmacopoeia of the United States*, the bark's astringent value might be used to clear up mouth sores. Constantine reports that the plant's essence is still served up in whisky as a home remedy. The Indians obtained a scarlet dye from the bark of the smaller roots, and small branches were once used as toothbrushes.

ELM, AMERICAN (gray elm, soft elm, swamp elm, water elm, white elm) *Ulmus americana*

This is the largest and best known of the various elms. Its popularity as an ornamental, however, is on the wane, for the Dutch elm disease has taken great numbers of the species. At one time, it was the favorite tree for lining streets in the Northeast.

The brown heartwood is very tough and difficult to split. The wood must be dried with care to prevent warping but is easily bent to make barrels and curved parts of furniture. Elm veneer is marketed as prinz wood and apatalae. Quarter-sliced elm is especially attractive and is a good choice for inlay work. Chairs used to be caned with elm bark; when macerated in water and rendered supple by pounding, it can be twisted into a strong cord.

The wood of the other principal elm species is much the same as that of the American elm. The inner bark of the slippery elm (*Ulmus rubra*) can be brewed into a tea that's comforting to a sore throat. A food for infants and invalids was made from a flour of the ground, dried bark mixed with milk and arrowroot. The primary uses for the wood are in various containers, poultry and beekeeping supplies, and caskets. It was used to build many of the ships that plied the Ohio River.

FIR, BALSAM (Canada balsam, eastern fir, fir tree) *Abies balsamea*

Wood of this medium-sized evergreen is not very durable, but it is used for food containers and as pulp. The assets of this tree don't

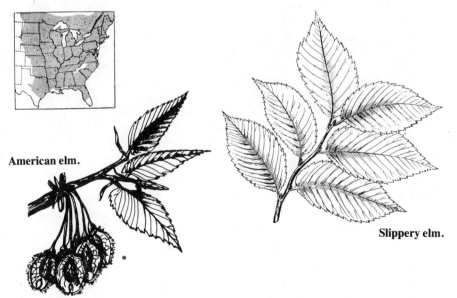

American elm.

Slippery elm.

stop there—this is one of the most valued species to be found in the Northeast. The balsam fir is a popular Christmas tree, because of its blue green foliage, its excellent shape, and fine aroma. The aroma lasts a good while, and it is the foliage of this species that one sniffs in balsam pillows. Because of its index of refraction, resin is collected from blisters on the bark to make a glass cement used on optical instruments and microscopic slides. Artists use a resin varnish to finish watercolors. Knots of the tree are rich enough in resin that they will serve as candles and were used as such by the Colonists.

Medicinally, the resin was applied by American Indians to burns and cuts; however, some sources say that this practice may actually aggravate an inflammation. An oleo resin known as balsam of Gilead or Canada balsam is made from this tree. It was used in cases of pulmonary complaints and once commanded a high price on the American and English markets.

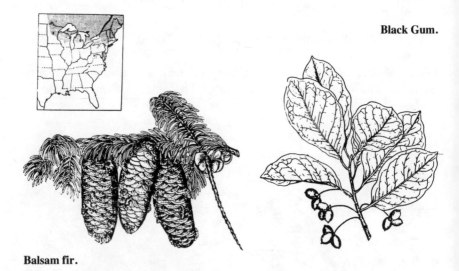

Black Gum.

Balsam fir.

FIR, DOUGLAS (Douglas spruce, fir, Oregon pine, red fir, red pine, red spruce, yellow fir) *Pseudotsuga menziesii (P. taxifolia)*

This tree is one of the most valuable sources of timber in the West. The growth rings are very prominent in rotary cut lumber, adding interest to fir plywood. While the wood is difficult to work with hand tools, it is suited to machining and glues well. It does not have a good surface for painting. The Indians wove baskets from the roots. A tea rich in vitamin C can be made from the fresh needles, and lumberjacks staved off scurvy with this dark brew.

GUM, BLACK (bettlebung, black tupelo, bowl gum, horn pine, pepperidge, snag tree, sour gum, stinkwood, wild peartree, yellow gumtree) *Nyssa sylvatica (N. multiflora)*

A swamp tree that grows to seventy-five or one hundred feet in height, the black gum can be grown north along the Atlantic seaboard to Boston, and all the way south to Florida. It is pyramidal in shape and is distinguished by branches that often droop at the tips. The shiny, dark green leaves turn a brilliant scarlet or orange in fall. Black gum produces a dark blue fruit approximately the size of a small cherry.

Like the other woods of the tupelo family, black gum has an interlocking grain that makes it hard to split and nail, and promotes warping. Because the wood is so hard to split, it was despised by early farmers who tried to fashion the logs into fence rails. The wood takes a good finish, and logs are turned into good-looking veneer. Naturalist and author Nelson Coon relates that "bettlebung" is a very local name derived from the use to which black gum was put in Martha's Vineyard. When whaling supported the local economy, the wood was used to make beetles, or mallets, with which bungs of whale-oil barrels were driven. A slow-burning wood, the tupelo played a part in plantation traditions in the Old South, whereby the slaves enjoyed a Christmas holiday that lasted as long as the life of the back log of the master's fireplace. As soon as the sap stopped its downward flow in fall, they would cut a tree and sink it underwater until Christmas, by which time it was fairly well saturated. In such a condition, the log might smoulder for several weeks.

Because the wood is hard and difficult to work, only a few special applications have been found for it. An early use was as pipes to carry salt water to the salt works in and around Syracuse, New York, still known as Salt City and served by a passenger train of that name. The sturdiness of these log pipes precluded the need for iron reinforcing bands at the ends, which of course would have soon rusted away. The wood has also been used to make wheelhubs, rollers, wooden shoes, crates, bowls and other woodenware, gun stocks, tool handles, and flooring. If you would like to make a durable wood-block floor for a patio, you might check at a railroad yard—the disposable flooring of boxcars is often made of black gum.

The tree is difficult to transplant, especially when dug from the wild, and your chances are better with balled and burlapped nursery plants. It requires low, moist soil having a pH of from 6 to 7. Apply a thick mulch to conserve soil moisture. If you would raise the tree from seed, stratify the seed as soon as it ripens, placing it in moist sand at 30° to 50°F. for ninety days before planting.

GUM, SWEET (alligatorwood, American styrax, bilsted, gum tree, liquidambar, red gum, starleaf gum) *Liquidambar styraciflua*
A large timber tree, the sweet gum has foliage that smells fragrant when crushed, a sign that it is a member of the witch-hazel family. The wood is sometimes commercially known as starleaf gum and sapgum, and a number of "absurd" names, according to one seventy-year-old source, such as satin walnut and California red gum. The wood is not so much valued for its own appearance as for its ability to mimic other woods when painted or stained. Often what appears to be oak, walnut, cherry, maple, or mahogany is actually stained sweet gum veneer. The wood is used in cabinetry, for shingles and clapboards, wooden plates, boxes and, as it is tasteless, for barrel staves. The light brown, darkly streaked veneer is used by marquetry picture makers, as highly figured pieces look something like mountainous landscapes.

The gum that exudes from wounds in the bark was once used in wartime as a perfume base in place of gum imported from the Orient. The gum was also used as the source of storax, an expectorant and mild antiseptic. One writer claims that wild animals rub their wounds on lumps of the gum, and it is known that American Indians were aware of the healing properties of the tree. The leaves were a common ingredient in diet drinks, wrote George Barrell Emerson in 1846.

HACKBERRY (bastard elm, common hackberry, false elm, hack tree, hoop ash, nettletree, one-berry, sugarberry) *Celtis occidentalis*
This tree of the eastern United States does best in moist rich soils and may reach a height of well over a hundred feet in ideal locales. Isolated hackberries have been locally famed as "unknown trees"; one of these stood near Palatine Bridge and another near Schuylerville, both upstate New York towns. The wood is sometimes

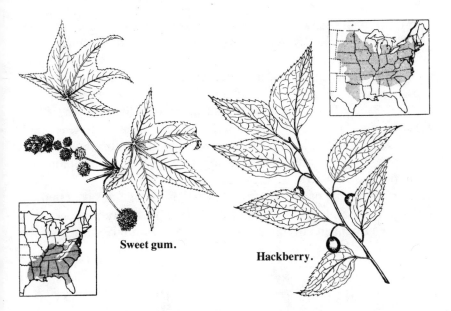

Sweet gum.

Hackberry.

sold as ash or elm, looking similar and having the same properties. It is a handsome, easily worked wood, suited for cabinetry and furniture. Formerly it was relegated to cheap furniture and common chair bottoms. Many birds feed on the dark purple, cherrylike fruit. Humans can eat the fruit, too; it tastes something like dates and hangs on the tree well into winter. The kernel within the pit can also be eaten.

In the northern area of its range the hackberry should be propagated from seed of trees native to the region's climate, as the resulting trees will likely be hardier than those from southern seed. The seed should be stratified for sixty to ninety days, although you'll have to be patient—they may take two years to come to life.

HEMLOCK, EASTERN (Canada hemlock, hemlock spruce) *Tsuga canadensis*

While hemlock is now milled for cheap lumber, it was once passed by because of its brittle, splintery nature. In the 1800s cities of the East Coast used it for hexagonal paving blocks. Pulp is made of the wood, and tannin, used in tanning hides, is obtained from the bark. The trees are very graceful when young and are suited for hedges because they prune well. Should you lose your way in the woods, take note of the terminal shoot—it typically points east, away from the prevailing winds. Hemlock is not the best choice for a campfire, as it throws sparks and may set a tent ablaze. It is sometimes used in closed stoves, however. The pink layer of inner bark will dye cloth a dull red.

The eastern hemlock has medicinal value. A tea of the inner bark was used by American Indians to bring on a sweat that would relieve colds. For a time, hemlock pitch was listed in the *Pharmacopoeia of the United States* as a counterirritant to relieve rheumatic suffering. Bathing in hot water in which boughs have steeped is supposed to produce a soothing effect. Veterinary liniments sometimes contain oil of hemlock, distilled from young branches. Poison hemlock, used by Socrates to commit suicide, is actually a small roadside plant, unrelated to the tree. You may make a tea of hemlock boughs in complete safety—in fact, you'll benefit from the vitamin C within.

Eastern hemlock.   **Western hemlock.**

HEMLOCK, WESTERN (Alaska pine, hemlock spruce, Pacific hemlock, West Coast hemlock) *Tsuga heterophylla*
This largest of the hemlocks produces a wood that works much like pine—it is straight grained and has a fine texture, unlike the eastern hemlock, above. The western species ranks as an important timber tree, much of the wood going into pulp.

HICKORY *Carya*
The several hickory species are known for their edible nuts and distinguished wood.

Shagbark hickory.

Shellbark hickory.

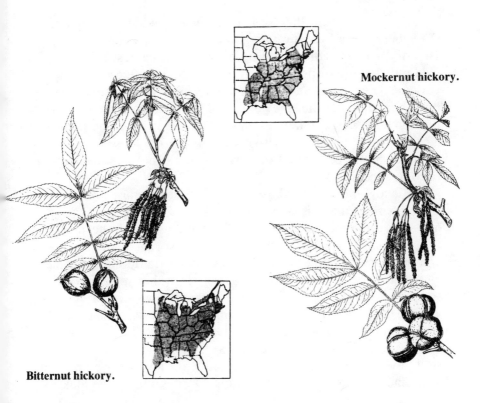

Mockernut hickory.

Bitternut hickory.

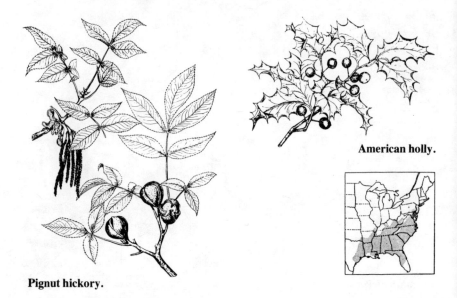

American holly.

Pignut hickory.

The seed within the nut is more or less edible, depending on the species—the best for eating are the shagbarks and shellbarks. Hickory nuts are considered by many to be the best tasting of the wild nuts but are difficult to extract from the shell. Some imported varieties have larger nuts with thinner shells. To preserve the nuts, pick them up soon after they drop and lay them on screens to dry in the shade. When the kernels have become crisp, place them in a mesh bag in a cool, well-ventilated place. This preservation method should be carried out promptly, as the nuts are liable to become rancid.

Hickory wood is hard, tough, and resists damage from shocks; these qualities make it an excellent choice for axe handles (and, at one time, automobile spokes). The light wood of the shagbark (*Carya ovata*) is suited for skis, walking sticks, hoops, veneers, and the manufacture of bent plywood. It has traditionally been employed for the screws of presses, the rings that hold the sails of small vessels to the mast, cogs of gristmills, wagon springs, light wagon shafts, ox bows, and on and on. The seasoned wood of some pignut and mockernut varieties is equal in durability to ironwood or lignum vitae and serves well as mallet heads. Shellbark splits the easiest of the hickories and was chosen for whip stalks and goads (sticks used to herd animals). In extolling the hickory's value Constantine says that, while there are woods stronger and harder, "the combination of strength, toughness, hardness, and stiffness possessed by hickory has not been found to the same degree in any commercial wood." And this comes from a man who is familiar with over three hundred woods, imported and domestic. Hickory must be dried carefully to prevent warping. A stand of hickory is a valuable asset to the homesteader, as the wood has a very high fuel value. It is good wood for a campfire, leaving coals ideal for baking or broiling. Hickory charcoal is of the best quality, and the ashes do well in soapmaking. The wood is widely used to smoke meat.

The nut of the shagbark is sweet; the bitternut, bitter; the nutmeg hickory, sweet and thick shelled; the water hickory, bitter and thin shelled; the red hickory, sweet and thin shelled; the pignut hickory, usually bitter and thick shelled. The Indians made an oil by boiling the nuts; it was administered to relieve stomach complaints. A fermented drink was made by pounding the nuts and letting them sit for a time in water. The nuts were also added to venison soup. An interesting wine can be made from the leaves with honey, raisins, and water.

HOLLY, AMERICAN (evergreen holly, holly, white holly) *Ilex opaca*

This is a medium-sized to large tree with elliptical evergreen leaves. The tree is best known as a Christmas decoration, and eastern Maryland sees a considerable harvest each season. The berries are eaten, and the seed distributed, by many species of birds. The ivory-colored wood is the whitest of any American tree, and small pieces are used to fashion piano keys, inlays on musical instruments, high-quality brush backs, toy boats, small pieces of furniture, and engraver's blocks. Constantine notes that the wood is cut in the winter and manufactured before the weather warms, as heat spoils the pale ivory shade.

Hollies must have an acid soil, ideally about 5 pH but as high as 6 if other conditions are met. Winter winds may dry out the broad leaves of this evergreen if planted in an exposed position. You can grow holly from seed but it is slow to germinate, taking at least two or three years. It's faster to take cuttings of the ripe wood. Plant males and females close by if you want the hollies to produce their bright red berries.

One species, *Ilex vomitoria,* served a ceremonial and perhaps somewhat practical role in the lives of the Indians of the Eastern Seaboard. As the Latin name indicates, a dark tea made from the leaves causes the imbiber to vomit furiously. Why drink it? The Indians found that the unpleasant experience left them able to travel free from hunger and thirst.

HOPHORNBEAM, EASTERN (hardhack, hophornbeam, ironwood, leverwood) *Ostrya virginiana*
This small tree bears clusters of nutlets that look much like hops. The wood is often known as ironwood, as it is heavy and hard. It somewhat resembles hickory, and it has occasionally been used as cogs for machinery, turnery, sled runners, bows, handles, mallets, and wedges. The bark is a good source of tannin but is seldom used commercially. As an ornamental, this hornbeam is best suited for shady areas and can be propagated from seed.

HORNBEAM, AMERICAN (blue beech, hornbeam, ironwood,
water beech) *Carpinus caroliana*
A low and spreading tree, this species is grown as an ornamental for its strangely ridged bark, brilliant fall foliage, and interesting catkins. It is, however, difficult to transplant. The wood has the same uses as the eastern hophornbeam. The buds are eaten by several bird species.

American hornbeam.   **Juniper.**

JUNIPER

The several varieties of juniper are bushes or small trees and are not an important source of lumber. What wood that can be wrested from the trunk is used for novelties (the Rocky Mountain juniper has an attractive red and white wood suited for this purpose), pencils, fence posts, and fuel. The berries of the alligator juniper, native to areas of Arizona, New Mexico, and Texas, were ground and dried by Indians to make a cake flour. The berries of the western juniper are sweet and edible.

Juniperus communis, known simply as the juniper, has been called the most widely distributed tree of the Northern Hemisphere, spreading throughout North America, central and northern Europe, and from the Mediterranean across Asia to the Himalayas. It is more shrub than tree, rarely lifting itself higher than a few feet off the ground. Its sweet fruit is used to flavor gin, and the French once flavored a barley beer with it. Not long ago, a juniper-flavored beer appeared briefly on the market in this country.

LARCH, WESTERN (hackmatack, larch, Montana larch, mountain larch, red American larch, tamarac) *Larix occidentalis*

This mountain tree produces a wood similar to Douglas fir in appearance but inferior to that wood in quality. Hence, it is used for

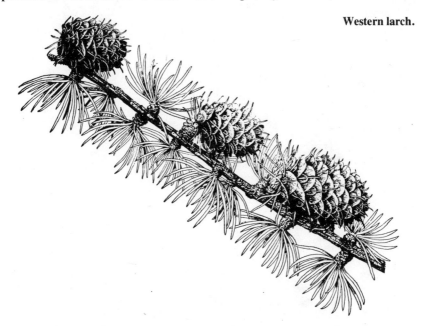

Western larch.

low-grade furniture, poles and posts, railroad ties, flooring, and in the production of fiberboard and kraft paper. The heartwood is light red, the sapwood lighter, and the grain is coarse. The gum, known as gelactin, is sometimes used to make baking powder. Another species, the European larch *(Larix decidua),* is tall and graceful and has been introduced to this country for its ornamental value. The wood is durable and has been used for underwater planking on ships and for posts.

LAUREL, CALIFORNIA (acacia burl, bay tree, California bay tree, California olive, California sassafras, mountain laurel, myrtle, Oregon myrtle, pepperwood, spice tree) *Umbellularia californica*

This small- to medium-sized tree produces an expensive cabinet wood known for its beautiful variety of figuring and color. The burls are the source of valuable myrtle veneer. The wood is hard, heavy, and strong, takes a fine polish, and is an excellent choice for turning. The shiny, leathery leaves are aromatic when crushed and can be used to flavor soups in place of basil leaves. The leaves' aroma will put off flies. Both foliage and wood give off a pungent medicinal oil under distillation.

California laurel.

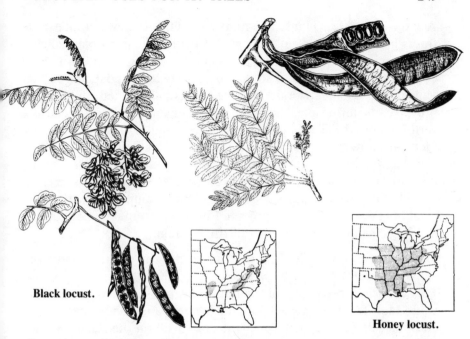

Black locust.

Honey locust.

LOCUST, BLACK (acacia, common locust, false acacia, green locust, honey locust, pea flower, pea-flower locust, red locust, shipmast locust, white locust, yellow locust) *Robinia pseudoacacia*

This is the most common locust in the United States, valued for its hard, strong, and durable wood, its role as a windbreak, and as an ornamental. Pole constructed houses and outbuildings are often of locust. The heartwood is brownish, and the sapwood a light greenish yellow; black locust is difficult to work by hand, but machine tools can do the job. The heartwood proves durable when used as posts or in fences. Formerly the wood was of some importance to shipbuilders, being preferred for floors and floor timbers. The Indians used the wood for bows. The leaves have been suggested as a substitute for indigo as a blue dye.

The tree is often planted as an ornamental in the eastern United States but is short-lived and very susceptible to damage from the locust borer. The fragrant, pealike flowers appear in June. Parts of the tree are poisonous, so don't try nibbling at the pods.

LOCUST, HONEY (acacia, common honey locust, confederate pinetree, honeyshucks, sweet bean tree, sweet locust, thorny locust, three-thorned acacia) *Gleditsia triacanthos*

A large tree often planted as an ornamental, the honey locust attracts bees with its sweet flowers. Young trees can be planted as a fast-growing hedge. The wood is heavy, strong, and durable in contact with the soil, and so it finds use as fence posts as well as veneer and cabinet wood. This tree is usually armed with an impressive cluster of long thorns, sturdy and sharp enough to cause a serious wound if run into or if a broken one is stepped on. This locust is more resistant to insects than the black locust.

The flat beanlike pods contain a sweet pulp that is worth a nibble early in summer. Later in the year, the seed can be soaked and sprouted or ground into a meal that is quite compatible with cornmeal. Fresh pods can be fermented in water to make beer. Cattle and hogs will feed on this free, nutritive forage.

MADRONE, PACIFIC (laurel, madrona, madrone, madrove, manzanita) *Arbutus menziesii*

This beautiful tree is one of the finest of broad-leafed ornamentals, valued for its white flowers, orange berries, and handsome leaves. Although difficult to transplant, it does well on the Pacific Coast and can be started from young seedlings. The pale brown wood is heavy and strong but checks seriously in seasoning. Still, it is handsome and well suited to turning. Madrone burls produce a beautiful inlay. Otherwise, the wood has been used to make gunpowder, charcoal, and textile shuttles.

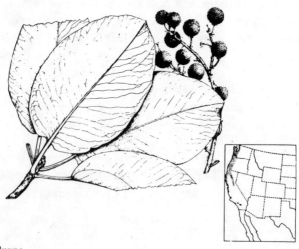

Pacific madrone.

MAGNOLIA, SOUTHERN (bat tree, big laurel, bullbay, evergreen
magnolia, laurel, sweet magnolia) *Magnolia grandiflora*
This is one of several magnolias native to the East. Most magnolia
timber comes from the southern magnolia and is used for cabinetwork, furniture, packing crates, and fuel.

MAHOGANY, WEST INDIES (baywood, Honduras mahogany,
madeira, mahogany, Mexican mahogany, redwood, Spanish
mahogany) *Swietenia mahagoni*
This finest and best known of all cabinet woods just barely qualifies
as a tree of the United States, as a few are found as ornamental and
shade trees in Florida. The rich, reddish brown wood is similar to
that of the other mahoganies. Among its attributes, the grain is attractive and is shown off to good advantage with stains; there is
much individuality between individual trees and between trees of
different localities; the crotch wood is especially eye-catching; and
few woods serve as well as veneers, as mahogany glues easily and
shrinks and distorts little. Of this species, Spanish woods rank
first, and Mexican woods second. Mahogany was once used in
place of oak in shipbuilding but is too valuable for such large-scale
usage today. The wood found great favor with cabinetmakers because it could be gotten in wide enough pieces that one or two
planks would suffice for a table top.
Phillipine mahogany is generally coarser than American and
African trees and must therefore be sanded a good deal to get the
desired smoothness. It is used in pieces of lower quality.

MAPLE *Acer*
Maple wood is characterized by fine texture, strength, and
variable appearance. Figures are described as bird's-eye,
blister, and curly—these are not woods of different species but
the favorable results of fiber distortions. The family's leaf
shape is the best-known characteristic, and maples are
popularly known as the source of maple sugar. The winged
fruit is also familiar to many.

MAPLE, RED (red flower, scarlet maple, shoe-pet maple, soft
maple, swamp maple, water maple, white maple) *A. rubrum*
The twigs, stems, blossoms, and fall foliage are red on this species.
It is classified as a soft maple, and as such the wood is cheaper and
plainer than that of sugar maple, a hard maple. Red maple is easily

worked and is used in cheaper furniture, general woodwork, and turnery. It occasionally shows a curly figure but rarely an attractive bird's-eye. Curly maple, sawed lengthwise, shows longitudinal fibers travelling in a serpentine course. The effect has been likened to the luster of silk, and this figure has been used for gun stocks and ornamental utensil handles. Landscape and mountain figures are created by the irregular line of color change between sapwood and heartwood and were used for the footboards and headboards of beds, door panels, and on other decorative pieces.

The bark, used with an aluminous mordant, produces a cinnamon color on wool and cotton. The effect is black when the bark is combined with ferrous sulfate. The leaves produce similar colors. Into the last century, the bark was used by schoolchildren to make a blue black ink. The trees are occasionally tapped, although they produce a relatively small amount of sugar. Red maple provides a fine fuel for heating the house. In sum, "Its virtues not its sins are as scarlet," as Henry David Thoreau wrote.

MAPLE, SILVER (river maple, soft maple, swamp maple, water maple, white maple) *A. saccharinum*
Shunning the Atlantic and Gulf Coasts, the silver maple is found just about everywhere else in the eastern half of the country. This is a soft maple, and its wood is much like that of the red maple. The leaves turn an unspectacular yellow in fall.

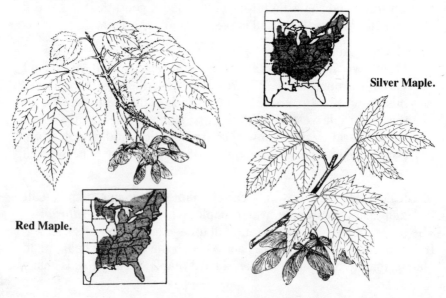

Silver Maple.

Red Maple.

Sugar maple.

MAPLE, SUGAR (black maple, hard maple, rock maple, sugar-tree
  maple, sweet maple, white maple) *A. saccharum*
The sugar maple is both beautiful and useful. It is tall and stately
and turns brilliant scarlet or orange in fall. This species accounts
for most maple syrup and sugar and produces the most valuable
and abundant wood of the native maples.

  The wood is tough and strong, polishes well, and is the source
of occasional blister, bird's-eye, curly fiddlehead, leaf, and burl
figurings, all of which are available as veneers. The bird's-eye
maple is the most sought after. In this figure, the fibers give the appearance of a roundish projection rising from within a slight cavity.
In shipbuilding, sugar maple was used, along with white oak, for
the keel. According to an old test, you can tell this wood from that
of the red or river maple by putting a few drops of sulfate of iron
(ferrous sulfate) on it; sugar maple will cause a greenish reaction
while the other two will turn the liquid a deep blue. Special uses for
this wood are first-quality dance floors, bowling alleys, piano-
actions, and old wooden type for show bills. It works and machines
well. In *Our Native Trees,* Harriet L. Keeler remembers " . . . a
country home where the kitchen stove was fed one entire winter
with the most beautiful curled and bird's-eye maple, carefully cut
into cordwood eighteen inches in length. Of course the owner knew
nothing of the existence of these trees until they confronted him in

his woodpile, and his anger and dismay may be imagined as he bewailed the stupidity of his workmen.''

MESQUITE, HONEY (algaroba, honey locust, honeypod, ironwood, prairie mesquite, screw bean) *Prosopis glandulosa (P. juliflora)*

This is a small tree of the southwestern plains that yields a rich, dark brown heartwood looking somewhat like walnut. The wood and roots are both used for fuel, and lumbered mesquite also finds its way into house beams, fencing posts, ties, and charcoal. Honeybees flock to the flowers, and cattle will feed on the pods. The sweet pulp within the pods was once eaten by Indians, and a meal made from the seed known as pinole, was an ingredient in their bread.

Red mulberry.

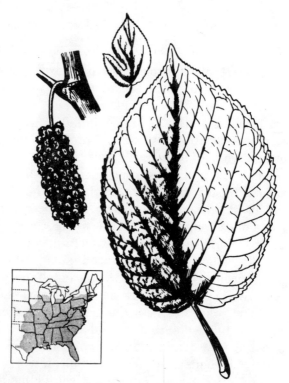

MULBERRY, RED (black mulberry, Virginia mulberry tree) *Morus rubra*

Although mulberry trees are valuable both for their red or purple fruit and for their wood, some people dislike them because of the dark droppings of mulberry-eating birds. Today, mulberries are largely ignored by humans, and little of the enormous crop from wild and ornamental trees is made use of. The berries eaten straight off the tree are sweetish and less interesting in taste than look-alike blackberries, but you can perk up their flavor with a bit of lemon. Lemon juice improves a mulberry pie and is an ingredient in most mulberry wine recipes. In quantity, the berries have a mild laxative effect. Mulberries can be dried and used like raisins in cookies and muffins or ground up into meal or flour for baking. In the South, hogs and poultry feed on the fruit.

Indians once wove strips of the inner bark. The wood is light, soft, and not especially strong. The heartwood is colored light orange yellow. Country chairmakers still use mulberry wood; it has also been used for local shipbuilding (especially in the South), fencing, and cooperage.

The black mulberry *(Morus nigra)* is a similar tree, but its wood is inferior. The berries of the white mulberry *(Morus alba)* are a milky white color, marked with black tubercles, and don't look or taste all that good. But the tree wasn't introduced from eastern Asia to this country for people food—the Colonists had hoped to establish a silkworm industry using the leaves as worm food. Naturalist Edwin Way Teale recounts that before the Revolution each parish of Connecticut was given a half ounce of white mulberry seed to foster silkworm culture. Worms were fed the leaves in the attics of many Connecticut farmhouses.

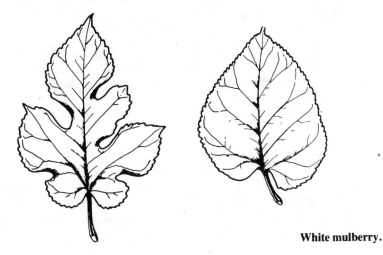

White mulberry.

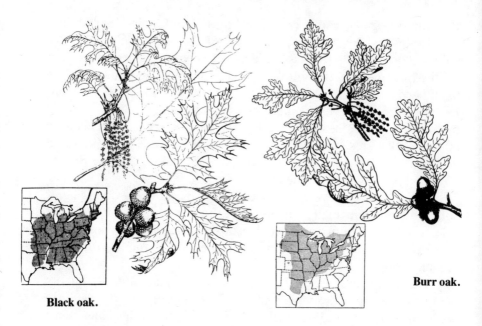

Black oak.

Burr oak.

OAK *Quercus*

The oaks are a paradigm for the qualities man attaches to trees—they're large, strong, beautiful, and long-lived. The oaks of this country can be divided into either of two groups, white oaks and red (or black) oaks. The former have more commercial value, their leaves generally have rounded lobes, and their nuts mature in one season and are lower in tannin. The second group nevertheless is the source of much valuable timber and is characterized by pointed leaf lobes; the nuts take two years to mature and are bitter from tannin.

In man's journey to wherever it is he's going, it may be that acorns have fed him longer than has wheat. Most acorns are high in tannin and bitter to the taste, unless this agent is leached out. Generally, acorns from white, burr, chinquapin, and chestnut oaks are more flavorful than acorns from red or black oak varieties.

One way to use acorns is to grind them into a meal. Hull the acorns, and then grind the meats in a hand mill or food chopper. Mix with hot water and pour into cheesecloth or a jelly bag. The water will leach out the bitter tannin; however, you may need to repeat the leaching process with a change of fresh water. Use the acorn meal in place of cornmeal.

OAK, BLACK (black jack, Dyer's oak, jack oak, quercipron oak, spotted oak, tanbark oak, yellow-bark oak) *Q. velutina (Q. tinctoria)*

This is one of the black oak family, and produces wood inferior to the white oaks. It is used to make cheap furniture, in construction, and in cooperage. The yellow inner bark imparts a yellow shade to wool and silk; the color is modified with iron salts. The kernels are bitter, so if you want to experiment with acorn dishes, try the white oaks. The bark is a source of tannin (the stuff that makes the acorns unpalatable).

OAK, BURR (blue oak, mossycup white oak, overcup oak, scrub oak) *Q. macrocarpa*

Although taller than most oaks, this species lacks the splendor of the white oak. It is a member of the white oak group, and its large acorns have a sweet white meat. The wood is very similar to that of the white oak but is said to be less elastic and more solid. As a fuel, burr was often preferred to white oak.

OAK CHESTNUT (rock chestnut oak, rock oak, swamp chestnut oak, tanbark oak, mountain oak) *Q. prinus*

One of the white oaks, this tree's nuts mature in one year and are free enough of tannin to be palatable. The wood is heavy, hard, and

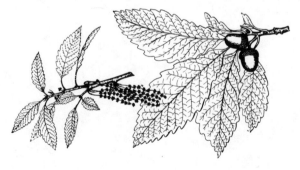

Chestnut oak.

strong, and is as useful as the similar wood of the white oak. The bark is especially rich in tannin.

OAK, CHINQUAPIN (chestnut oak, yellow oak) *Q. muehlenbergii*
Because of its small size, the wood of this species is only of moderate importance, even though similar to white oak in quality. What wood that is lumbered goes into construction work. The acorns are reputed to be sweeter than those of any other oak.

OAK, LIVE *Q. virginiana*
This is a short, wide spreading oak used often as a shade tree. The leaves stay on the tree the entire year, explaining the name live oak. Its acorns are sweet. The heavy, durable wood was used in shipbuilding—curved timbers could be fashioned from the tree's knees, where the trunk sections off into the roots. Constantine says that the mighty *Constitution,* known also as *Old Ironsides,* was made from Georgian live oak. But the short, stubby trunk yields only small straight pieces of lumber, and the live oak is very seldom used today.

OAK, NORTHERN RED (Canadian red oak, eastern red oak, gray oak, red oak) *Q. rubra*
This large tree is the most important of the black oak group for lumber. The name red oak is appropriate, as the midrib and veins

Chinquapin oak.

of the leaves, and then the leaves themselves, turn a rich red in fall. As with the other black oaks, the acorn is bitter, although it is good food for cattle and hogs.

To the author of the 1846 Report on the *Trees and Shrubs Growing Naturally in the Forests of Massachusetts:* "Like some individuals in a higher field in creation, [the red oak] compensates in some measure for its comparative uselessness, by its great beauty." The wood was considered inferior to black oak for fuel and timber. A 1914 source, *Pennsylvania Trees,* says that "the wood of this species . . . is relatively poor but is coming into more use daily. The despised species of today may be prized tomorrow." Indeed, modern writers have come to put more practical value on this oak. Although its wood does not measure up to that of the white oak, the premium species, red oak is widely used today for furniture and flooring.

The northern red oak is a worthy ornamental, growing more rapidly than any other of the *Quercus* clan.

OAK, OREGON WHITE (California post oak, Garry's oak, Pacific white oak, prairie oak, western white oak) *Q. garryana*
The wood of this western tree is the best regional substitute for eastern white oak. The light brown to yellow heartwood is hard and tough, works well with tools, and takes a good polish. The wood

Oregon white oak.

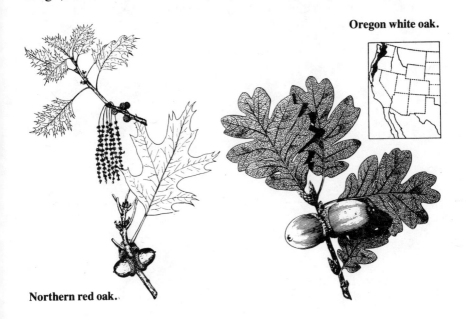

Northern red oak.

was formerly used in shipbuilding and carriage construction, and now ends up as cabinetry and good furniture.

OAK, PIN (swamp oak, water oak, water Spanish oak) *Q. palustris* This is a medium-sized oak with numerous pinlike branches evident in winter, possibly explaining the species' most popular name; it also could be that the tree was so named because it is the source of pins used to hold together squared barn timbers. The many branches on the trunk cause the wood to be quite knotty, reducing its ornamental value, and most pin oak ends up as shingles, clapboards, and in construction. Pin oak galls can be snipped off and soaked in water with iron nails to make a potent black ink. The active substance in the galls will work on steel nibbed pens, so you'll have to use a quill, instead.

William M. Harlow suggests in *Trees of the Eastern United States and Canada* (Dover, 1957) that this is one tree that can be identified with the eyes closed, just by listening to the characteristic sound of the windblown foliage. While it would take much practice to cultivate the necessary sensitivity, experience, and even patience, it does seem logical that an angular, deeply lobed tree would make a different sound than a tree with elliptical, unlobed leaves. Compare the pin oak with a poplar—the former should have a ragged sound, while the latter makes a quiet hiss. So, instead of familiarizing yourself with bird calls next summer, you might work on an ear for trees.

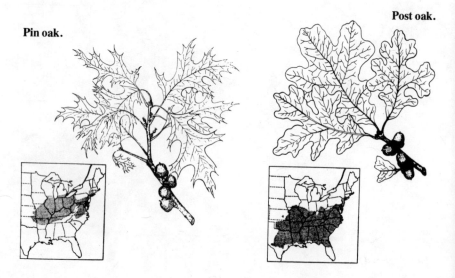

Pin oak.

Post oak.

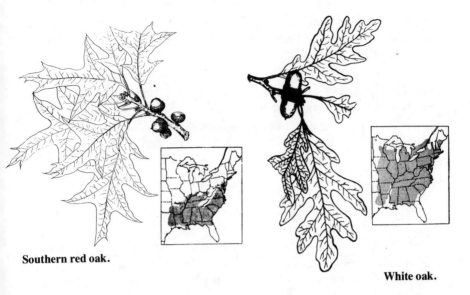

Southern red oak.

White oak.

OAK, POST (box white oak, brash oak, iron oak, overcup oak, white oak) *Q. stellata*
This is a small- to medium-sized oak that may grow to no more than a shrub in the northernmost edge of its range. The wood is heavy, hard, and strong, but checks badly in drying. All in all, the wood is seldom distinguished commercially from white oak, and goes into railroad ties, construction timbers, fencing, and cooperage.

OAK, SOUTHERN RED (finger oak, hill red oak, Spanish oak, spotted oak) *Q. falcata*
This is a large tree with foliage of varying shape. The hard, heavy, strong wood is suited to construction, although it checks badly in the process of drying. The bark is very rich in tannin. The southern red oak does best in dry, barren soils and is a rapid grower.

OAK, WHITE (forkedleaf white oak, stave oak) *Q. alba*
Though last to be treated here, the white oak is the most widely used of all American oaks, and from it comes the most and best lumber and veneer. It is also one of the most attractive of trees, the leaves turning dark purplish red in fall. Wild animals scoop up and hoard the nuts—so many nuts that writers of seventy-five and a hundred years ago feared that the species might become extinct. The wood is of a reddish tint, very heavy, compact, and close

grained. The annual markings are clearly visible. White oak takes a good polish and is often used for paneling of the best quality and fine furniture.

White oak was once the favored source of ship timbers, namely the upper and lower floor timbers, keel, kelson, stem and stern posts, timbers, and lower deck beams. For sturdiness, the ribs, knees, and gunwhales of whale boats were of this wood. It was commonly used for treenails and was the first choice of carriage builders for spokes. Wrought in a green state, it is still much used for barrels; the pores are filled with a substance that keeps liquids from penetrating the wood.

The wood of the lower trunk of young trees can be stripped into narrow ribbons and woven into baskets. The bark was used by tanners. White oak charcoal is inferior only to that made from chestnut, hickory, and chestnut oak. The nuts can be roasted and eaten, but if they are to be milled for baking you should first soak them in water.

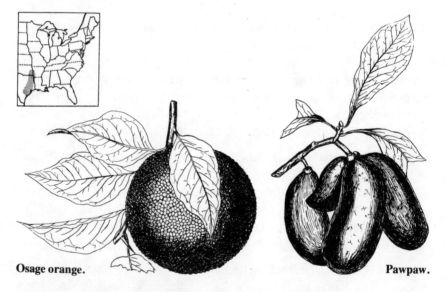

Osage orange.   Pawpaw.

OSAGE ORANGE (bodark, bowwood, hedge plant, mock-orange,
        Osage apple tree, yellowwood) *Maclura pomifera*
A medium-sized tree, the Osage orange produces small logs of a yellow green to orange color. It is a hard, strong, and flexible wood, and holds up well in contact with the soil. The Indians made bows of it (the common name bodark is a corruption of *bois d'arc*),

and the tree is still used for this purpose. Its durability is such that the erstwhile Kansas City, Ft. Scott and Memphis Railway once maintained a bodark plantation in Farlington, Kansas, as a source of ties. The wood occasionally shows an attractive mottling, and it takes a beautiful polish. A yellow dye for cloth is released by boiling wood chips.

The Osage orange bears formidable spines and can be grown into an impenetrable hedge. No use has yet been found for the curious green fruit.

PALMETTO, CABBAGE (cabbage tree, Carolina palm, swamp cabbage, tree palmetto) *Sabal palmetto*
The tender leaf bud at the top of the tree indeed tastes like a cabbage when cooked, but trees usually die when robbed of this part. Still, there are places in the South where you can buy the canned delicacies. Brush bristles were made from the sheath of young leaves. The light brown wood is soft and light, but fibrovascular bundles make it hard to work. Constantine says that cross sections of the trunk make good-looking table tops, but most of the wood is relegated to fence and telegraph poles and wharf-work (it repels the shipworm). The tree is best known for its role on Palm Sunday.

PAWPAW (banana tree, custard apple, custard banana, Indiana banana, Nebraska banana, poor man's banana) *Asimina triloba*
Although it is of little commercial value today, the pawpaw's fruit was once sent to the market in large quantities from the Mississippi Valley. Before the fruit ripens it emits a disagreeable odor, as does the rest of the tree. This fruit is yellow when young and turns dark brown when mature; the pulp within is delicious and sweet, with a taste somewhere between that of a banana and a pear. You might try using the fruit as pie filling.

The wood is little used commercially, some of it going into firewood, but it is fairly attractive and works and turns well. The fibrous inner bark was long ago used to make cord for fishing nets. In sum, the pawpaw is an excellent choice for an ornamental, considering its fruit, attractive foliage, and beautiful early spring flowers. It can be propagated by seed in fall or by stratified seed in spring; you can also start it by layering or from root cuttings.

PEAR *Pyrus communis*
Pears have long been pressed into a cider known as perry, a mild

drink. The *History of the Manufacture and Use of Enebriating Liquors* of 1838 reported that, in Europe, fermented perry was often passed off as champagne.

Pear wood is very attractive, colored a rosy pink, and possessed of a very fine and close grain. It once ranked second only to boxwood for engraving and has been stained black to imitate ebony. Pear wood turns well. Today it is used in marquetry work and appears in fine furniture. The Museum of Modern Art in New York has featured a gracefully fashioned desk made largely out of pear. Should the wood not be in good enough shape for handiwork, it will make an excellent fire. The leaves and bark were once used as the source of a yellow dye.

PECAN *Carya illinoensis*

This is the largest of the hickories, reaching a height of 160 feet. If the nuts do not separate from their shucks, knock them from the trees onto sheets or drop cloths spread below. Shelled nuts don't keep as well as unshelled and should be stored under refrigeration. With their shells, they can be kept in a cool cellar until a week or two before they are to be used.

Reddish brown, close-grained pecan wood is valuable either as a veneer or as lumber. The wood goes into heavy-duty chairs and is used to smoke meat. Pecan veneer usually ends up in furniture or paneling.

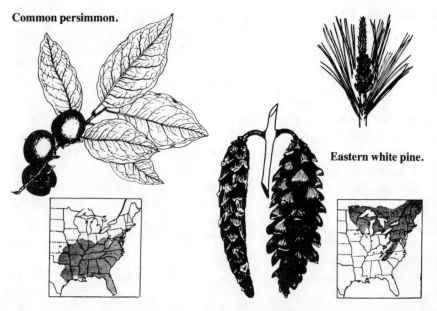

Common persimmon.

Eastern white pine.

PERSIMMON, COMMON (boawood, butterwood, date plum, possumwood, simmon, sugar plum) *Diospyros virginiana*
Diospyros means heavenly fruit, and ripe persimmons are a tasty, if rather unknown, native delicacy. They can be turned into a butter or baked in a pie. But beware of the unripe persimmon—its high tannin content will pucker your mouth. Let the fruit ripen on the tree (it will still be good well into winter) or pick it early and allow it to ripen in the house. The dried leaves will make a spicy tea. Long ago, persimmon butter was made by mixing the dried pulp with honey and then cooking the result over a low fire. The seed have been roasted and ground as an ersatz coffee. The fruit is well off in vitamins A and C and iron, and the leaves offer much vitamin C. Grafted trees are commercially available. The fruit was at one time listed in the *Pharmacopoeia of the United States* as an astringent.

Persimmon sapwood is light brown, strong, and tough, and finishes nicely; the heartwood is dark brown or black and very thin. The sapwood is used to make golf club heads and shuttles, and once was made into plane stocks and shoe lasts.

PINES *Pinus*

The three dozen or so pine species can't all be discussed here, but the most representative and important species will be mentioned. They are softwoods, usually evergreens, and have needles instead of broad leaves. The woods are characterized by the presence of resin and are lightweight and easy to work. The trunks are typically smooth and straight.

PINE, EASTERN WHITE (balsam pine, Canadian white pine, cork pine, northern white pine, patternmaker's pine, pumpkin pine, soft pine, spruce pine, Weymouth pine) *P. strobus*
This is a tall, impressive pine of the East, reaching a height of two hundred feet. The wood is creamy white to pale brown, with a close, straight grain and compact structure. It is comparatively free from knots and resin. White pine seasons well, is easy to work, nails without splitting, is fairly durable, and paints well. While it ranks as the lightest and weakest of eastern Unites States pines, this is the number-one wood for carpentry. And so it has been since colonial times, when the tree was pictured on the flag. At that time, there was an estimated 750 billion square feet of white pine growing in virgin stands; today, but 15 billion remain.

Aside from carpentry, white pine has been used for pattern-making, matches, spars, and boxes. This tree is the source of white pine tar cough remedies. The Indians used a bark tea to relieve coughs and colds. A tea of the needles supplies much vitamin C and vitamin A. When other food was not available, Indians of New York State ate the inner bark. In fact, "Adirondacks" is a somewhat garbled version of the Indian term for bark eaters, an insulting name attached to a defeated tribe that took refuge in these mountains and subsisted on bark, the only food available.

PINE, JACK (black pine, gray pine, Hudson Bay pine, northern scrub pine) *P. banksiana (P. divaricata)*
This is regarded as one of the less valuable species of pine. The wood is cut for pulp and is occasionally used for ties, posts, and lumber. Because it is so knotty, a good deal of it goes into knotty pine veneers and plywood. The Indians used it for canoe frames.

PINE, LOBLOLLY (among the adjectives attached to this pine are Basset, bastard, black foxtail, black slash, bull, cornstalk, frankincense, Indian, longshat, longshucks, longstraw, meadow, North Carolina, old field, rosemary, sap, shortleaf, slash, spruce, swamp, torch, Virginia, yellow) *P. taeda*
The length of this list of common names suggests the utility of the Latin tag. It also suggests that this pine has no dominant feature that sticks in the mind, and in fact it loses its identity when used with other southern pines. The yellow brown wood resembles shortleaf pine, while selected pieces rank with longleaf pine in quality. Loblolly is made into veneer, boxes, and pulp and is used in construction.

PINE, LODGEPOLE (black pine, coast pine, scrub pine, shore pine, tamarack pine) *P. contorta*
The lodgepole pine once served as the poles that held up the shelters of western Indians. The soft, fine-textured, knotty wood is now a moderately important source for fences, local outbuildings, ties, mine timbers, and poles. The tree grows very slowly, reaching maturity in about two hundred years. Lodgepoles spring up after forest fires, forming dense stands.

PINE, LONGLEAF (this species has been labelled as brown, fat, Florida, Florida long-leafed, Florida yellow, Georgia, Georgia heart, Georgia long-leafed, Georgia pitch, Georgia yellow, hard, heart, long-leafed pitch, long-leafed yellow, longstraw,

North Carolina pitch, pitch, rosemary, southern, southern hard, southern heart, southern pitch, southern yellow, Texas king-leafed, Texas yellow, turpentine, yellow) *P. palustris*

Again, here is a tree species best referred to by its Latin name for identification purposes. Longleaf is perhaps the most descriptive name—the needles range from six to twenty inches long, dropping off every two years. As the orange heartwood develops when the tree reaches about eighteen years, the off-white sapwood is correspondingly wide in young trees. It is one of the strongest and stiffest of pines and is used in heavy construction, shipbuilding, docks, beams, ties, flooring, house trim, and pulp. The tree is also a source of much turpentine and pine oil.

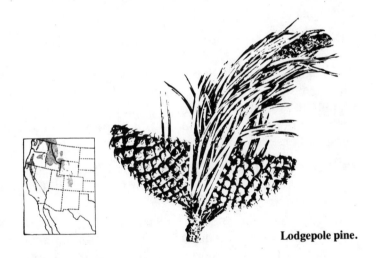

Lodgepole pine.

PINE, PINYON (Colorado pinyon, nut pine, pitch pine, scrub pine) *P. edulis*

The most notable thing about this tree is that the thin-shelled seed is easily cracked by the teeth and tastes delicious when baked. This crop, known as pine nuts, has been harvested for ages by the Indians of the Southwest. The nuts are rich in fat, protein, and the B complex vitamins, and have a high fuel value (3,205 calories per pound). Next to pecans, the pinyon is the most commercially valuable wild nut tree. The nuts can be eaten cooked or raw and have been ground into bread flour and cereal meal. Bumper crops occur every three or more years. The wood is very knotty and finds local use as telephone poles and in construction.

PINE, PONDEROSA (big pine, bird's-eye pine, foothills yellow pine, heavy pine, heavy-wooded pine, long-leafed pine, Montana black pine, Oregon pine, pitch pine, prickly pine, red pine, southern yellow pine, western pitch pine) *P. ponderosa*
The Latin *ponderosa* means heavy, referring to the trees' great size. They reach up to three hundred feet and may grow to twelve feet in diameter. The coarsely grained heartwood is a light red, the sapwood nearly white. A fungus introduced by feeding beetles sometimes turns the wood of dead trees a bright blue, and this lumber has its own special uses in cabinetry. Occasional logs have a bird's-eye figure, much like that of maple. The wood is cut for cabinetwork, general millwork, knotty pine paneling, pulp, posts, and poles.

PINE, RED (Canadian red pine, hard pine, Norway pine) *P. resinosa*
Although the Latin name suggests that the wood is resinous, red pine is more valuable for its lumber. It has long been the choice of shipbuilders for masts, spars, and decking. It is also used for wainscotting, flooring, and general construction. The long sheaths are such that children can make chains of the leaves.

PINE, SCOTCH (Danzig fir, deal, Memel fir, northern fir, northern pine, redwood, Rigi fir, Stettin fir, Swedish fir, yellowwood) *P. sylvestris*
The proper common names above refer to places of shipment early in the century and are no longer in common parlance. In Europe, where it is of prime importance, the tree is known as redwood. It is a tough, elastic, easily worked wood used to fashion beams, planks, masts, and heavy timbers. The wood is reddish white to yellowish, and even and straight in grain.

PINE, SHORTLEAF (other adjectives are bull, Carolina, hard, North Carolina yellow, old field, pitch, poor, rosemary, shortleafed yellow, shortshot, slash, spruce, Virginia yellow, yellow) *P. echinata*
The wood of this large, erect tree once served as masts on naval sailing vessels of the United States and Britain. It now serves a more mundane function, as lumber in construction and as knotty

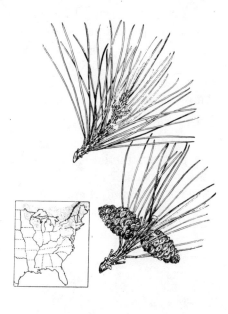

Red pine.

Ponderosa pine.

Shortleaf pine.

Scotch pine.

pine paneling in basement recreation rooms across the country. It affords considerable pitch and turpentine.

PINE, SUGAR (big pine, gigantic pine, great sugar pine, shade pine, white pine) *P. lambertina*
Growing up to three hundred feet, this is the largest of the pines. From it comes a light, soft, easily worked wood that resembles eastern white pine. Sugar pine lumber is made into interior finish, doors, and sashes, and is used in general carpentry. A sugary exudation is known as American false manna and acts as a purgative.

PINE, WESTERN WHITE (finger cone pine, little sugar pine, mountain pine, mountain Weymouth pine, silver pine, soft pine, white pine) *P. monticola*
This northwestern species offers a pale reddish brown heartwood, marked with many knots, that looks something like eastern white pine and is put to the same uses.

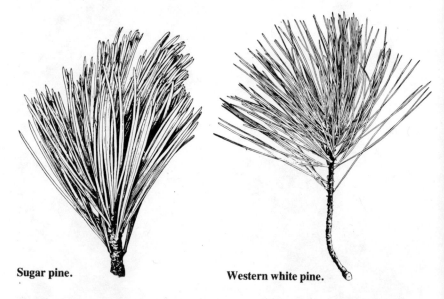

Sugar pine.

Western white pine.

POPLAR, BALSAM (balm of Gilead, balsam, tacamahac) *Populus balsamifera*
This tree is not a balsam, and is botanically not a poplar either, but a member of the cottonwood family. When the wind blows, the leaves of this attractive tree alternately show their dark top sides and light bottom sides. The light, soft, white wood is used for paper

making, lumber, and the manufacture of pails. It must be seasoned carefully so that it will not split.

POPLAR, YELLOW (blue poplar, canoe tree, cucumber tree, hickory poplar, popple, tulip poplar, tulip tree, whitewood)
Liriodendron tulipifera

This is one of the largest and most valued trees of the Atlantic States. The trunks may be free of branches to a height of a hundred feet, making a very impressive sight. It is often planted as an ornamental shade tree, the young poplars having a pyramidal shape and the older having an oblong head. The distinctive foliage and large tuliplike flowers add to the tree's appeal. Although classed as a hardwood, poplar is a soft wood, easily worked and carved. It is of a pale yellow green color that looks good without stain. Pianos, shelves, doors and sashes, and shingles are constructed of this wood; it formerly was used to make pumps and in shipbuilding. The pale sapwood sometimes is colored gray, purplish, or blue. Second-growth poplar has a very wide sapwood. Virgin stands are fast diminishing; a British woodworking book laments that, while it was once common to receive logs with a diameter of four or more feet from America, the timber now rarely measures more than two feet across. Poplar is a good foundation wood for veneer, and itself finds considerable use as a veneer. But it's an indifferent firewood.

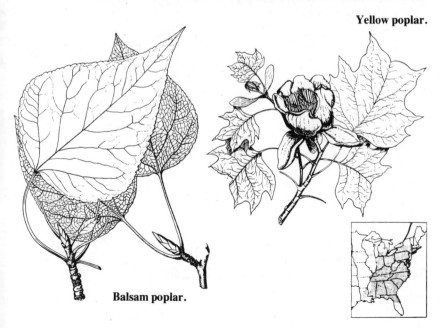

Yellow poplar.

Balsam poplar.

As an anonymous poet wrote, "Poplar gives a bitter smoke, fills your eyes and makes you choke."

One very old source recommends the root bark and branches as being remarkably pungent, bitter, and aromatic to the taste, acting on the system as a stimulating tonic and sudorific (sweat inducer). It was used successfully to treat chronic rheumatism and fevers. A more recent source suggests that a heart stimulant can be made from the bark of the inner root, but this tree disappeared from the *Pharmacopoeia of the United States* in 1882. The bark will produce a golden dye.

As the name canoe tree indicates, the tree was used by Indians for canoes—not made of sewn bark, but from the dugout trunk of the huge trees themselves. Some such vessels were reportedly large enough to carry twenty or thirty people.

To grow this tree, plant a balled and burlapped young poplar in a cool, moist site.

Eastern redbud.

REDBUD, EASTERN *Cercis canadensis*
This species occurs either as a small tree or shrub. It is often planted because of its early bloom, the pink flowers appearing on the bare twigs in April or May. One variety has white flowers, and another has double flowers. Constantine says that redbuds are to be found at Mount Vernon, planted there by George Washington and Thomas Jefferson. The hard brownish lumber is of little com-

mercial value but is fashioned into small pieces of furniture by craftsman of the Appalachians. It is suited to turning.

The seed are eaten by several bird species. In the South, blossoms and buds are incorporated in salads and the young pods are made into fritters, while in Mexico the flowers are fried and the bark is used for its medicinal value. Indians once wove the bark.

If you would like to grace your lawn or hedgerow with a redbud, choose a somewhat shaded place having a sandy loam. The tree does poorly in very moist sites.

REDWOOD (California redwood, coast redwood, sequoia) *Sequoia sempervirens*
The thick heartwood of this huge tree is red, changing to reddish brown as it is seasoned. It is a fairly lightweight wood, is very durable (often finding its way into picnic tables), and can be easily worked. It is used for framing, shingles, heavy construction, and interior decoration. Redwood burl veneers are highly figured and are used in furniture.

SASSAFRAS (cinnamon wood, red sassafras, sassafrac, saxifrax) *Sassafras albidum*
Sassafras was "probably the first contribution of America to the drug counters of the Old World, " notes Nelson Coon, and old books abound with uses for the tree. One continuing use has been as an ingredient in soups by southern cooks. Known locally as gumbo file, the leaves are picked when mature but still green, dried and powdered so that the stringy parts are separated, and then sifted. The powder makes soups turn ropy and gives them a characteristic flavor. From Virginia south, sassafras was once popularly used to brew a beer. Young shoots were boiled in water, molasses added, and the result fermented.

One of the most popular of folk teas is made from the root, usually dug up in spring. It's best to pick on a small sapling, as the roots of bigger trees are hard to unearth. Sassafras is easily identified, even before the leaves come out, by the bright green twigs. To confirm this clue, scratch and sniff a twig—it should have the unmistakable spicy odor. There's no doubt about the identity of the roots, either, as they exude a powerful smell of root beer. A few roots left to simmer on a back burner will make enough pinkish orange tea for a few days; as the tea runs low, just add more water. The tea tastes good iced, too. The young leaves are edible, having a

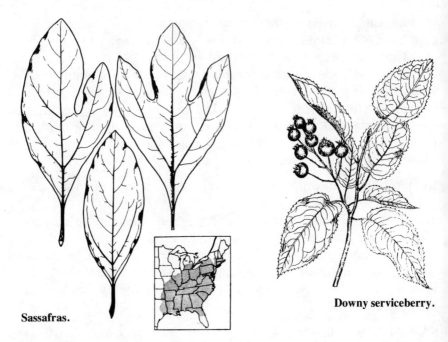

Downy serviceberry.

Sassafras.

mucilaginous quality and a somewhat lemony scent—quite a bit different than the roots.

Although sassafras is still spoken of as the source of a spring tonic, the tree isn't quite the cause of celebrity it once was. Sassafras roots were on board the first cargo exported from Massachusetts, according to George Barrell Emerson, and it was regarded as a panacea. In Arkansas and Mississippi, bedsteads were fashioned from the wood to ensure a sound sleep. In time, the claims for this tree have become much more modest; by the 1800s, it was recognized as but a warm stimulant and diaphoretic (that is, it induces sweat). The dark blue fruit, not very pleasant to the tongue, was once made into a wine by the Pennsylvania Dutch to treat colds.

The active principal of the tree seems to be the volatile oil safrole, obtained by distilling the roots and root bark. Because the oil is volatile, says the 1890 *Pharmacopoeia of the United States,* it should be kept in well-stoppered bottles, protected from the light. It is used to scent soaps and lotions and also to flavor medicines and candy.

The wood is soft and reddish, resembling both ash and chestnut. When marketed, it is usually sold as ash. As might be expected, sassafras wood is somewhat aromatic, and it resists decay when out in the weather. It was used to fashion the smaller joints of fishing rods in the 1800s, and as the odor was supposed to be disagreeable to insects and worms it was used to make trunks and drawers. Craftsmen of the Appalachians make handsome, pale-finished rockers from the wood. As fuel, sassafras earns low marks, since it snaps a good deal. The bark will impart a durable orange color to wool.

Native to this continent, the sassafras has been planted in Europe as an ornamental. The tree will grow in poor soils, matures quickly, and has attractive berries and leaves that vary a good deal in shape.

SEQUOIA, GIANT (bigtree, mammoth tree) *Sequoia gigantea*
Giant is right. One of these evergreens measured 273 feet high and 36 feet around at the base. Typically billed as the largest living things, sequoias would certainly seem to qualify—unless you consider the box huckleberry, a low bush which can spread over several acres. The sequoia is also reputed to be the oldest of living things—unless you consider lichen colonies, which some naturalists view as one on-going plant whose life is not confronted by the debilities of old age. Edwin Way Teale mentions that there are lichens in Europe reported to be more than ten centuries old. Regardless, the sequoia is a very impressive tree in its native stands. The purplish brown wood is seldom used, as the mammoth trees are protected.

SERVICEBERRY, DOWNY (currant tree, grape pear, Juneberry, may cherry, saskatoon, shadberry, shadbush, sugar pear, sugar plum, wild Indian pear) *Amelanchier arborea (A. canadensis)*
This is a small, graceful tree growing fifteen to thirty feet high. It is planted for its beauty, the blossoms appearing in early spring, and because the black berries attract birds. The berries attract people too, as they can be made into pies, jams, jellies, wines, and muffins. They can be eaten raw, but their flavor lacks until they are cooked. You can put them up by freezing or canning, or you can preserve their goodness as the Indians did—by pounding the dried fruit into pemmican.

The wood is hard, heavy, and flexible, and is turned to make handles and, under the name lancewood, is made into fly rods.

SMOKETREE, AMERICAN (chittim wood, Venetian sumac)
  Cotinus obovatus
The smokelike visual effect of this little tree is caused by plumes of fruit and flowers. The tree is not common and is little used on the market. However, the light, soft, and durable wood is an attractive light yellow to orange shade, and it can be finished clear to show off the color. Smoketree wood is also used as fence posts and is a source of an orange dye.

SOURWOOD (arrowwood, elk tree, lily-of-the-valley tree, sorrel
  gum, sorrel tree, titi tree) *Oxydendrum arboreum*
The sourwood is an attractive ornamental, by virtue of its form, late flowering, and bright scarlet fall foliage. It takes is name from the acidic flavor of the leaves and branchlets, which are said to have refrigerant, tonic, and diuretic properties. Extracts made from the sap are used to compound medicines. The hard and heavy wood is difficult to work with tools, but can be turned.

SPICEBUSH (Benjamin bush, downy spice, feverbush, feverwood,
  souther, spicewood, wild allspice) *Lindera benzoin*
This is an aromatic shrub, fond of wet woods, that signals the advent of spring with its sprays of tiny yellow flowers. Before any plant but the skunk cabbage has shown signs of life, the woods develops a transparent haze of yellow. A sure way of identifying

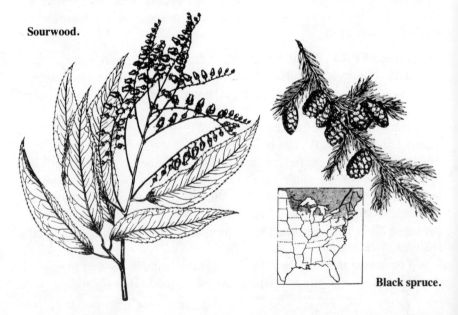

Sourwood.

Black spruce.

the bush is to scratch a twig or crush a leaf or berry and sniff. The good smell suggested a couple of uses to the Colonists; they made tea from the twigs, leaves, and bark, and also ground the dried red berries as a substitute for allspice. The principal of the tea was used to treat coughs and colds. The berries, which ripen from bright green to lipstick red by fall, are eaten by many birds.

SPRUCE, BLACK (blue spruce, bog spruce, double spruce, spruce
  pine, water spruce, white spruce, yew pine) *Picea mariana*
  (P. nigra)

Becoming scraggly and, to the eye of the landscaper, unsightly as it grows older, this spruce is not often planted as an ornamental. It has several other qualities to recommend it, however. For one, it is this species that is most often mentioned in recipes for spruce beer, although red spruce and Scotch pine will also work. The Indians of the Northeast taught the settlers how to boil the young twigs with honey to make the beer. In the 1800s spruce beer was made commercially, rivalling porter and ale for popularity. According to one recipe of that time, the fresh young twigs are boiled in water until the bark is loosened, and to this decoction are added roasted oats or barley and toasted bread or biscuits; brown sugar or molasses is added for sweetness, and the whole is fermented with yeast. Maple sugar has also been named as a sweetener. The beer served a medicinal function, its vitamin C staving off scurvy.

The black spruce is also valued for spruce gum (made into a confection), a yellow orange dye from the roots, and turpentine from its resin. You may have chewed commercial spruce gum, but don't try to eat it right off the tree—you'll gum up your mouth in an awful way. To make the manageable, crystalline product occasionally seen at old-fashioned candy counters, heat up spruce gum in a pan until it has liquified into a syrup, and pour dollops onto buttered cookie sheets to cool.

The wood of the black spruce is used as a substitute for white pine, and finds employment as lumber, flooring, piles, posts, ties, paddles, oars, sounding boards, and paper pulp. Black spruce was an important shipbuilding wood, serving as masts, knees, and the smaller spars.

SPRUCE, BLUE (Colorado blue spruce, silver spruce) *Picea pun-
  gens*

The silver blue needles, symmetrical shape, and hardiness of this spruce have earned it a place in many yards. The trees grow quickly from seed. Beautiful in its youth, the tree becomes scraggly and loses its lower branches with age, and it is often taken out after twenty years. The wood is weak and of little or no value.

SPRUCE, ENGELMANN (balsam, mountain spruce, white pine, white spruce) *Picea engelmannii*
This is a valuable tree of the central and southern Rockies, thriving at high altitudes. The blue green needles put off a disagreeable odor when crushed. The wood is very light and colored pale reddish yellow. It has been used in glider construction and is also made into lumber, sheathing, and high quality paper pulp. The bark is rich in tannin and has been used for tanning.

Engelmann spruce.

Norway spruce.

SPRUCE, NORWAY *Picea abies*
This European tree is often planted in this country as an ornamental and as a forestry crop. The yellowish white wood is medium hard, and works well; it is used for general construction, interior finish, paper pulp, basket making, and to fashion oars and masts on small vessels.

SPRUCE, RED (spruce pine) *Picea rubra*
This is a medium-sized tree that is the common spruce in the mountains of New York east through New England. It is an important

source of pulpwood in the Northeast. The wood is resonant and is suited to making sounding boards on musical instruments. Spruce beer is made from the young shoots and needles. Red spruce can be planted in soils too moist for other species.

SPRUCE, SITKA (sequoia silver spruce, tideland spruce, West Coast spruce, western spruce, yellow spruce) *Picea sitchensis* Once used for shipbuilding, this tree is now favored for wood aircraft construction. The wood is pinkish yellow in color, darkening with exposure. Pieces of Sitka are used for guitar tops, as the wood is very resonant.

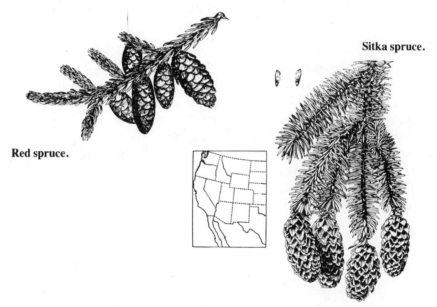

Sitka spruce.

Red spruce.

SPRUCE, WHITE (Adirondack spruce, blue spruce, bog spruce, cat spruce, single spruce, skunk spruce) *Picea glauca (P. canadensis, P. alba)* This is the principal spruce of the Arctic forests. The wood is used for lumber, flooring, carpentry, interior finishing, furniture, lightweight oars and paddles, and piano sounding boards.

SUGARBERRY (honey berry, Mississippi hackberry, southern hackberry, sugar hackberry, thick-leafed hackberry) *Celtis laevigata (C. mississippiensis)* This is a handsome tree found planted along streets and in parks in the South. The edible purple fruit sweetens as the weather turns cold; the white kernel within tastes something like a date. The wood is made into furniture and boxes.

SWEETBAY (laurel magnolia, swamp magnolia, swampbay, sweetbay magnolia) *Magnolia virginiana*

Typically a small tree or shrub to the north of its range, this magnolia may grow to a height of seventy-five feet in Florida. Consequently, wood of commercial size is produced only in the South. It is most often found along creeks or in moist bottomlands. It would serve well as an ornamental, having interesting fruit and fragrant white flowers, although it grows slowly. The sweetbay's wood is similar to that of the cucumber tree and goes into furniture and boxes.

SYCAMORE, AMERICAN (button-balltree, buttonwood, ghost tree, plane tree, water beech) *Platanus occidentalis*

The stately sycamore was so venerated by the Romans that they fed it with wine. It is still valued and still impressive with regard to size and distinctiveness. The bark is incapable of stretching to accommodate the growing tree's expansion, and so young trunks and branches have a pied and somewhat serpentlike mottling.

The heartwood is reddish brown, the sapwood shaded lighter, and it is an attractive furniture wood when quartered. Sycamore is not easy to work and is apt to warp on seasoning. It is cut into

Sweetbay.

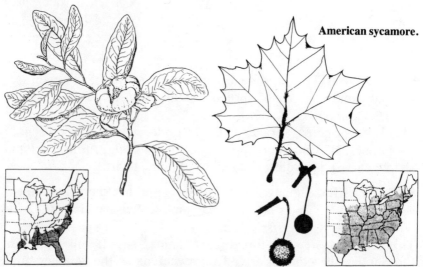

American sycamore.

lumber and veneer, and used for cabinetry; at one time, it was made into tobacco boxes and ox-yokes. Because the wood does not readily split, butcher blocks are often made of it.

Large sycamore trunks are often hollow. The Roman Licinius Mucianus set up an apartment in the trunk of a huge sycamore sleeping there and once served dinner within to nineteen companions. The early French in Illinois made a sixty-five-foot sycamore dugout that could carry a load of nine thousand pounds.

There is record of the sap being made into a wine.

Tamarack.

TAMARACK (American larch, black larch, eastern larch, hackmatack, juniper, larch, red larch) *Larix laricina (L. americana)*
An early use for the tamarack is mentioned by Longfellow in Hiawatha: the roots were used to bind the ends of birch bark canoes together. This is a distinctive needle-bearing tree, its foliage soft and fine and colored a bright yellow green that sets it off from other pines. It also is the only pine of the Northeast that loses its leaves each fall. The tree grows best in low, wet places, often along the boggy banks of a lake or stream. To some, the tree lends a lugubrious atmosphere to a setting. This is the case along the shores of Big Moose Lake in the Adirondacks, where the murder of Dreiser's *American Tragedy* was witnessed only by the tamaracks on shore.

The wood varies from a yellowish red to brown in color and is among the most durable of woods. Shipbuilders distinguished between red and gray heartwoods, preferring the most durable red-hearted logs for knees, beams, and top timbers. Tamarack is seldom cut into lumber for fine purposes as most of it is used for railway ties, posts, and telephone poles.

Although larches prefer swampy sites, they will also do well on drier land and are sometimes planted for ornamental effect. Wildlife is attracted to the seed, foliage, and branchlets.

TUPELO, WATER (bay poplar, cotton gum, gray gum, large tupelo, olive tree, pawpaw gum, sour gum, swamp tupelo, tupelo gum, white gum, yellow gum) *Nyssa aquatica*

This tree is quite similar to the black gum in as far as appearance and uses that have been found for the wood. The wood has a contorted vein, and is weak and difficult to work; it has been used for turnery, woodenware, pulp, veneers, and cheap furniture. Constantine says that one special use is as the veneer to which cedar is glued in cigar boxes. The roots were once used as net floats in place of corks.

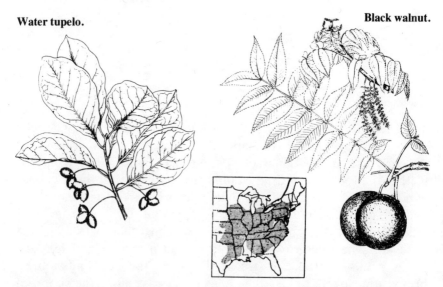

Water tupelo.

Black walnut.

WALNUT, BLACK (American walnut, eastern black walnut) *Juglans nigra*

The walnut is a beautiful tree, inside and out. A cut log is unmistakable, as the heartwood is a dark purply brown. The tree takes an especially attractive form when found growing apart from other trees.

The value of the walnut's wood has long been recognized, and the timber was exported to England in the early 1600s. Stands of the trees came down in the Civil War to provide wood for gun stocks. New trees weren't planted to replace these, and by World War I walnut had become so scarce that small stands and even individual trees were sought out for gun stocks and airplane propellers. The wood has more peaceful uses, of course. It is probably the most sought after native wood for cabinetry, and there are cases of trees being poached from private woodlots. Walnut is hard, heavy, strong, and easily worked, planing, sawing, and finishing well. Particular figures are featured in veneers; Constantine says that available figures include butts, crotches, burls, fiddleback, leaf, and straight stripe.

Walnuts were a valuable source of food for the Indians, and each fall you can still see nut gatherers by the roadsides. The nuts should be shelled soon after harvest, as the rind holds a stain that will in time go through the shell to the meat, coloring it and giving it an off taste. The hulled nuts can be washed down with a hose and spread out on a screen to dry in the shade. Walnuts are tricky to crack. A cookbook by the Michigan Nut Growers Association suggests that if the nuts are very dry they should be soaked overnight in a bucket of water, as this will cause the kernels to swell and permit the shell to crack easily without shattering. (The water in the pail can then be poured on the ground to bring earthworms to the surface—a useful trick for the fishermen to keep in mind.)

This cookbook also tells how to dye with walnut hulls. The hulls are stored until needed by placing them underwater and out of the light. The dye is prepared by soaking the hulls overnight and boiling them for two hours before straining the liquid into the dye bath. Wet wool is dyed by immersing it in lukewarm bath, and then heating the bath slowly to a boil. The wool is simmered for one hour, then rinsed and dried. The color can be darkened by adding a few sumac berries and a pinch of ferrous sulfate. A brown wood stain is made by mashing and boiling walnut (or butternut) hulls in one gallon of skimmed milk with five pounds of lime and one-half pound of powered alum or salt. Strain and dilute with skimmed milk until you achieve the desired color. Walnut or butternut hulls make a brown ink, too. Boil them in water and add vinegar and salt. If you desire a black ink, add indigo or soot.

Walnut sap has been tapped and boiled down into a sweet syrup and sugar (this has also been done with beech, butternut, and hickory). An early source says that "valuable and abundant" oil expressed from the kernels can be used for cooking and as lamp oil. Bread has also been made from the kernels.

Don't place a black walnut near valued plants, as the roots exude a substance that some neighbors will find toxic.

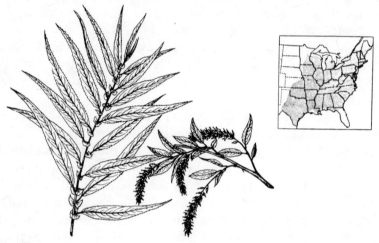

Black willow.

WILLOW, BLACK (pussy willow, swamp willow, willow) *Salix nigra*

This is the largest and most abundant of our willows. While most of the family are smaller trees or shrubs, forest black willows may grow to over a hundred feet in height.

Its wood is the most important of the willows and the gray brown, light, strong wood has found a special use in the manufacture of artificial limbs. However, willow wood is difficult to work with tools and checks badly in drying. A bitter decoction was once made from the roots, which contain salicylic acid, related to aspirin. Once largely obtained from plants, the decoction was supplanted by synthetic preparations and later by aspirin itself. The bark is rich in tannic acid and was once used as a substitute for quinine in relieving fevers. Willow sap has been made into wine.

Various willow species have special uses. The heart-leafed

willow *(Salix cordata)* furnishes twigs suited for basket making. The white willow *(Salix alba)* was planted in line at regular intervals to grow into barbwire posts. Fevers were treated with a tea máde of this species' leaves. In general, willows are used to make charcoal and are planted along streams to prevent the banks from washing out.

YEW, PACIFIC (California yew, Oregon yew, western yew) *Taxus brevifolia*
The wood of this western species has been called the best of all American trees for making bows, followed by Osage orange, white hickory, elm, cedar, and apple. The Indians valued it for making paddles and fishhooks, as well. The wood is tan, darkening to brown with exposure. There isn't much of a commercial market for it, as the tree is quite scarce, but yew is occasionally used for small works of cabinetry and the burls produce a very attractive veneer.

Index